D1601714

Admiral Lord Keith and the Naval War against Napoleon

New Perspectives on Maritime History and Nautical Archaeology

UNIVERSITY PRESS OF FLORIDA

Florida A&M University, Tallahassee
Florida Atlantic University, Boca Raton
Florida Gulf Coast University, Ft. Myers
Florida International University, Miami
Florida State University, Tallahassee
University of Central Florida, Orlando
University of Florida, Gainesville
University of North Florida, Jacksonville
University of South Florida, Tampa
University of West Florida, Pensacola

New Perspectives on Maritime History and Nautical Archaeology
James C. Bradford and Gene A. Smith, Series Editors

The Maritime Heritage of the Cayman Islands, by Roger C. Smith (1999; first paperback edition, 2000)

The Three German Navies: Dissolution, Transition, and New Beginnings, 1945–1960, by Douglas C. Peifer (2002)

The Rescue of the Gale Runner: *Death, Heroism, and the U.S. Coast Guard*, by Dennis L. Noble (2002)

Brown Water Warfare: The U.S. Navy in Riverine Warfare and the Emergence of a Tactical Doctrine, 1775–1970, by R. Blake Dunnavent (2003)

Sea Power in the Medieval Mediterranean: The Catalan-Aragonese Fleet in the War of the Sicilian Vespers, by Lawrence V. Mott (2003)

An Admiral for America: Sir Peter Warren, Vice Admiral of the Red, 1703–1752, by Julian Gwyn (2004)

Maritime History as World History, edited by Daniel Finamore (2004)

Counterpoint to Trafalgar: The Anglo-Russian Invasion of Naples, 1805–1806, by William Henry Flayhart III (first paperback edition, 2004)

Life and Death on the Greenland Patrol, 1942, by Thaddeus D. Novak, edited by P. J. Capelotti (2006)

X Marks the Spot: The Archaeology of Piracy, edited by Charles R. Ewen and Russell K. Skowronek (2006)

Industrializing American Shipbuilding: The Transformation of Ship Design and Construction, 1820–1920, by William H. Thiesen (2006)

Admiral Lord Keith and the Naval War against Napoleon, by Kevin D. McCranie (2006)

Admiral Lord Keith and the Naval War against Napoleon

Kevin D. McCranie

Foreword by James C. Bradford and Gene A. Smith, Series Editors

University Press of Florida

Gainesville · Tallahassee · Tampa · Boca Raton
Pensacola · Orlando · Miami · Jacksonville · Ft. Myers

11 10 09 08 07 06   6 5 4 3 2 1

Frontispiece: *Admiral Lord Keith, K.B.*, engraving after a painting by John Hoppner, from Alexander Allardyce, *Memoir of the Honourable George Keith Elphinstone, K. B. Viscount Keith, Admiral of the Red*. Edinburgh: William Blackwood, 1882.

Library of Congress Cataloging-in-Publication Data:
McCranie, Kevin D.
Admiral Lord Keith and the naval war against Napoleon / Kevin D. McCranie;
foreword by James C. Bradford and Gene A. Smith
p. cm. —(New perspectives on maritime history and nautical archaeology)
Includes bibliographical references and index.
ISBN 0-8130-2939-2 (acid-free paper)
1. Elphinstone, George Keith, 1746–1823. 2. Admirals—Great Britain—Biography.
3. Great Britain—History, Naval—18th century. 4. Great Britain—History,
Naval—19th century. I. Title. II. Series.
DA88.1.E46M43 2006
940.2'745092—dc22
[B]   2005056303

The University Press of Florida is the scholarly publishing agency for the State
University System of Florida, comprising Florida A&M University, Florida Atlantic
University, Florida Gulf Coast University, Florida International University, Florida
State University, University of Central Florida, University of Florida, University of
North Florida, University of South Florida, and University of West Florida.

University Press of Florida
15 Northwest 15th Street
Gainesville, FL 32611-2079
http://www.upf.com

To my parents, for support and love I can never begin to repay

Contents

Figures and Maps

Figures

Maps

Foreword

Water is unquestionably the most important natural feature on earth. By volume the world's oceans compose 99 percent of the planet's living space; in fact, the surface of the Pacific Ocean alone is larger than that of the total land bodies. Water is as vital to life as air. Indeed, to test whether the moon or other planets can sustain life, NASA looks for signs of water. The story of human development is inextricably linked to the oceans, seas, lakes, and rivers that dominate the earth's surface. The University Press of Florida's series New Perspectives on Maritime History and Nautical Archaeology is devoted to exploring the significance of the earth's water while providing lively and important books that cover the spectrum of maritime history and nautical archaeology broadly defined. The series includes works that focus on the role of canals, rivers, lakes, and oceans in history; on the economic, military, and political use of those waters; and upon the people, communities, and industries that support maritime endeavors. Limited by neither geography nor time, volumes in the series contribute to the overall understanding of maritime history and can be read with profit by both general readers and specialists.

Biography, one of the largest genres of naval history, has been dominated by studies of men victorious in combat. Such studies vary in tone and intent. Before history and biography emerged as modern academic disciplines, most biographers wrote primarily to eulogize their subjects or to entertain their readers. During the late nineteenth century many writers sought the lessons of history. Exemplified by Alfred Thayer Mahan, they attempted to divine the causes for the rise and fall of nations, the factors that brought victory and defeat in battles and wars, and the qualities that engendered greatness in leaders. Biographers probed whether leadership is innate or learned, the product of one's youth or implanted by a system. As a genre biography became more critical and analytical than hagiographic. Still, most biographers continued to select as their subjects individuals who, as in previous centuries, achieved fame through victory. A steady supply of books on Lord Nelson and John Paul Jones appeared in publishers' lists, and each war led to multiple biographies of major commanders. During the late twentieth century an interest in the common person and in "history from the bottom up" engendered an interest in enlisted personnel. The lives of junior officers, and of those operating just below the highest levels, and even of those who held high commands but to whom the opportunity never came to distinguish themselves, have been largely overlooked.

George Keith Elphinstone, Viscount Keith, is just such a man. Commissioned in Britain's Royal Navy during the latter half of the eighteenth century, Keith saw service afloat and ashore during the American Revolution before distinguishing himself at the siege of Toulon around the time of the outbreak of the hostilities between Britain and France that would last a quarter century. During that time Keith held four major independent commands and, as an admiral, commanded British forces in the North Sea and the English Channel. Well known during his lifetime, Keith then fell into relative obscurity. With biographers deterred, perhaps, as much by the volume of papers Keith left behind as by his failure to obtain a signal victory such as those that placed Lords Nelson and St. Vincent in the pantheon of naval heroes, Keith has not until now received the attention he merits.

In this biography Kevin D. McCranie explains how Keith rose to high command in the Royal Navy, assesses his strengths and weaknesses as an administrative and combat leader, and measures his achievements against those of his contemporaries. Keith's life provides a lens through which to view the difficulties Britain faced in subduing her rebellious American colonies, the challenges faced by commanders forced to respond to situations without the benefit of consultation with higher authorities, the role of political patronage in the careers of senior officers, and the inner workings of Whitehall. McCranie's description of the tensions that developed when Keith had to coordinate naval operations with the operations of military commanders ashore in North America, Iberia, and Italy has implications for the modern military's focus on "jointness." The Keith who emerges in these pages is a complex character, a man with strengths and weaknesses, and one who is inherently interesting.

James C. Bradford and Gene A. Smith
Series Editors

Preface and Acknowledgments

During the wars of the French Revolution and Napoleon, the British navy dominated its rivals. To accomplish this, Britain needed competent and steady officers such as George Keith Elphinstone, later Viscount Keith (1746–1823). Although he earned distinctions and a fortune in prize money and even commanded fleets for longer periods than notable contemporaries such as Admiral Lord Nelson, Keith's story remains obscure. Perhaps this resulted from his failure to command a fleet in a major sea battle, but this was not unusual, because there were only six fleet engagements during the Revolutionary Era. Keith served a lifetime at sea, gaining experience as a captain during the American Revolution and then, between 1795 and 1815, holding four independent commands: the Eastern Seas, 1795–96; the Mediterranean, 1799–1802; the North Sea, 1803–7; and the Channel, 1812–14, 1815. The diversity and longevity of his naval service meant that he played a major, if underrecognized, role in the implementation and the crafting of British naval policy.

The geographic diversity of Keith's commands was matched only by the range of his objectives. In the Eastern Seas, he captured the Cape of Good Hope from the Dutch. He commanded the Mediterranean Fleet while the French occupied Egypt and, as the capstone of this command, he witnessed their expulsion from Egypt. In the North Sea, Keith's fleet served as the primary defense against the invasion flotilla being organized by Napoleon in the French Channel ports. And when he commanded the Channel Fleet, his cooperation with Wellington in the Iberian Peninsula proved necessary for the British war effort. Even though he was never spectacular and lacked a killer instinct, Keith was extremely competent and steady. His success resided in his ability to administer large naval forces and understand the intricacies of joint operations. Few admirals of the period matched Keith's experience in operating in conjunction with British or allied land forces. While he generally registered success in his commands, he had several notable failures, including the British operation at Cádiz in 1800.

This study of Keith does not merely encompass his commands; available source material allows for the examination of his standing in British society.

Although Keith's father was a Scottish peer, the family faced financial distress and had limited connections. However, Keith, largely on his own, developed a series of important patrons. These bonds allowed him to secure a series of naval appointments that few in the period could match. Through trial and error, he came to understand the patronage system and to manipulate it to his advantage. In the end, he mixed self-interest, dedication, and ability to reflect a composite image of an ambitious, well-connected, and rich officer who, though never brilliant, generally proved steady, capable, and able to meet the challenges he faced.

This project is the culmination of work begun in May 1996. Little did I know then that the study of a single man would involve nearly a decade's work. Yet, I still find Keith a fascinating, complex, and difficult character who in many respects epitomized the British navy in the late eighteenth and early nineteenth centuries. In the process of researching and writing this book, I have received the assistance of numerous individuals and organizations.

I have visited many libraries and archives, where I have found people always willing to help. Although small, the library at Brewton-Parker College has proved yet again that a proverbial David can slay a Goliath. The director of the library, Ann C. Turner, may be proud of her staff. Particularly, I wish to thank Barry Bull for hours of assistance as a reference librarian; Ruth Stewart is amazing with interlibrary loan given the obscure books I order; and Michael Bonnard has cataloged more books for me than he wishes to admit. In addition, the librarians at Florida State University's Strozier Library were notably helpful, allowing me to make extensive use of the library's French Revolution and Napoleon Collection. Overseas, Daphne Knott, manuscripts archivist, National Maritime Museum, Greenwich, has provided permission to reproduce material found there.

Numerous people have assisted in this book's completion. Since my arrival at Brewton-Parker College in 2001, I have received considerable financial assistance from the school's Faculty Development Committee and the generous patronage of the school's president, David R. Smith, as well as the provost, T. Ronald Melton. At the University Press of Florida, the kind and helpful staff, particularly Meredith Morris-Babb, have made the construction of this book as painless as possible. Also, I would be remiss if I did not thank Gene A. Smith for inquiring about my plans for the dissertation and encouraging me to submit the manuscript to the Press. Among the historians I must thank for assistance, comments, or criticisms are James C. Bradford, Brian DeToy, William Henry Flayhart III, and David Syrett.

It is a pleasure for me to thank the faculty and staff of the history department at Florida State University both for their scholarly influence and for their aid in procuring financial assistance for my studies and research. Jonathan Grant and Paul G. Halpern in particular made a substantial difference. But by far the greatest thanks must go to Donald D. Horward. Without his direction, this project would still be a hazy dream. I will be forever grateful for his guidance at every step of the dissertation process. More broadly, the Institute on Napoleon and the French Revolution, founded by Dr. Horward, has proved an enduring influence in sustaining my interest in the period's history. This organization's value exceeds the sum of its members and patrons. Specifically, the Institute on several occasions provided essential monetary support through the generosity of such individuals as Margo deVeres and Ben Weider. Fellow members of the Institute including Hal Blanton and Karen Greene offered encouragment and commiseration while I cut my teeth as a historian.

The annual meetings of the Consortium on Revolutionary Europe, 1750–1850, have also been of great importance. At the 1997, 1998, and 1999 meetings, I presented papers on aspects of Keith's career. Although the papers do not appear verbatim in this book, I have reutilized some of the information, and I appreciate the Consortium's permission to do so.

On a personal level, I am especially grateful to my parents, Charles Larry and L. Suzanne McCranie. They have never ceased to provide encouragement and have always supported my decisions, even when they did not understand them. My sister, Sara McCranie, deserves special thanks for generating the maps used in the book. I also especially thank Lydia Farmer for the hours of often tedious secretarial work she put into the manuscript. To these and to the many others who aided in my research and writing, I am grateful; however, I alone am responsible for any mistakes.

Lastly, I must salute the forgotten men of the Royal Navy. Sailors and marines served by the thousand aboard Keith's ships. Although rarely mentioned, their sacrifice and attention to duty allowed Keith to achieve prominence, making him an excellent subject for a book.

Introduction

"A man of rank in society"

A breeze carried through the sails as the first rays of sunlight cut through the darkness on the morning of 4 May 1799. This followed a very long night. The officers and men had slept little and received no hot food. It was not a storm that had kept the men at their stations; rather, almost a day had elapsed since their commander had issued orders to clear for battle. With this, the sailors had stowed their hammocks, broken down the barriers that cordoned off the officers' quarters from the rest of the ship, and readied the guns for firing. The excitement had begun on the previous morning when two warships joined the British squadron off Cádiz after sighting a massive French battle fleet. The squadron commander, a vice admiral, then pondered his situation, testing his lifetime of experience. He was a tall man, imposing and dignified, "with the appearance of what he really was, a man of rank in society." Only his gray hair betrayed Lord Keith's fifty-three years. The daunting task before him offered the chance of glory and renown, yet the odds were set against him. A French fleet reportedly of thirty-one ships sailed toward his squadron of fifteen similar ships. However, this was only half the equation. His squadron's mission was to blockade the Spanish fleet in Cádiz. If the French and Spanish united, they would outnumber his squadron by nearly three to one. Even for the Royal Navy, the most experienced in the world, these were near impossible odds.[1]

On the morning of the fourth, the weather seemed almost perfect for a battle, with a light breeze and a clear sky. However, the glass was falling. This drop in barometric pressure signaled the approach of a storm, though it could be hours away. As the light rolled back the darkness, British lookouts peered through the morning mist and found their prey. "At dawn of day" they sighted "3 sail west, and shortly after 3 more." Soon seventeen unknown ships could be seen, and by 9:30 a.m. the number had risen to twenty-seven. Keith described them as "suspicious and of the line, going large with the wind." Private signals from the British squadron received no response;[2] the ships appeared to be the enemy, probably French. At 11:00 a.m. signals broke out on Keith's flagship directing his ships to form line of battle. By noon, fifteen miles separated the two fleets, and lookout ships maneuvered closer to gather intelligence. Perplexed, Keith watched as the unknown fleet maintained "the same wary distance." Early that afternoon "it came on to blow and rain hard." The chance of an engagement quickly faded and then disappeared as both fleets attempted to save their ships from being pounded to pieces on the storm-swept Spanish coast, which had become a dangerous lee shore.[3]

This was almost a great naval battle, and the word "almost" best sums up the career of George Keith Elphinstone, Viscount Keith. Although he earned distinctions and a fortune in prize money, he never participated in a major sea battle—the closest he came was that morning off Cádiz. Yet he commanded fleets for longer periods than any of his "more notable" contemporaries including Lord Horatio Nelson and the Earl of St. Vincent, the two admirals often considered the most important of the period.[4]

Between 1795 and 1815, Keith held four major independent commands: the Eastern Seas, 1795–96; the Mediterranean, 1799–1802; the North Sea, 1803–7; and the Channel, 1812–14, 1815. The sheer fact that he held four commands on five occasions necessarily influenced the implementation and, to a lesser degree, the crafting of British policies. This was especially true of Keith's commands in the East Indies and the Mediterranean, where he often had to operate on his own initiative without recourse to instructions from the Admiralty. Even in the North Sea and the Channel, much was at stake. By 1815, Keith had commanded Britain's two most important British fleets.[5] This leads to the main point of the book—Keith was much more important than the cursory treatments provided by most historians would suggest. Even though he never achieved a spectacular victory, he was extremely competent and steady. His success rested on his ability to administer extensive commands, cooperate with the army, and maintain a precarious control of the sea. However, he lacked the killer instinct of men such as Nelson, and for posterity this has diminished his standing among both historians and enthusiasts.

If Keith's career was almost great, and if he almost commanded the British fleet in a great naval battle, "almost" also describes the treatments of his career by historians. Only three biographies of Keith exist, and all are inadequate. The first was written in the early 1820s by James Meek, Keith's former secretary.[6] It was neither completed nor published. While the completed part provides a unique insight into Keith's life and motivations, the text abruptly ends in 1803. It is probably true that Keith financed and oversaw the writing, since Meek stopped working on the biography about the time of Keith's death. Today the handwritten text exists as part of the Keith Manuscripts at the National Maritime Museum in Greenwich. The second biography, by Alexander Allardyce, dates from 1882.[7] It contains no citations or bibliography, and it was written by a friend of the family. Moreover, it relies heavily on Meek's earlier work for the organization and source material. Overall, the book by Allardyce is neither scholarly nor objective. This contention is supported by John Knox Laughton, the author of Keith's entry in the *Dictionary of National Biography*, who describes Allardyce's book as "a clumsy, crude, and inaccurate compilation."[8] The final biography is inadequate for a different reason. Although the scholarship is sound and the argument objective, it is a mere chapter of a larger book on eighteenth-century British admirals.[9] The part about Keith encompasses less than twenty-five pages and only whets the appetite for more information about this important naval officer.

In addition to the biographies, several primary sources prominently feature Keith and provide insights into his attitudes and motivations. Admiral Sir John Markham's published papers contain more than one hundred private letters from Keith written during 1803 and 1804.[10] The Earl of Kerry, Keith's descendent, also published over sixty letters relating to the surrender of Napoleon in 1815.[11] Of greater importance, the Navy Records Society published a selection of Lord Keith's papers in three volumes containing some 1,200 documents.[12] The information in these volumes deals almost completely with Keith's naval campaigns, and there are few details on his personal life or on such important aspects of his service as patronage. However, these volumes are merely a fraction of the entire Keith collection, bequeathed in 1930 to the National Maritime Museum. It is the largest personal collection in the museum's archive, consisting of 168 bound volumes and 350 boxes of loose papers, totaling more than 100,000 documents. The shelving for the collection runs 124 feet.[13] Numerous other collections in the United Kingdom also contain information relating to Keith. The Admiralty Office Papers, deposited in the National Archives at Kew, Richmond-upon-Thames, is the largest of these. With such a wealth of information on a single person coupled with a career spanning more than half a century including Britain's most important wartime naval commands, a biography of George Keith Elphinstone, Lord Keith, fills an important void in the period's scholarship.

"My liking the sea very well"

Education and Advancement—His Early Naval Career (1746–82)

In August 1761 a young man of fifteen hailing from Stirlingshire, Scotland, met his cousin Charles Gascoigne in London. Gascoigne, several years older, soon realized to his consternation that his teenage cousin had no definite career possibilities and that, in fact, the young man's father was relying on some unnamed benefactor to advance his interests. The young man, whose full name was George Keith Elphinstone, had an ancestry with a long and proud heritage, but his family had fallen on difficult times. Debt and mismanagement had reduced his ancestors' estates so that they no longer brought in a revenue worthy of the Elphinstone name. Still, his father, Charles, clung to a lifestyle befitting his position as 10th Lord Elphinstone, a title he had inherited four years previously in 1757. To exacerbate the family's financial difficulties, Charles and his wife, Lady Clementina Fleming, had consistently demonstrated their fertility; Keith Elphinstone was one of fourteen children. While not all survived, four male children reached adulthood. The youngest of these, Keith, who entered the world on 7 January 1746, seemed an afterthought. His father had purchased commissions in the army for his two oldest sons. Although this represented a considerable investment, Charles Elphinstone wanted the prestige of an army commission for his heir. John, the oldest, stood ready to inherit the title, but the second oldest, Charles, had perished while sailing to join his unit at Gibraltar—he had been aboard the *Prince George* (90) which sank on 13 April 1758. William, the third oldest, eventually pursued employment with the English East India Company.[1]

Charles Gascoigne understood the Elphinstone family's financial circumstances and requested Lord Elphinstone's permission to secure employment for Keith. The naval service, in Gascoigne's opinion, offered several distinct advantages for one without financial backing. There was no purchase of a commission, as in the army, and Keith's education would be provided without cost to the family; he would even be paid for his service aboard a man-of-war. Communications proved slow, and Keith spent several months awaiting his father's permission as the days grew shorter and the season changed from summer to autumn. Finally, in early November 1761, Gascoigne received Lord Elphinstone's consent to act on Keith's behalf. In the eighteenth century, finding a patron, or a superior with the power and means of reward, was necessary to advance one's career. This held particularly true in the navy, and Gascoigne secured an audience with a family friend, Vice Admiral Francis Holburne, the port admiral at Portsmouth. On 5 November the admiral visited London and met Keith. Afterwards the teenager enthusiastically explained that Holburne "bid me to go to get everything ready and come to him and he would give me a letter to the Captain of his own ship at Portsmouth who would take care of me till he came to Portsmouth and then he would send me out in the first Frigate that went on a good cruize so I go on Saturday." Being assigned to a small ship, particularly a frigate, was important. It was generally believed that flagships and ships-of-the-line were poor places for those entering the navy, since it was only on small ships that one could master the art of seamanship. In joining the navy, Keith's resembled the experience of many of his contemporaries, particularly with regard to finding a patron; however, at almost sixteen, he was older than average.[2]

In Portsmouth, Holburne attempted to find a suitable appointment for young Elphinstone, and on 1 January 1762, Keith finally received orders to report to the *Gosport* (44) under Captain John Jervis. Although not a frigate, this small two-decked fifth rate proved an excellent choice. Jervis, in his mid-twenties, was a rising star in the navy. Thirty-five years hence, Jervis would be created an earl in recognition of his 1797 victory over the Spanish at Cape St. Vincent and would thereafter be known as the Earl of St. Vincent. Elphinstone would again serve his first captain in 1798 and 1799. However, this was years in the future, and Keith was not even a midshipman when he first met Jervis. On 7 January, Keith's birthday and merely a week after he first stepped aboard the *Gosport*, his new captain rated him a midshipman. This led Keith to write to his mother: "I am with a very good Captain who conterery to all custom Rated me midshipman which intitles me to pass for Lieutenant in three years where as it ought to be six." Although slightly mistaken in this comment, Keith should have officially entered the ship's books as a member of the lower deck. Several reasons could account for this departure from standard practice. First, records were easy to manipulate, especially for a captain. If a well-connected father was considering sending his son to sea, it was not uncommon to ask a friend who served as a naval captain to enter the boy on his ship's books while the boy remained at home. This would provide valuable "sea time" allowing for an immediate appointment to midshipman and reducing the requisite six years of service before the boy could take his lieutenant's exam. Another possibility involved Keith Elphinstone's comparatively advanced age. A midshipman could take his lieutenant's exam for the first time when he was nineteen, and becoming a lieutenant at a young age meant improved career opportunities.[3]

Although Elphinstone lacked experience, he compensated with enthusiasm and an eagerness to learn his new profession under the watchful eye of Captain Jervis. To his parents he wrote of "my liking the sea very well." During March 1762 the *Gosport* sailed off Rochefort with the British blockade squadron. And as Jervis spent much of this period escorting convoys, Elphinstone sailed to Halifax, Bermuda, and the Thirteen Colonies.[4] One tense moment occurred in May 1762 while the *Gosport* sailed as part of a three-ship squadron under the command of Commodore Sir Joshua Rowley escorting a 105-ship convoy to the American colonies. On the afternoon of the tenth, lookouts sighted three sail hull down on the horizon. For Elphinstone, the chance of action and adventure far outweighed any nervousness. The British captains positioned their ships between their convoy and the unknown ships. Night fell and, Elphinstone wrote, "We . . . lay a stern all night thinking they would come up with us in the night." The next morning the lookouts spotted the ships again, this time to leeward. "We made the signal to the Superbe [*Superb* (74)] of an enemy and she made ours to chace which we did." As Jervis closed, he saw that the unknown ships were bearing down on the convoy with a full press of sail "with French pendants flying." These ships consisted of two ships-of-the-line and a pair of frigates under the chevalier de Ternay transporting 1,500 soldiers for a raid on the British fisheries in Newfoundland. Jervis signaled the other escorts that they were French, and the outnumbered British formed line of battle. "[We] in great spirits cleared ship for engagement by this time they were in ½ mile of us," Elphinstone recounted. "We was resolved to fight." Even with their superior force, the French ships came about and withdrew. The British ships pursued the French for seven hours before they lost sight of their own convoy. Ternay failed in his endeavor, and the British convoy and its escorts arrived safely in the colonies.[5]

At the end of the Seven Years' War, the *Gosport*'s crew was paid off. This left Elphinstone unemployed. However, he found service aboard the *Juno*

(32) before being transferred into the *Lively* (20) for service in the Mediterranean under the command of Captain the Honourable Keith Stuart on 29 May 1763. On 20 November 1763, "in a hard Gale of wind" off Corsica, the *Lively* lost her masts and nearly foundered. Some six months later Elphinstone recounted the incident to his parents, stating that "in cutting away our main mast I had a strouke on my eye which cut it and threw me into a fever of which I was very bad for six weeks." Elphinstone acknowledged, "Captain Stuarts good behavior to me in that time has put me under great obligations." He ended the letter by asking for his parents to pay his bills, including £2 owed to the schoolmaster for teaching him navigation, "which I could not do the service without." Elphinstone served aboard the *Lively* until 21 February 1765, and then he transferred to the *Arcturus* (Tender) as a lieutenant's servant. Employment was difficult to find, and this was probably the only position available.[6]

Pressures from Keith's family also influenced his desire to remain on active service. In particular a granduncle, George Keith, 10th Earl Marischal, for whom George Keith Elphinstone was named, consistently acted as his great-nephew's benefactor. Although they rarely saw one another, significant correspondence occurred between and about the two. The earl had been exiled from Scotland for opposing the British government in the wake of the 1715 Jacobite Rebellion. Eventually Marischal settled in Prussia and became a confidant and courtier of Frederick the Great. He had a certain fondness for his great-nephew, affectionately referring to him as "little Ben," and he made it very clear that any employment was better "than that he remain idle at home."[7] Marischal particularly worried about his nephew's future. When he learned that Keith was planning to leave the navy to find employment with his brother William in the East India Company, Marischal pleaded, "It would have cast him into company not fit for one of his birth. Can not an Ensigncy be bought for him at a moderate price?" Although William had decided to pursue a career in the East India Company, Marischal wished for his namesake to remain in the more honorable service of his country.[8] Without opportunities in the navy and lacking funds for an army commission, Keith was forced to take employment as third mate in the East India Company ship that William commanded, the *Tryton*, sailing to India in 1767.[9]

Upon Keith's return to England in August 1768, he lost his position as the *Tryton*'s third mate. Marischal voiced his concern to William: "I am very sorry little Ben can not go with you, I hoped that those in the service once of the

Company were sure of being always employed . . . if he goes to Edinburgh to his mother, it will be idling away his time."[10] Instead of Scotland, Keith joined the *Emerald* (32) and served for nearly a year before receiving an offer to serve under Commodore Sir John Lindsay in the East Indies as a captain's servant, with the understanding that Keith would be appointed lieutenant at the first possible instance. Keith had the six years of service needed to be considered for lieutenant, but in the peacetime navy this promotion was difficult to attain. Unsure what to do, he went to see his uncle Marischal in Prussia. There the young man was presented to Frederick the Great. Moreover, Marischal approved of Lindsay's offer, and his nephew returned to Britain, arriving at Spithead barely in time to join the commodore aboard the *Stag* (32) on 28 September 1769.[11]

In early December the ship reached the Cape of Good Hope. It was standard practice in those days for ships operating in the East Indies to carry an extra lieutenant, since these officers often served on detached duty.[12] Lindsay planned to make Keith Elphinstone one of these additional lieutenants, so he ordered the young man to stand on 24 December 1769 before a committee consisting of three captains to test his competence. During the examination, Elphinstone established that he had six years, seven months, one week, and two days of experience aboard ships of the Royal Navy and a further one year, eight months, and one week with an East India Company ship. The committee approved of Elphinstone's abilities and concluded, "He can knot, splice, reef a Sail, keep a Reckoning of a ship's way by plain sailing and Mercator, observe by sun or star, find the Variation of the Compass, Shift his Tides, and is in every respect perfectly qualified to do the Duty of an able seaman and midshipman."[13]

Afterwards the newly passed lieutenant wrote his mother, "I have this day been made 3rd Lieutenant of the *Stag* and my commission is sent to England for confirmation of Admiralty which will perhaps require some interest."[14] At twenty-three, he showed both savvy and an understanding of the system. He had secured Lindsay's patronage to secure a lieutenancy. Then he had his family members use their connections to obtain the confirmation of his commission, all the while taking advantage of an Admiralty regulation that allowed commanders in chief on foreign stations to appoint officers to fill vacancies. However, Elphinstone's scheme contained an additional wrinkle, and he declared, "As soon as I hear of my commission being confirmed I will return to Europe."[15] Although string-pulling occurred, Elphinstone had the necessary qualifications to become a lieutenant. He had served for the requisite six years, and he had kept journals of his service.[16] Overall, he used patronage, and his career was enhanced, rapidly surmounting the promotion barriers endemic to a peacetime navy.

While in the East Indies—which to the Admiralty meant the Cape of Good Hope eastward including the Indian Ocean—awaiting confirmation of his commission, Elphinstone sailed to Muscat and the Persian Gulf working on a hydrographical survey of the coast. During this mission he became very ill with a digestive ailment and occasional fever, a condition that would be chronic for the remainder of his life. Described as his "East India complaints," the malady would assail him most often at sea and during periods of great stress.[17] Because of it, he obtained passage home on 12 October 1770, arriving in London on 22 March 1771. During this period he learned that the Admiralty had confirmed his appointment as lieutenant, effective 28 June 1770. Although the illness would recur, it did not preclude further service, and two months after his return to England he received orders to serve as second lieutenant of the *Trident* (64), the flagship of Admiral Sir Peter Denis's Mediterranean Fleet. This was an advantageous appointment, since close proximity to the admiral allowed young officers to demonstrate their competence on a daily basis. If vacancies in the fleet occurred, the lieutenants were often the recipients of the admiral's patronage, in accordance with custom and Admiralty regulations. On 18 September 1772, Elphinstone, then first lieutenant of the *Trident*, received a commission from Denis to serve as master and commander of the *Scorpion* (14). Until April 1774, Elphinstone plied the waters of the Mediterranean learning the art of command, successfully conducting routine patrols along the southern coast of France and the western coast of the Italian peninsula, and even to Algiers.[18]

Two years after assuming command of the *Scorpion*, Elphinstone received orders to carry Admiral Denis's dispatches to London.[19] Upon his return to England he remained unemployed, and on 10 November he unsuccessfully stood for Parliament for the county seat of Dunbartonshire, where his family had some interest. Although he tried to appeal the election's outcome, the Admiralty recalled him to service as a post captain on 11 May 1775.[20] Several factors may have contributed to this key promotion. His father was a peer, and his family had substantial influence in Stirlingshire and Dunbartonshire.[21] In addition, problems in the American colonies led the Admiralty to commission new ships, which needed capable captains. Elphinstone had

already proved his ability while commanding the *Scorpion*, and now he would
have a chance with a larger post ship. He received command of the *Romney*
(50), the flagship of Rear Admiral Robert Duff, commander of the Newfoundland Station. It was not unusual for a newly posted captain to serve
as a flag captain, because the admiral provided oversight. In addition, a post
captain's pay was based on his largest command, and post captains like Elphinstone often benefited from the practice of being appointed to a large ship
for a short period to qualify for a higher pay rate and then being transferred
to a smaller ship. After one voyage the Admiralty removed Elphinstone from
the *Romney* on 24 March 1776, and on the following day the captain received
command of the *Perseus* (20), a small, newly commissioned copper-bottomed
sixth rate.[22]

After several months of working up his new ship for active service, Elphinstone was ordered to escort a convoy of twenty victuallers and troopships to
New York City, where he was to join Vice Admiral Lord Richard Howe's
North America Squadron. The *Perseus* sailed from Spithead in late July, but
the task of controlling the convoy became an ordeal for the young captain as
the ships slowly traversed the Atlantic. Conflicts soon developed with the
masters of the merchant vessels. To Elphinstone's consternation, they proved
inattentive to his signals, and on 16 August he wrote in the *Perseus*'s log that
he "Rebuk'd the masters for their conduct." According to Elphinstone, several of the captains did little to disguise their hostility and would rather have
sailed alone. In addition, some of the victuallers were nearly hulks; Elphinstone, in disgust, described one as "unfit for any purpose except that of burning."[23]

On the night of 25 September the convoy scattered in the darkness. In
the early morning light the *Perseus*'s lookouts sighted an unknown vessel
among the dispersed ships. Elphinstone ordered his men to set a full press of
canvas, and the *Perseus* bore down on the interloper, which made to escape.
Hours after the chase had begun, Elphinstone ordered his men to fire the
bow chasers. The unknown vessel quickly struck her colors to the *Perseus*.
She proved to be the *Viper*, a sloop of war commissioned by the Continental Congress. Finally, on 14 October, the *Perseus* arrived in New York with
her much depleted convoy, having lost nine out of twenty transports during
the eleven-week passage. The majority of these ships were lost on the Grand
Banks of Newfoundland when the convoy encountered a storm and thick

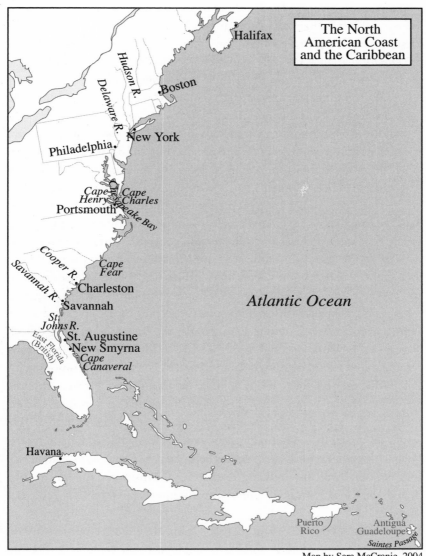

The North
American Coast
and the Caribbean

Halifax

Hudson R.

Delaware R.

Boston

Philadelphia

New York

Cape
Henry

Cape
Charles

Chesapeake Bay

Portsmouth

Cooper R.

Savannah R.

Cape
Fear

Charleston

Savannah

St.
Johns R.

East Florida
(British)

St. Augustine

New Smyrna

Cape
Canaveral

Atlantic Ocean

Havana

Puerto
Rico

Antigua

Guadeloupe

Saintes Passage

Map by Sara McCranie, 2004

Map 1. The North American Coast and the Caribbean.

fog which scattered the transports. After the weather cleared, the dispersed convoy became easy prey for American privateers. The excessive losses among the convoy were potentially damaging to Elphinstone's career. Particularly, Howe ordered an investigation of the circumstances surrounding the loss of the *Dinah*, victualler, since her master charged Elphinstone with negligence. Howe eventually determined that these accusations against the young captain were groundless and attributed the convoy's losses to the weather and to inattentiveness aboard the transports.[24]

Following Elphinstone's inauspicious debut, Howe found an alternative assignment for the young captain and ordered him to patrol the coast for colonial shipping. Elphinstone would be enforcing the American Prohibitory Act, which had been passed by Parliament on 22 December 1775 and which ordered the Royal Navy to prevent maritime trade from occurring in the colonies. Any ship defying this regulation was subject to seizure and confiscation as a prize of war. After capture, adjudication occurred in an Admiralty court to establish the legitimacy of the prize; then the ship and cargo were sold. Although the proceeds of the sale technically belonged to the Crown, tradition and various Orders in Council allowed for the distribution of this money to the officers and men involved in the capture. A post captain received three-eighths of the proceeds, and if serving under the command of a flag officer, the captain forfeited one-eighth of his share to his superior.[25] Elphinstone demonstrated a combination of luck and skill by consistently positioning his ship in the right place to capture colonial merchant ships. Eighteen months before he assumed command of the *Perseus*, his uncle Earl Marischal had expressed concern about Elphinstone's finances, writing, "Keith is poor."[26] He would no longer be so after taking numerous prizes while commanding the *Perseus*. Overall, Elphinstone's services between 1776 and 1779 provide ample evidence that the British inflicted heavy losses and disrupted American trade, though the Royal Navy never proved capable of sweeping the seas of colonial shipping.

Following several successful patrols, Elphinstone received orders in December 1776 to cruise off the southern colonies with the *Camilla* (20) before sailing to English Harbor, Antigua, where the two ships would refit and avoid the severe winter weather along the American coast. The voyage was uneventful until the two British warships arrived off the busy port city of Charleston. The *Camilla* and the *Perseus* pursued several colonial ships, which they drove "ashore on the Bar, where they were beat to pieces." Furthermore, they made prizes of four vessels and recaptured two British merchant ships.[27] Elphinstone also exchanged prisoners with the government in South Carolina. When the British former captives arrived aboard the *Perseus*, they claimed mistreatment by the Americans. The ship's purser became enraged and struck Lieutenant Joshua Barney, one of the remaining colonial prisoners. Barney struck the purser in return "& knocked him over one of the Quarter-deck guns & from thence down the after Hatchway." The two were taken to the captain's quarters, and the prisoner recorded that Elphinstone "ordered the purser to go down on his knees & beg my pardon . . . for the disgrace he had caused his majesty's service but this the purser absolutely refused."[28] The captain then placed the purser under arrest. This unusual incident sheds light on Elphinstone's character and his sense of honor, as he supported Barney, an American prisoner, against his own purser.

On arrival at English Harbor on 23 February 1777, Elphinstone was given temporary command of the *Pearl* (32), whose previous captain had died. Tropical diseases had thinned the crew, and the *Pearl*'s new captain received orders to press additional seamen to make up the deficiency in the ship's complement. Because of the winter storms along the Atlantic coast of America, Elphinstone did not return to the colonies until March, but in the next two months his ship captured ten colonial vessels.[29]

On 21 May, Elphinstone anchored the *Pearl* in the Delaware, and on the following day he reassumed command of the *Perseus*, which was anchored nearby. He immediately sailed on a new cruise. Between June and October 1777 the *Perseus* plied the southern American coast. Sometimes Elphinstone sailed alone, while at other times he acted as part of a small squadron including the *Daphne* (20), *Brune* (32), and *Galatea* (20). By late June, the British ships were neither healthy nor well manned. The *Perseus* suffered an outbreak of yellow fever and smallpox, with thirty-four crewmen ill as of 8 July.[30] A lack of supplies aggravated the situation; near the end of the month Elphinstone complained there was "at this time Scarce a Biskit in the Ship fit to eat."[31] Matters did not improve, and the men continued to face intolerable conditions. On 7 September, ten of the *Perseus*'s men stole the ship's cutter and sailed up the Chesapeake. When Elphinstone learned of the desertion, he ordered his ship to give chase, and at six in the morning the lookouts spotted the cutter along the western shore. The remaining boats pursued the cutter, but they returned empty-handed later that morning. This incident should not have been surprising. Many among the crew were pressed into service, and they were then expected to survive on unpalatable food in an unhealthy environment.[32]

In late October 1777 Elphinstone received orders to serve under Captain Robert Fanshawe of the *Carysfort* (28), patrolling the waters from the Carolinas south to Florida. The *Perseus*, accompanied by the *Lizard* (28), cruised off Charleston, and by early December, after six weeks at sea, these ships had accounted for eleven captures. However, both ships sailed shorthanded and could not spare prize crews to man their prizes, so all eleven were burnt and sunk. The morale aboard both ships certainly plummeted as valuable ships and cargoes went up in flames with no prize money to be shared. On Christmas 1777 lookouts on the *Carysfort* and the *Perseus* sighted two sail pressing to gain Charleston harbor. Frustrated by a lack of wind, Elphinstone ordered the men to man the sweeps, temporarily transforming the ship into a hybrid galley. After six and a half hours of grueling labor, the *Perseus* closed with and captured the *Marquis de Pezay*, a rich prize from Bordeaux laden with powder, arms, and dry goods.[33] Elphinstone then sailed to St. Augustine to revictual, but he was detained. Captain Fanshawe recounted the reason: "I found that an accident had necessarily detained the *Perseus* at St. Augustine. The victualler going into the harbour was cast on the bar and with difficulty got off; it was owing to the personal attendance of Captain Elphinstone with assistance from the *Perseus* that the vessels and stores were not entirely lost."[34]

In May 1778 Elphinstone returned to the Delaware, and on 3 June he received instructions to take his ship to sea with the *Otter* (14) and a naval victualling transport. The small squadron sailed five days later, and by early July they had arrived in the waters off the British province of East Florida, where Elphinstone had orders to assist Governor Patrick Tonyn and Brigadier General Augustin Prevost in the defense of the colony. The American military units in South Carolina and Georgia included approximately three thousand troops along with several naval vessels and posed a grave threat to East Florida, which remained loyal to the Crown.[35] The arrival of Elphinstone's squadron led Prevost to declare, "I think now that the 'Perseus' and 'Otter' are arrived to our assistance in guarding the coast [,] I may venture to assure your Excellency that we shall preserve the Province until reinforcements arrive."[36]

Elphinstone took charge of the naval defense of East Florida, which was made difficult by the many islands, inlets, and lagoons that formed a series of inland waterways. In addition to the *Otter*, the naval command included several row galleys guarding the entrance to the St. Johns River. During the months he remained on the coast, the American force was rendered inactive by disease and a general lack of commitment in the face of Elphinstone's naval squadron. However, in mid-August a storm caused extensive damage to the *Perseus*.[37] Before repairs were completed, reports arrived that a colonial privateer had conducted a slave raid at New Smyrna, south of St. Augustine at Mosquito Inlet. Elphinstone dispatched the *Otter* to intercept the privateer. While searching for the colonial vessel, the *Otter* attempted to weather a storm off Cape Canaveral on 24 and 25 August. At 7:00 a.m. on the twenty-fifth the storm, described by her commander as "a perfect hurricane," drove the *Otter* ashore and dashed her to pieces; however, the entire crew survived.[38] Prevost reported, "The loss is serious, as a naval force is absolutely necessary for the defence of this Province."[39] Elphinstone's squadron, now reduced to a single warship, had nearly exhausted its provisions, so he ordered the *Perseus* to sail for New York in late August. Although no serious attempt was made to capture St. Augustine during the summer of 1778, the appearance of British ships provided a strong deterrent, given the lack of roads in the region, which necessitated that any invasion force maintain control of the inland waterways and the offing.

The *Perseus* arrived at New York on 11 November, and Elphinstone grudgingly placed his ship under the command of Rear Admiral James Gambier, whom he considered incompetent. James Meek, who later served under Elphinstone's orders, described the relationship as acrimonious; however, this was not an unusual complaint, as another contemporary claimed, "I have seldom heard any seaman speak of Gambier as a good naval officer or one who deserved to be trusted with any important command."[40] The rear admiral ordered the *Perseus* to patrol the coast between Cape Canaveral and Cape Fear, but while sailing south she encountered a pair of gales. The violent weather sprung her masts, caused many of the shrouds and cables to part, and carried away most of her yards. The battered *Perseus* remained afloat but was little more than a hulk and needed a dockyard for repairs. Since it was late in the season, she could not return to New York for fear that she would be trapped by ice. Instead Elphinstone sailed to Antigua. He did not return to the American coast until 9 May 1779, when he assumed command of a small squadron operating out of Savannah. However, disease struck both the British and American camps, and no significant military operations ensued before Elphinstone sailed for New York in early August.[41]

When Elphinstone returned to New York, he found that the complexion of the war had changed from the previous year. France, with her powerful navy, had entered the war. Rather than American privateers and merchant shipping, the British North America Squadron had to contend with French warships and possibly a French fleet. On 23 November 1779, while on patrol near Hog Island off Virginia, the *Perseus*'s lookouts sighted a "strange ship." Elphinstone ordered his ship cleared for action and then ran down on the unknown vessel. As the *Perseus* closed, the unknown ship hoisted French colors and fired a broadside. Rather than engage his opponent in a distant cannonade, Elphinstone continued to close with the French ship until 1:30 p.m., when he brought his broadside to bear. During the exchange of volleys, a French cannonball wounded the *Perseus*'s foretopmast and another took away a yard, while numerous shots holed the sails and sliced through the rigging. Suddenly, fire threatened. Along the sides of the ship, the men of the *Perseus* would place their hammocks when they were not asleep, forming a netting that, it was thought, afforded protection in combat; however, during the engagement with the French ship some of the hammocks caught fire—a potential catastrophe aboard a wooden ship. After several tense minutes, Elphinstone's men brought the fire under control, but not before some twenty hammocks burned. On the other hand, the French gunfire only wounded a single British seaman, and at 2:15 p.m., after forty-five minutes of engagement, the French ship struck. She was *La Thérèse* (22), a privateer. Elphinstone claimed that "the Enemy was very much shattered" and had sustained one dead and two wounded.[42] This action furthered Elphinstone's career by demonstrating his capacity and ability to command in combat, in addition to furnishing the latest in a string of valuable prizes. Elphinstone had continued to capture American merchant ships, taking twenty-four in the thirteen months prior to the engagement. By this point in the war, his ships had accounted for nearly seventy prizes, and although most were smaller vessels involved in coastal trade, the combined total made Elphinstone a wealthy man.[43]

The French naval strength on the American coast increased during 1779 when a squadron under Vice Admiral Charles Hector comte d'Estaing arrived in the region. This paralyzed the British naval commander, Vice Admiral Marriot Arbuthnot, and his ships at New York, but as winter descended, intelligence arrived that the French had sailed from the coast. On 26 December, Arbuthnot's squadron of fourteen warships and ninety transports, with 8,700 soldiers embarked, sailed from New York amid heavy ice floes. The *Perseus* led the convoy, bound for Charleston, the center of the rebellion in the southern colonies. Almost unabated adverse weather made the job of escorting the transports a nightmare. On more than one occasion the *Perseus* assisted transports in distress. One had lost her main and mizzen masts. Worse still, on 17 January 1780 the transport *George* signaled distress. "Being found too leaky she was scuttled and sunk," but not before Elphinstone's men spent a grueling day in their boats transferring the transport's men and baggage. By the time the fleet reached the southern colonies, the weather had scattered many of the transports. Thus Arbuthnot regrouped his ships at Tybee Inlet at the mouth of the Savannah River in preparation for the attack on nearby Charleston.[44]

Arbuthnot and General Henry Clinton, the army commander, then formalized the plans for the amphibious landing. They soon asked Elphinstone's advice, since he had spent months sailing off the southern colonies earlier in the war and Arbuthnot had never even seen Charleston. The admiral proposed landing the troops at Stono Inlet. Elphinstone felt the landing should occur further south at North Edisto Inlet which, although nearly thirty miles from Charleston, provided a larger sheltered area for the transports. Arbuthnot agreed with Elphinstone's recommendation and placed him in command of the landing.[45] In early February the fleet arrived off North Edisto Inlet, and one of the officers with the invasion force reported, "Although the mouth of this harbor is so narrow that only two ships at a time can wind through the sandbars, Captain Elphinstone guided the entire fleet through safely."[46] The landing occurred on 11 February. During the next three months, Elphinstone remained constantly ashore. He acted as liaison to the army; he saw that the soldiers received adequate supplies from the ships; and he surveyed the inland waterways. In the week following the landing, the soldiers advanced toward Charleston, and by 18 February the British had gained control of James Island. From this vantage point Charleston was visible across the Ashley River.[47] Clinton needed additional naval assistance for the next phase of the operation, and Arbuthnot sent Elphinstone nearly five hundred officers and sailors to man both the flatboats and the longboats. However, the admiral

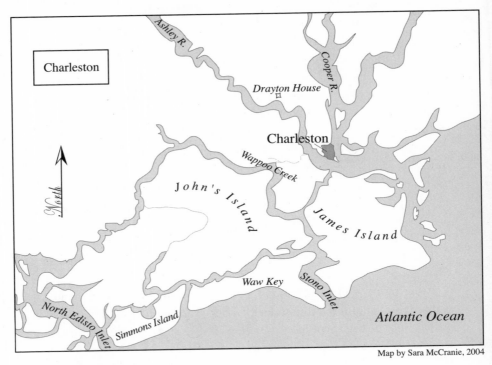

Map 2. Charleston.

insisted that these men were "always to be commanded by their own Officers and not by the Army."[48]

The decisive stage of the campaign began at 3:00 a.m. on 29 March. Sailors commanded by Elphinstone rowed seventy-five flatboats with muffled oars out of Wappoo Creek and headed up the Ashley River. When the seamen arrived at Drayton House, about thirteen miles above Charleston, they rowed to the southern bank of the river where, under the cover of morning fog, assault units consisting of the British combined grenadier and light infantry companies began boarding the flatboats. Once the men had embarked, armed row galleys opened fire on the colonial pickets covering the northern bank. Their cannons drove the Americans back, allowing an unopposed landing around 8:00 a.m. Elphinstone commanded the disembarkation points, overseeing the entire operation, and by 3:00 p.m. some five thousand troops, along with cavalry and artillery, had crossed the Ashley. The British quickly secured the bridgehead, cutting all land communication between Charleston and the interior. Formal siege operations began on 1 April with the construction of parallels and batteries.[49]

As the "sick season" neared and the threat of a French fleet arriving off Charleston increased, Arbuthnot became anxious to leave Charleston, and one of Elphinstone's subordinates relayed the crude message: "The Admiral . . . begs you will burn the Town as soon as possible and send 24 pound shot into the stomacks of the women to see how they will deliver them."[50] By mid-April the situation had become critical for the British. When Elphinstone requested supplies on 15 April, Arbuthnot filled the order but urged him to "be frugal for the ships are undone, having barely sufficient for our present demand."[51] To be sure, it could only be a matter of time before the Americans capitulated. Still, Major General Benjamin Lincoln, the colonial commander, held Charleston until 12 May.[52]

It has been claimed, "The capture of Charleston was the greatest defeat inflicted upon the Americans during the revolutionary war."[53] The naval officer who received the most laurels was not Arbuthnot, for he moved slowly and lacked vigor, even breaking his promises to Clinton.[54] Instead, Elphinstone received credit for the success. Clinton declared, "You are so much of a soldier that you know our wants and can best state them."[55] The general also maintained, "Nor must I neglect . . . my obligations to the officers and crews of the King's ships . . . , particularly to Captain Elphinstone and the officers and seamen acting under him on shore, whose professional abilities and indefatigable activity and zeal greatly facilitated the approaches of the troops to the object of our attack."[56]

Soon after the surrender, Elphinstone sailed for Britain. This was the first time he had been home in four years. Shortly after his arrival he relinquished command of the *Perseus*, and on 22 July 1780 he took charge of the *Warwick*, a fifty-gun fourth rate. While preparing his new ship for active service, Elphinstone briefly returned to Scotland and successfully stood for the Dunbartonshire seat in the Commons.[57] However, the Admiralty ordered the *Warwick* to sea before the new Parliament convened. Elphinstone's hasty departure was occasioned by the 20 December 1780 declaration of war by Britain on the United Provinces of the Netherlands. Elphinstone joined a small squadron consisting of the *Formidable* (98), *Active* (32), *Edgar* (60), and *Maidstone* (28) patrolling the northern approaches to the English Channel with orders to seize Dutch merchant vessels. After taking several Dutch prizes, the squadron broke up on 27 December. The *Warwick, Edgar,* and *Maidstone* under Elphinstone, the senior captain, continued to patrol the area. After taking several additional Dutch prizes, the *Warwick* parted company with her consorts. On the morning of 6 January 1781 her lookouts sighted one sail to the east and four to the northwest. Sighting so many ships in the constricted waters of the Channel was not unusual, but Elphinstone ordered his ship to bear down on the larger group. Soon it became apparent that one of the four was a large warship, and the *Warwick's* men "made the private signal which was not answered." Having ascertained that the warship was not English, Elphinstone had his men make "the signal with a gun for an Enemy of superior force." Around 1:00 p.m. Elphinstone ordered his men to hoist the English colors, while his opponent, another two-decked warship, hoisted the Dutch colors at 2:00 p.m. Rather than a brutal encounter, this action began with a degree of sport and honor. At 3:30 p.m. the Dutch ship opened the action with a nine-gun salute. Elphinstone then had his ship tack and come up beside his opponent, where he hailed the Dutch captain to surrender but was refused. The *Warwick* then opened fire. An hour later, at half past four, the Dutch captain struck his colors. The vessel Elphinstone had captured was the *Rotterdam* (50) with three hundred men, eleven days out of the Netherlands. Although the *Warwick* survived the engagement without human loss, the sails, masts, and rigging were "cut to pieces." Afterwards, in his report, Elphinstone praised his command: "The ship's company, notwithstanding their being young in the service, and reduced in number by the several Dutch vessels [prizes] we had manned and sent into port, conducted themselves with becoming activity and spirit." Elphinstone returned to Spithead the next day with his prize.[58]

In March, Elphinstone sailed from Cork to America escorting a convoy transporting three regiments of infantry and four hundred recruits. On their voyage the *Warwick* captured two small prizes, and the convoy arrived without incident at Charleston on 4 June. Elphinstone landed the three regiments of infantry and escorted the remainder of the convoy to Portsmouth, Virginia. Then Elphinstone proceeded to New York. Whereas the convoy had arrived healthy and intact, his own ship suffered considerably from fever. Twelve died before reaching New York, and upon arrival he immediately sent one hundred to the hospital, making his ship temporarily unfit for service. The fever ran its course, and in late August, Elphinstone received orders from

Rear Admiral Thomas Graves, who now commanded the North America Squadron, to escort a convoy bound for Quebec and then Halifax.[59]

While he was sailing to the north, a series of events occurred in which Elphinstone had no part but which would influence the *Warwick's* operations for the remainder of the war and would condemn the British to defeat in America. The Americans and their allies, the French, concentrated their land and naval forces at the Chesapeake, trapping the British army under General Lord Charles Cornwallis. Part of this operation involved Admiral François Joseph comte de Grasse, who sailed from the Leeward Islands with twenty-four ships-of-the-line, arriving at the Chesapeake on 30 August 1781. On the following day Graves sailed from New York with nineteen British ships-of-the-line. On 5 September he arrived off the Chesapeake and fought an indecisive engagement with de Grasse. However, this would prove a brilliant strategic victory for the French since Cornwallis remained trapped at Yorktown.[60]

Graves returned to New York and, now with General Clinton, began to prepare a stronger relief expedition. During this period the *Warwick* returned from Halifax. When Elphinstone learned of the situation, his mood soured, and to a friend in Scotland he complained, "Every circumstance which I mentioned before has turned out true. . . . We are going to attempt his [Cornwallis's] relief with twenty-seven ships and 6,000 men. The stake is deep—and the odds are against us. Victory gives peace. Defeat loses America."[61] After much delay, the fleet consisting of twenty-five ships-of-the-line, three fifty-gun ships, and eight frigates transporting 7,149 soldiers proceeded to sea on 19 October.[62]

On the twenty-fourth, the expedition encountered a schooner whose captain informed Graves that Cornwallis had surrendered. Still Graves continued with the mission, and on 27 October he ordered the *Warwick* and the *Nymphe* (36) to stand into the Chesapeake to reconnoiter the French. Elphinstone sailed between Capes Henry and Charles. With Cape Henry about three miles west by southwest, Elphinstone mounted the top and sighted forty-five sail. On the following day Graves again ordered these two ships into the bay. This time a French ship-of-the-line "was under sail to meet them," two other French ships sailed down the bay showing their colors, and one fired a gun before Elphinstone retired. Graves decided not to chance an engagement and returned to New York.[63]

The defeat at Yorktown signaled a change in British policy. The majority of Graves's fleet sailed for the West Indies soon after the Chesapeake operation, and Rear Admiral Robert Digby assumed command of the depleted North America Squadron, which still included the *Warwick*. After remaining in New York Harbor during the winter months, Elphinstone spent the spring and summer of 1782 off New York and Delaware. For six weeks beginning in late April he patrolled the mouth of the Delaware River to intercept the *South Carolina* (44), an American warship built in France. Supplies began to run low in early June, and Elphinstone sailed for New York. Two days later the American ship slipped into the Delaware with a valuable convoy from Havana.[64]

Following the debacle at Yorktown, Clinton resigned, and General Sir Guy Carleton replaced him in early 1782. On land, the British controlled four scattered positions: Charleston, Savannah, New York, and St. Augustine. With perhaps the exception of the last, Carleton had orders to slowly evacuate these bases. However, the British navy lacked transports to immediately remove the soldiers, loyalists, and military stores from each of these places.[65] Elphinstone understood the transport problem and was familiar with Savannah, Charleston, and St. Augustine, so Carleton sought his advice and recorded that Elphinstone thought it best to postpone evacuating St. Augustine "till after the evacuation of Savannah and Charleston, as it would require more tonnage than is at present at their command." This advice influenced Carleton; in July 1782, Savannah was evacuated, and the last British soldier left Charleston in December.[66]

Meanwhile, Elphinstone received command of a small squadron consisting of the *Warwick*, *Astrea* (32), and *Carysfort* (28) with orders to sail off the Chesapeake. Under cloudy skies with a light breeze, the squadron sighted four sail on 15 July 1782. As the British ships closed, the adversaries turned out to be a two-decked ship, a frigate, and two schooners. Elphinstone pursued. At 1:30 p.m. he ordered his ship cleared for action and soon signaled for his squadron to form a line of battle with the *Carysfort* in the van. At 3:00 p.m. Elphinstone watched as the enemy squadron began to disperse, with the schooners sailing to the northwest. An hour and fifteen minutes later the unknown frigate broke away from her larger consort to escape. At 5:00 p.m. the two-decked ship hoisted the French colors, and soon she engaged Elphinstone's squadron with her stern chasers. At 5:55 p.m., the *Warwick*'s log noted, the "Carysfort Hoisted her colours & began firing on the Enemy." However, night fell and the French ship escaped.[67]

These ships were likely part of de Grasse's French fleet which Admiral Rodney had defeated at the Battle of Saintes on 12 April. Following this battle, a detachment of the fleet sailed for Boston to avoid the hurricane season, and in early August they appeared off New York causing great anxiety, for the British did not know about Rodney's victory or French intentions. To oppose this fleet, the British at New York had only the *Warwick*, *Centurion* (50), *Lion* (64), and several frigates. Digby instructed Elphinstone, the senior captain, to undertake the unenviable assignment of defending the bar at the mouth of New York Harbor.[68] The admiral declared, "[I] am quite satisfied (as you are better acquainted with the bar than I can be or can make myself in a short time) that you will place everything better than I could direct."[69] The French squadron did not try to force a passage into New York; instead they sailed for Boston. During this period Elphinstone was not well, and he lamented, "The heat and cold after eight years has hurt me much, and brought on my East India complaints though not with violence." He asked Digby for leave to return to Britain, but the admiral denied his request.[70]

Although Elphinstone's health remained questionable, his luck improved, and he received command of a small squadron consisting of the *Lion* (64), *Vestal* (28), and *Bonetta* (14) with orders to cruise off the Delaware River. On 13 September the squadron captured the French armed merchant ship *La Sophie* (22). The following morning the *Lion*'s lookouts sighted two French frigates. Elphinstone's squadron immediately pursued. As the day passed, the chase brought the warships toward the shoal water at the mouth of the Delaware. Elphinstone had the *Vestal* and the *Bonetta*, his two smaller vessels, in the lead because they drew less water and could operate more effectively in the shallows. At 5:30 p.m. the British and the French anchored about six miles apart. In the morning Elphinstone sent a boat over to the French ships with one of his officers and a flag of truce. The French refused to surrender, but the ships remained at anchor until 3:30 p.m., when both the French and the British weighed. The possibility of an engagement appeared slight, given the French lead. However, the larger of the French ships, the *Aigle* (44), ran aground at 5:30 p.m. Her commander dismasted his ship and attempted to scuttle her. Meanwhile the *Aigle*'s boats carried Anne-César, chevalier de La Luzerne, the French minister to the United States, and General Antoine Charles du Houx, baron de Vioménil, ashore with the equivalent of £50,000 to pay the French army in America. When the British squadron arrived, the *Aigle* surrendered. However, there were still more than six hundred men aboard, along with a great deal of equipment and £4,000. The second frigate, the *Gloire* (36), escaped upriver. Afterwards the commander of the British North America Squadron declared, "Had it not been for Captain Elphinstone's great vigilance and knowledge of the Delaware, they would never have been able to have either taken or brought out the Aigle."[71]

Even though there was talk of commissioning the *Aigle* in the British navy with Elphinstone as her commander, he received permission from Digby to return to England. After an uneventful voyage, he arrived home at the end of November 1782.[72] Elphinstone had commanded the *Warwick* for more than two years, mostly with the North America Squadron. Although he captured fewer prizes during these years, this was to be expected, since fourth rates were neither as fast nor used in the same manner as the smaller sixth rates such as the *Perseus*. Elphinstone had still captured two large ships, the *Rotterdam* and the *Aigle*, though his captain of marines wrote that next time "I hope to be more fortunate than in the *Warwick*."[73]

The British defeat in America cannot be ascribed to Elphinstone, for his role was small. Rather, his service illustrated at the ship level many of the problems that Britain faced in fighting for America. It became obvious that American merchant shipping could never be swept from the seas, even after tremendous losses. With some exceptions, the army and navy had not cooperated effectively, and Elphinstone saw the effects of this. The question remained in 1782: Would he recognize the mistakes made by senior British officers in both services and better deal with the rigors of joint command if he should be faced with the same situation in the next war? Another concern lingered with Elphinstone: The British navy had failed to gain command of the sea, never destroying the French or even the American naval forces. Personally, Elphinstone had demonstrated skill and dedication as a naval officer, learning the art of command, and by the end of the war he had become a senior post captain. Now, in his mid-thirties, he had nearly twenty years of almost continuous service and had made a small fortune in prize money. After returning to Britain, he was prepared to sit in Parliament, collect his half pay, and live the life of a country gentleman.

"If I were well it would be a wonder"

Personal and Career Prospects (1774–94)

A successful naval career entailed more than professional competence; it demanded political savvy, wealth, and, most important, contacts. Beginning in 1774 when Keith Elphinstone first stood for Parliament, he began a lifelong process of diversifying his career. Although it took years to develop connections, he eventually became involved in a wide range of activities from naval service to politics to winning the favor of several members of the royal family. Even so, the development of those friendships, alliances, and associations included several glaring miscalculations along with the occasional, and often unexpected, success.

In 1774, before Elphinstone sailed to war for the first time, his family decided to contest the House of Commons seat for Dunbartonshire during the General Election. The incumbent, Sir Archibald Edmonstone, had the powerful support of John Campbell of Mamore, the Duke of Argyll, who dominated politics in western Scotland; however, several of the forty eligible voters in the county contended that Edmonstone had failed to represent their interests in Parliament. The Elphinstone family, with the backing of Sir Lawrence Dundas, another major figure in Scottish politics, decided to unseat the incumbent.[1] Although Keith's older brother William was chosen to contest the seat, he declined. Lord Elphinstone then approached Keith, who responded, "I think it would be a pitty to lose so great an interest in the county, and am of opinion my brother [William] should be declared candidate whose natural right it is, but should he for any reason decline, I shall be very ready to attend."[2] Although Keith took leave from the naval service to be present during the election, at least one member of Parliament believed that Edmonstone would easily win.[3] Keith also predicted defeat when he commented, "This is a very delicate affair to manage I mean to oppose a strong party without almost a certainty of success." Showing both youth and brashness, he ended with a challenge—"bring on contempt."[4] Unsurprisingly, he captured only 14 of 40 votes. Keith Elphinstone appealed to Parliament, contending that Edmonstone should not sit in the Commons because he received some of the proceeds from the Office of the Receiver General of the Customs in Scotland, held in the name of another person. Parliament admitted the appeal, but before the matter reached a vote, the Admiralty on 11 May 1775 appointed Elphinstone post captain in command of the *Romney* (50). Even as Elphinstone reported for duty, his supporters failed to receive an extension from Parliament and the appeal failed.[5]

Undeterred, his family and their allies prepared for the next election by crafting a new political alignment in Dunbartonshire. They acquired the support of the Marquess of Graham, who controlled the Lennox estates in the area. Graham attempted to limit the Duke of Argyll's influence by creating thirty new freeholders. Given the formidable opposition, Argyll withdrew Edmonstone and supported Lord Frederick Campbell, since familial connections made him a more powerful contender. Because the new freeholders could not vote until a year and a day after they were placed on the voting registry, the county sheriff, an Argyll supporter, scheduled the election on the day before the freeholders became qualified to vote. To gain time and thus their voters' eligibility, the Elphinstone faction began a heated debate lasting until four or five o'clock the following morning. The county sheriff maintained that only those eligible at the start of the polling could vote, and Campbell won by a tally of 27 to 19 votes. The Elphinstones again appealed the outcome to the House of Commons. With the election results in doubt, Captain Elphinstone received orders from the Admiralty to proceed to sea in the *Warwick* (50). For unknown reasons, Campbell did not seriously contest the appeal, and on 14 February 1781 a select committee of the Commons declared Elphinstone the winner.[6]

For the next two years Elphinstone remained on active duty and could not take his seat in Parliament; however, he maintained correspondence with friends in Britain and began to believe, from firsthand experience, that the American War was lost. He lamented after the failure at the Chesapeake and commented to his sister, "We make but a bad hand of war. . . . I wish for peace."[7] With these feelings, he increasingly identified with those who opposed George III and sought to end the war. Although this was not a party in the modern sense of the word, it was one of two major factions in Parliament; the other quasi-party supported the Crown and the royal prerogative. Family connections also proved important, since William Adam, a prominent member of the Opposition, had married Keith's sister Eleonora in 1777.[8] Personal experiences and familial alliances rather than a naval officer's loyalty to the Crown colored Elphinstone's decision. This provoked the ire of George III, as became apparent when a vacancy opened for command of His Majesty's yacht. Elphinstone's name was presented. One of the king's supporters replied, "Captain Elphinston . . . has lately taken a part very opposite both Your Majesty's Government and to the Sense of his own Profession on the subject of the Peace." The king accordingly refused to entertain the idea of his appointment.[9]

While Elphinstone posed a minor inconvenience for the king, the Opposition proved more troublesome. In an attempt to limit their power, George III in December 1783 chose William Pitt the Younger to head the government, and the following year the king dissolved Parliament. The resulting election was the most bitterly contested of the century. In Dunbartonshire, Keith Elphinstone's brother John, now 11th Lord Elphinstone, managed the election with the assistance of William Adam. Chances of reelection appeared slim for Keith, since he had alienated the Marquess of Graham by supporting the Opposition even though it was Graham's assistance that had allowed him to carry the 1780 election. It appeared that he would "certainly be turned out and a friend [of Pitt] brought in," but at the last moment Lord Elphinstone and Graham brokered a deal. Keith Elphinstone would be elected on the condition that he not contest Dunbartonshire in the following election.[10] Thus he remained in Parliament until the election of 1790, but he was hardly an active member.

Although Elphinstone remained almost a nonentity in Parliament, destined to lose his seat at the next general election, he developed connections with several members of the royal family. The first step came accidentally during the American Revolutionary War when Prince William, the third son of King George III, served for several months as a midshipman aboard the *Warwick*. William grew to respect and appreciate Elphinstone. To be sure, the presence of royalty caused the captain considerable grief; the commander of the ship's marines recorded that the prince was "a very fine youth" but he probably would never sail in Elphinstone's ship again "as he got a Fall a Fortnight ago and put his right Shoulder out, but is recovering very fast."[11] Still, Elphinstone developed a relationship with William based on respect rather than deference, and this began a lifelong connection between the captain and the royal family.

Through William, Elphinstone probably became acquainted with the heir to the throne, George, Prince of Wales. In late 1782 Elphinstone provided him with accounts of William's experiences, and William likely wrote to his brother about service aboard the *Warwick*.[12] Elphinstone's association with the Opposition after the war mirrored the feelings of the Prince of Wales. In addition, he and many of Elphinstone's friends frequented Brooks' Club, where they could talk, dine, and participate in high-stakes gaming. The prince liked to gamble, as did William Adam, and both suffered financial difficulties because of this predilection. However, Elphinstone avoided serious losses either through luck at the tables or through a decision not to partake in these pleasures. At Brooks' his relationship with the Prince of Wales likely blossomed, and Elphinstone was appointed his Scottish Secretary in June 1783.[13]

While he developed a lifelong friendship with the Prince of Wales, Elphinstone did not forget Prince William and recognized that "if he continues to be as attentive to this profession [the navy] as he is at present there will not be a better officer in the Universe."[14] William in turn trusted Elphinstone, who during the 1780s became his advisor and troubleshooter. In late 1785 and early 1786 the prince, while still in the navy, became a regular visitor at Commissioner Henry Martin's house in Plymouth, where he fell in love with Martin's daughter and decided he should marry her. This was of course impossible; it was totally inappropriate for a one of royal rank to become involved with a commoner. But the prince, a ladies' man, was smitten, describing her as "an unfortunate and virtuous girl." The king and queen instructed Elphinstone to deal with the problem before it became public. With orders to separate the two lovers, he persuaded the prince to travel to London for his sister's birthday and in the process took the blame of allowing William to go absent without leave from his naval appointment. Elphinstone later claimed the king "was quite pleased with my taking the blame of bringing Prince William up [to London] under the pretence of seeing his sister and staying to the birthday."[15]

William also turned to his former captain in a professional matter after assuming command of the *Pegasus* (28). In February 1787 Prince William demanded the court-martial of Lieutenant Isaac Schomberg for disrespect. In a letter to his brother the Prince of Wales he explained, "I have to request the utmost secrecy on your side in this business, as it is of consequence to the

Naval service in general. . . . Elphinstone you may communicate the matter to. . . . Do not shew this to any other officer but him." William ended by asking his brother to solicit Elphinstone's professional opinion. His former commander promptly responded, "H.R.H. [His Royal Highness] will in time be convinced that he who has charge and command over many must at times give offence to some." Elphinstone advised against a court-martial for two reasons. First, they "are at all times disagreeable," and second, it would be humiliating if the defendants were acquitted or lightly punished.[16] William dealt with the incident quietly; Schomberg was removed from the *Pegasus* and the incident was largely forgotten.[17] On the other hand, Prince William's trust in his former commander grew.

When a new problem arose, he again turned to Elphinstone. George III had given an annual allowance of £3,000 to William, whose spending habits far exceeded that sum. The young man needed someone in Britain who understood the financial obligations of a captain of royal rank and who could act as his advocate in securing a larger allowance. He wrote Elphinstone, "At present I must trouble you with a request which will meet every obstacle from the King, and will require all your art to first enter upon. . . . it is to represent to his Majesty that my allowance is really too small."[18] Elphinstone sympathized with William's plight, declaring, "Upon the whole wretched system that has been persued all along with regard to [the] Prince is astonishing! That he to whom the nation looks up to in his line should be suffered to tumble up and down the sea from station to station upon three thous^d pounds a year without any establishment, or even a person of rank and experience about him with whom he might advise or communicate his sentiments to when at a lose, it is really surprising at his time of life that his conduct has been so well as it is."[19] Since the prince had no conception of the exact amount of his debt, Elphinstone tried to ascertain the state of the young man's finances. He then asked for a larger allowance, citing unavoidable entertainment expenses on account of William being royalty. A rejection immediately arrived in the form of a "stiff letter,"[20] but Prince William nevertheless continued to depend on Elphinstone.

In late 1788, George III suffered a bout of insanity. The Opposition, including Elphinstone, used this as a grounds to support the Prince of Wales in his bid to become regent for the ailing ruler. This event, known as the Regency Crisis of 1788–89, resulted in a new and bitter dispute between Pitt and the Opposition. During the crisis Elphinstone became an active member in Parliament, voting on several bills. In each instance he voted against Pitt and for the heir. While he supported the Opposition, the best explanation for his voting record was his loyalty to the Prince of Wales, but he was careful to voice his displeasure quietly, since the majority of the Commons supported Pitt in the regency question.[21] When George III recovered and learned of Elphinstone's actions, it upset the king. This displeasure surfaced when Prince William, now the Duke of Clarence and of St. Andrews, named Elphinstone to his permanent household as controller and treasurer. George III contended that he had supported the Opposition against the royal prerogative, and this could not be tolerated. The Duke of Clarence successfully defended his selection, claiming that Elphinstone "for these four last years, without profit or emolument, which I had indeed no means of bestowing, faithfully and diligently filled a similar situation to that to which I now propose to appoint him."[22]

While Elphinstone's relationship with the Duke of Clarence and the Prince of Wales matured, the forty-one-year-old officer sought companionship in marriage. For someone seen as a perpetual bachelor, this startled his friends and caused the Duke of Clarence to declare, "I received a letter from Elphinstone in Scotland who says he is by this time a Benedict. Who would have thought it?"[23] Although it surprised his friends, marriage at such an age was not unusual; a large proportion of eligible men either remained bachelors or married late. This was especially true of those in the services. Elphinstone married Jane Mercer, coheiress of William Mercer of Aldie, on 10 April 1787. Jane was also in line of succession to the barony of Nairne, which had been under attainder since the 1715 Rising. Heiresses often married younger sons of peers, so any estates the bride brought to the marriage remained distinct and would not be amalgamated into the traditional estates of the husband's family.[24]

The marriage contract allows some insight into Elphinstone's financial status. He agreed to provide "a jointure to the wife of £500 a year to be payable from lands to be purchased." Until this occurred, Elphinstone supplied Jane's trustees with a bond of £10,000. Furthermore, he agreed to acquire £16,000 or the equivalent security to his wife and any children in the event of his death. This was "all the wife and children can claim." In return Elphinstone received a £2,000 portion by the contract. This was a small portion in relation to the size of the jointure because there was great competition to obtain a favorable marriage with an heiress. The entailed estates of Aldie would pass through his wife and then to any children resulting from the marriage.[25]

A little more than a year after their wedding, Jane gave birth on 12 June 1788 to their first and only child, Margaret Mercer Elphinstone. However, all was not well in the young family. With his daughter less than six months old, the new father became deathly ill. The Duke of Clarence told his brother, "I received a letter from Elphinstone which has hurt me much. He is in a dangerous way and I am afraid we shall loose him. As he, poor fellow, is unable to write . . ." Elphinstone's illness involved serious irregularities in the functioning of his stomach and bowels and was a continuation of the chronic health complaint contracted years before in the East Indies.[26]

Even in poor health, Elphinstone decided to seek reelection to Parliament in 1790, but he had to look outside Dunbartonshire, where he had agreed not to contest the seat. Instead he became interested in the Glasgow burghs. In this he represented part of a larger trend wherein the Opposition became better organized to more effectively contest parliamentary seats. Elphinstone's brother-in-law Adam was at the forefront of this movement, managing election funds, and he promised to support Elphinstone if money was available.[27]

Elphinstone found that Scottish burgh elections were more corrupt and complex than county elections, since they occurred in the council of each burgh, which then cast a single vote in the final district poll. Because the Glasgow district had only four burghs, a tie would be broken by the "returning burgh," which in the general election of July 1790 was Rutherglen. Two other burghs, Dunbarton and Glasgow, were controlled by those who backed the Crown. Opposition supporters believed that Elphinstone could capture Rutherglen and the fourth burgh, Renfrew, and thus win the election.[28] Adam and Elphinstone looked to John Morthland, a leading barrister, for support. He was an ardent member of the Opposition more adept at cursing Pitt with such tirades as "O damn him! damn him damn him! damn him" than effectively securing votes. Still, Morthland was the Opposition's best connection in the burghs, and he explained that the Rutherglen Council had voted 12 to 6 to support the Prince of Wales in the Regency Crisis. While this indicated strong Opposition leanings, Elphinstone received warnings of the council's fickleness. Morthland held higher hopes for Renfrew, since "our friend" Archibald Speirs of Elderslie was powerful enough to decide the vote in that council.[29]

With the election nearing, Elphinstone decided to travel from London to Scotland in December 1789 even though he had yet to recover from his East India complaints. The journey proved miserable, and on the eleventh he declared, "We are a sad set." He lamented, "Jane continues to suffer prodigiously and incessantly with pain and vomiting. Margret is getting eye-teeth and is a very bad travelling companion indeed. . . . If I were well it would be a wonder."[30] The day after he posted this letter, Jane died. His family and friends mourned her death and worried about the widower. A friend wrote Adam "to enquire after poor Keith Elphinstone, whom I really pity beyond Measure, & confess that in his present very Weak state, I dread the Worst of Consequences."[31] The combination of ill health, mourning, and a lack of support in the Glasgow burghs caused Elphinstone to withdraw his candidacy prior to the 1790 election.

His illness lingered for a year, keeping him out of the public eye. In late 1790 he traveled to London, met with the Prince of Wales, and then sailed for the Mediterranean in hopes that the warmer climate would improve his health. He arrived at Gibraltar in January and then proceeded up the Mediterranean.[32] Listlessly he reported "not much recovered by this fine climate but not less."[33] However, he became stronger soon after arrival at Nice, where he decided to stay. By early March he wrote, "My bowels are rather better," and he even celebrated with the local inhabitants during the Carnival season. The parties and festivals drained him, and he commented, "I hope to get some sleep when Lent begins." In early April he reported, "I had an attack of wind last night and passed a bad one"; still, he went on, "upon the whole I have not a tenth part of the complaint I had."[34]

During his stay in Nice, the French Revolution concerned Elphinstone because of its proximity and its increasing radicalism. Still, he dismissed the Revolution in a letter as "nothing to interest you." Cynically he declared, "We deal on the great scale—French Revolutions, invasions from all quarters, war with Spain, Naples and the Emperor, England and Russia etc. etc. I am sick of their nonsense."[35] Elphinstone departed Nice on 6 April and, despite the Revolution, returned to England overland. The jolting of the carriage made the trip uncomfortable. To avoid further sickness, Elphinstone claimed, "on the road I dare not eat." He traveled through Lyons and Paris during May, eventually returning to England in mid-1791.[36]

Elphinstone soon realized that the Revolution was more than mere "nonsense." In England, both popular and government opinion turned against

France by late 1792 as the upheaval became more radical and violent. The British government on 26 November quietly ordered the commissioning of warships. By mid-December, naval vessels were at sea "observing" French-controlled ports, while diplomatic negotiations between the two countries yielded nothing and tensions escalated following the execution of Louis XVI. On 1 February 1793, France declared war on Britain. This ended speculation, and most Britons firmly sided with George III and his government under Pitt.[37]

While Elphinstone had previously identified with the Opposition rather than Pitt's government, this had not prevented the Admiralty from ordering him to take command of the *Robust* (74) on 29 January. His appointment should not be seen as surprising: he was a skilled and experienced post captain, and men of his ability were in short supply. Elphinstone immediately made arrangements for his sister Mary to care for his daughter, but preparing the *Robust* for active duty was a slow process. His ship was still only half manned in March when he wrote that he had "sent indignantly to the Adm[iralt]y" but still need 250 men. In mid-April he received orders to join the Mediterranean Fleet of Vice Admiral Samuel Lord Hood. Manpower problems persisted, and he was directed to replace his marines with a detachment of soldiers from the 30th Regiment. Elphinstone was not happy and described them as "wretched."[38]

Finally on 23 May the *Robust* sailed from Spithead with the nucleus of Hood's fleet. They arrived at Gibraltar in early June with the solstice near and the sun-drenched days intensely hot. Elphinstone left his wig off and put his long hair into "a fine tail tied upon occasions." To his sister, the captain described his men as "dirty and indolent" and claimed, "I make them bathe every day and do so too, but it is like bathing in the kail pot the water is so warm." This was unusual in the naval service, and in the absence of freshwater, these baths were in saltwater. Still, the rigors of the service proved difficult for the forty-seven-year-old captain, who reported, "Stomach some days well others ill."[39]

Once in the Mediterranean, the *Robust* maneuvered as part of Hood's fleet, and when the sailing order of battle was created, Elphinstone's was the lead ship. Although this was a mark of honor due to his seniority, it was also a curse when practicing for a fleet engagement, since it involved sailing in a line of battle. Wherever his lead ship steered, the rest of the fleet followed. This required perfect adherence to Hood's orders, and Elphinstone complained of the smallness of the signal flags, given the distance between the *Robust* and the relay frigate.[40]

On 10 June, Hood ordered Elphinstone to take six ships-of-the-line to water at Cádiz. Ashore, the captain related to his sister, he was "tormented with Spanish civility and heat. I was at a bull feast last night, a grand amphitheatre but the most truly barbarous amusement I ever saw. Ten bulls, three horses killed; ten men fell, three of whom seemed much hurt, one gored in the thigh." With Elphinstone was Captain Horatio Nelson of the *Agamemnon* (64), who concurred: "we English had certainly to regret the want of humanity in the Dons and Donnas. . . . Had they [the bullfighters] been killed it would have been quite complete. . . . The dead mangled horses with their entrails tore out, the bulls covered with blood, was too much." Hood approved of Elphinstone's conduct at Cádiz, and in August he ordered him to cruise off Toulon with four ships-of-the-line.[41]

Upon Hood's return, a series of extraordinary events occurred that would influence British operations and directly involve Elphinstone until late December 1793. Toulon and Marseilles had revolted against the French National Convention in July as part of a reaction against its radical policies. The Convention reacted swiftly, sending an army to crush the rebellion. Delegations from Marseilles and Toulon petitioned Hood for assistance, but negotiations were so slow that Marseilles fell to Republican forces before an agreement was reached. At Toulon, on the other hand, the commanders of the French fleet and the leaders in the town reluctantly agreed to let the British enter their harbor and assist in the defense of their city.[42]

At 9:00 a.m. on 28 August the *Robust* and five other warships stood into the outer roadstead at Toulon. Aboard these ships were all the soldiers and marines in the fleet along with additional sailors to man the harbor batteries. Elphinstone oversaw the landing operation, and the British quickly took control of the city's defenses. The following day the remainder of the ships anchored in the outer road along with a Spanish fleet consisting of seventeen ships-of-the-line and a frigate.[43] The seizure of Toulon was a coup for Britain and its allies, because the entire French Mediterranean fleet was now at their mercy. The major problem was the lack of soldiers and marines aboard Hood's ships—and few regiments were forthcoming from Britain. In addition, assistance from her allies, including Spain, proved suspect, which led Elphinstone to lament, "We have plenty of allies but no one friend."[44]

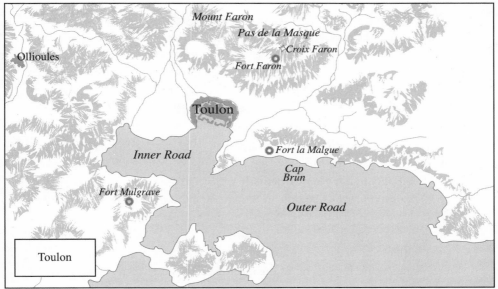

Map by Sara McCranie, 2004

Map 3. Toulon.

Hood appointed Elphinstone governor of Toulon, and several days later on 30 August a patrol reported that approximately 600 Republican soldiers and ten guns had arrived at the town of Ollioules, on a main road about three miles from Toulon. Elphinstone immediately abandoned his lunch, gathered 300 British and an equal number of Spaniards, and marched toward Ollioules. After securing his flanks, he went forward with an aide-de-camp to make a reconnaissance of the French position. He found 200 Republican soldiers supported by a pair of guns fortifying the town, which was located in a ravine. On the hill opposite the ravine were the ruins of a castle where the French had placed two more guns. Nearby they had deployed more of their infantry behind the walls of a vineyard. After the reconnaissance it was 6:30 p.m., and Elphinstone concluded that he had to either advance or withdraw to Toulon. He attacked. The detachments on each flank opened fire while the main force arrived undetected within two hundred yards of Ollioules. Elphinstone ordered these men to advance in column. His troops rushed the town, captured the guns, and advanced up the hill, taking two colors and many prisoners. The French retreated. Losses had been light: one British officer was killed and thirteen soldiers wounded, while the Spanish contingent suffered three killed and three wounded.[45] At first Hood "thought Elphinstone had rather acted rashly," but after receiving news of the victory, he approved of the action, since Ollioules was one of the few gateways between Toulon and the interior. On the day after the engagement, Hood appointed Rear Admiral Samuel Granston Goodall governor of Toulon. Although Elphinstone had shown himself capable, he had taken too many risks at Ollioules, and Hood wanted a more senior officer in command.[46]

Toulon proved difficult to defend. The city was located on a narrow coastal plain dominated by hills, the highest being the 1,700-foot Mount Faron. The western defenses were particularly weak, and after the arrival of a young artillery captain named Napoleon Bonaparte in mid-September, the French applied pressure to this area. With Goodall's appointment as governor of Toulon, Elphinstone received command of the city's eastern defenses, centered on Fort la Malgue. September passed quickly, but small arms were in short supply, and by the end of the month Elphinstone acknowledged, "We are still without success and nearly in the same state we were, excepting the enemy are closer on all sides and cannonading is without intermission."[47]

Elphinstone's next challenge occurred on the night of 1 October. General Jean Lapoype, the commander of the eastern wing of the French army, ordered his men to storm the allied positions on Mount Faron. In the darkness, Lapoype's troops seized the hilltop. Elphinstone considered this position "of such consequence as the possession of Toulon itself." From Fort la Malgue he described the allied defense: "I saw our pickets driven by great force towards a strong redoubt [Croix de Faron] but guess to my horror on observing this redoubt formerly held by Spaniards, empty, almost naked."[48] The British commanders reacted swiftly. Elphinstone marched his available soldiers to Fort Faron. General Henry Phipps, Lord Mulgrave, then the governor of Toulon, led his reserves in a counterattack and forced the French to withdraw to the Croix de Faron redoubt on the highest and easternmost crest. For the last assault, Mulgrave attacked with two columns directly approaching the redoubt, and a third column under Elphinstone advanced out of Fort Faron and maneuvered deep into the French left flank.[49] One observer, Thomas Graham, claimed, "The success of this attack was no doubt much owing to Elphinstone's attack, originally intended as a diversion only; but . . . he left only 30 men in the fort, and went out with 460; of these the Spaniards and French [Royalists] hardly ever came into action, but about 160 of the 30th and 69th [British] regiments behaved with uncommon steadiness, climbing up the face of the excessive rugged and steep hill . . . without returning a shot till near the top."[50] In this action Elphinstone was too weak to lead the attack in person, having been feverish and confined to bed for the previous four days. Instead he directed the assault from the rear. Graham acknowledged that this attack never could have succeeded had the other two attacking columns not occupied the attention of the French frontline.[51] With considerable loss, the remnants of the Lapoype's force withdrew.

After this, Elphinstone again settled into the drudgery of garrison command. He understood that the defenses were weak and claimed, "We are composed of too many nations to be strong." He concluded, "I can only tell you I am well for once but very thin and wasted with fatigue." Hoping to be replaced, he requested to return to the *Robust*. However, Elphinstone lamented, "The General said he could not let me go because he could not do without me and had no officer to put in my place if he could dispense with my services."[52] He was both worried and upset. His appointment as governor of Fort la Malgue had not come from the British government but had instead been made on the spot. Eventually this led Hood to discharge Elphinstone from the *Robust*, predated 28 August, so he could promote a master and commander to be the acting post captain of Elphinstone's former ship. The admiral had the power to fill vacancies, but he manipulated the system using his patronage to advance one of his protégés. Although Hood appointed another officer to command the *Robust*, this was not a mark of disparagement for Elphinstone. All evidence indicates that Hood was pleased with his actions. Still, Elphinstone was upset and ranted to his brother that he was "superseded without thanking me or even telling me of it." In addition, he complained to Graham, "I am displeased at being superseded." To add insult, service ashore proved costly, and by late November he had spent nearly £1,000 for food and other expenses.[53] This did not take into account the prize money that he might have garnered if his ship had been successful at sea.

Operations continued to go poorly for the British and their allies ashore, with the French concentrating their efforts against the high ground on both flanks of the outer roadstead. If the British lost either of these positions, Toulon could not be defended, and Napoleon Bonaparte developed his plan accordingly. Elphinstone came to a similar conclusion: "If we lose Cap Brun [on the east] the fleet must move, the same with Fort Mulgrave [on the west], neither very strong." Bonaparte's plan succeeded. He massed the French artillery against Fort Mulgrave and took it on 18 December. On the same day, Mount Faron fell. The senior allied officers recognized that their position was untenable and gave the order for evacuation on the following day. Military personnel and civilians began boarding the ships while the allies prepared to burn the arsenal and whatever French ships could not be evacuated. Bonaparte later described the scene as "sublime, but agonizing."[54] The British destroyed their half of the French fleet, but according to Elphinstone, "The damned Spaniards did not burn their half of the ships, I believe either from design or fear."[55]

While the arsenal exploded and the ships burned, the last of the allied bastion of Fort la Malgue was evacuated on 19 December. Bonaparte recorded that he expected the magazines in the fort to be detonated at any moment as the allied soldiers were escaping to the town. Instead, the boats from the ships in the harbor were rowed directly to the beach outside the fortress where the soldiers and residents of Toulon awaited evacuation. That night, 8,000 soldiers along with refugees arrived on the beach and were brought off without loss. Elphinstone was one of several naval captains tasked with coordinating the evacuation. In the last moments of darkness, Elphinstone boarded the final boat and was carried to the *Robust*, which proceeded to sea. When day broke on the twentieth, his ship was still in mortar range, but the French shells missed her and she safely joined Hood's fleet. The *Robust* sailed dangerously overloaded, with 3,060 persons embarked including her own crew, 2,000 soldiers, and 500 émigrés. For a seventy-four-gun ship with a normal complement of approximately 600, the numbers were daunting. Space was so scarce that eighty evacuees even received accommodation in the captain's private cabin.[56]

Elphinstone had performed unusual service during his time at Toulon. His duties did not involve nautical matters; instead he had demonstrated skill and daring in his several land engagements. At Ollioules he had defeated a French detachment of equivalent numerical strength but with complete superiority in artillery. Hood commended his performance even though he considered it rash. Elphinstone again proved his ability at Mount Faron on 1 October; it was his attack that had forced the French to retreat. Although his poor health caused him to remain in the rear during this attack, this was not detrimental. Indeed, at Ollioules he likewise did not lead from the front. On the other hand, he was close enough to the fighting in a later skirmish to have his sword struck by a musket ball.[57] In these engagements he acted commendably. Captain Horatio Nelson, then serving in the Mediterranean, concurred: "Every day at Toulon has hitherto afforded some brilliant Action on shore, in which Sea-Officers have made a conspicuous figure: Elphinstone in particular, who is a good Officer and gallant man."[58] For the entire siege, while other senior allied officers were replaced, Elphinstone remained governor of Fort la Malgue, even after he offered to resign. Overall, he demonstrated an understanding of land warfare, especially in the employment of battalion and weak regimental units.

After the evacuation, the fleet sailed to the Islands of Hyères, and Hood, through his patronage powers, offered to make Elphinstone captain of the fleet. He declined. Instead the admiral appointed him commodore, ordering him to raise the broad pendant aboard the *Robust* on 1 January 1794 and sail to England commanding a squadron containing three British ships-of-the-line and three French warships taken at Toulon. They escorted a convoy of 130 merchantmen from Malta and Naples which arrived safely at Spithead on 16 March. During the voyage Elphinstone enjoyed the company of a French countess whom he described as "a pleasant little woman." Although the convoy arrived safely, his digestion again caused problems. He commented coarsely to his sister, "The French [émigrés] say I have the winds under command and nothing can turn out ill in my hands; I am sure I have wind enough in my stomach."[59]

Upon his arrival in England, Elphinstone immediately traveled to London where he attended court and met with old acquaintances. He returned the hero with Hood's dispatches and several of the ships captured at Toulon. Moreover, he was a senior post captain, near the top of the navy list. Since captains were promoted strictly on the basis of seniority, he did not have long to wait for his admiral's flag. For the General Promotion of 12 April, the Admiralty advanced seventeen captains to the rank of rear admiral. This was a large number, and Elphinstone's was the last name on the list. Often the Admiralty "reached down" the list of captains to promote a specific officer to admiral—this time it was Elphinstone who received the distinction.[60] The day after his promotion, the king bestowed upon the new admiral the ribbon of a Knight of the Bath; thenceforth he would be known as Sir George Elphinstone. In these proceedings he described the king as "very complimentary." Still, he remained unemployed for several months awaiting a vacancy in the Channel Fleet of Admiral Richard Lord Howe. As a result, he missed the First of June, the war's first major naval battle.[61]

In London, Elphinstone renewed his friendship with his brother-in-law William Adam. He went to the opera and "almost melted" when he heard "Rule Britannia" and attended a charity play for the families of those who died in battle on the First of June.[62] However, he had returned to Britain in the midst of a political crisis. The Opposition, Elphinstone's political faction, fragmented over the war effort. A minority under Charles James Fox favored reconciliation with France, while the majority, under the Duke of Portland, abhorred the Revolution and wished to restore the French monarchy. The latter group had initially opposed Pitt, claiming that his actions against Revolutionary France were tardy and timid. Over time, Portland's supporters slowly gravitated toward a coalition with Pitt which was finally formalized on 11 July. Elphinstone and Adam had supported Portland since 1784, but Adam now joined Fox's faction. For his part, Elphinstone continued to support Portland, probably to advance his naval career. Because of the coalition with Pitt and his success at Toulon, his prospects were promising. Furthermore, John George, 2nd Earl Spencer, one of Portland's chief lieutenants, became First Lord of the Admiralty in December.[63] The newly promoted admiral now had a strong political ally to advance his interests.

Between 1774 and 1794, Elphinstone learned that powerful patrons were necessary for a successful career. During this period, his life had gone full circle. After receiving great praise for his service in the American Revolution, he had upon his return to England become associated with the Opposition. This had alienated Elphinstone from George III, precluding immediate employment. He had also become involved with several of George III's sons, and since they were often out of favor with their father, Elphinstone became guilty by association. Moreover, personal loss permeated these years. His father had died in 1781, and his wife's death weighed heavily. While Elphinstone stayed out of the public eye in the early 1790s, the war with France in 1793 led to large increases in the naval establishment. As a senior captain with extensive combat experience, Elphinstone received command of a ship. Then, at Toulon, his service ashore garnered much praise. Everything fell into place upon his return to England: he received an admiral's flag and knighthood, and a new political alignment foreshadowed handsome support from George III and Pitt's government.

"Things go remarkably well"

From the Cape of Good Hope to Mutiny (1794–97)

With powerful allies in Pitt's government and an impeccable combat record, the newly promoted rear admiral soon obtained employment. In mid-July, Elphinstone received orders from the Admiralty to become a subordinate admiral in the Channel Fleet and hoist his flag aboard the *Barfleur* (98). As was customary, he turned out the ship's captain, Cuthbert Collingwood, who had commanded her at the First of June, and chose John Elphinstone as his new flag captain. Although the two shared the Elphinstone name and Scottish ancestry, they were not related. In addition, both the admiral and his new flag captain brought their "followers," or those men they wished to promote.[1] To make room, part of the ship's complement was drafted into another ship, resulting in a "dangerous restlessness" that disrupted the naval life of a veteran crew. In this incident, Collingwood spoke highly of Captain John Elphinstone's ability to settle the problem but remained mute about the new admiral's actions. This was due to the division of responsibilities between the two Elphinstones. The flag captain ran the admiral's ship, while the flag officer commanded multiple ships. The transfer of men might unsettle the *Barfleur*'s original crew, but followers, not just servants and clerks and secretaries, were necessary, for captains and admirals had to attract competent officers and men to their commands, and they could do this only by being successful patrons.[2]

At the time Elphinstone raised his flag, the Channel Fleet numbered thirty-one ships-of-the-line under the command of Lord Howe, and Elphinstone took charge of a squadron consisting of the *Gibraltar* (80), *Arrogant* (74), *Orion* (74), *Barfleur* (98), and *Ramillies* (74). The fleet's operations were mainly defensive, with emphasis placed on protecting large convoys sailing to the East and West Indies, and Howe did not vigorously pursue the blockade of the French fleet at Brest.[3] For Elphinstone, service in the Channel Fleet proved mundane; however, one tense moment occurred in October. To calm his sister, he wrote, "Do not be alarmed if you read of the *Barfleur* being on fire, although it was the case in the night of the 10th; we got it out without much trouble. A little confusion at first. I got wet and some cold. Some sails burnt and that is all the damage."[4]

In January 1795 Elphinstone complained about Howe, "We at least were expected to have been at sea ten days ago, but our great Earl is as slow as a dray-horse, and I fear the French will get in ere we get out."[5] His words were prophetic: the Brest fleet had put to sea, severely disrupting British trade, while the Channel Fleet had remained at Spithead. Howe received blame for this and was eventually replaced for lethargy.[6] Because of Elphinstone's subordinate status, he escaped censure but decided to use his connections and obtain a different, and perhaps independent, command. By January 1795 he had offers. First, he disclaimed the rumor that he would be appointed to the Board of Admiralty. His previous political affiliation and lack of political experience precluded this appointment. As to service in the Mediterranean, he wrote, "I have had my share of evacuations and declined."[7] In late January, Elphinstone met with the cabinet ministers, whom he described as "distressed and at their wits-end." On his return, he claimed that Howe begged him to remain in the Channel Fleet, and he told his sister that he would unless the Admiralty offered him an independent command, since "it was better to be first in a village than last in a town."[8]

Elphinstone soon received his wish. The Dutch Republic (the United Provinces), an ally of Britain, had entered the war against Revolutionary France in 1793, but French military forces occupied the Netherlands in November 1794. Although the mother country was defeated, her ruler, the Stadtholder Prince William V of Orange, had escaped to Britain, and the control of her colonies remained undecided. This included the strategically important Cape Colony located astride the British route to India. Henry Dundas, a chief cabinet minister and president of the Board of Control for the East India Company, had negotiated with the Dutch since early 1793 to have the British defend the Cape. With the collapse of resistance in the United Provinces, Dundas feared that the French would use the Cape as a base to intercept British commerce. Dundas's position in the East India Company meant that he had wide-ranging authority over company affairs. He was also secretary of state for war and had extensive power to prosecute Britain's overseas war effort. At the cabinet meeting on 8 February 1795, Dundas used his influence to obtain approval for the capture of the Dutch colonies at the Cape and in the Indian Ocean.[9] One of the naval officers considered for command of this operation was Elphinstone. He was familiar both with the region and with the operations of the East India Company, though familial ties placed Elphinstone opposite Dundas in company politics. The admiral's brother William was one of Dundas's chief opponents in the East India Company. However, on issues relating to East India Company security, the admiral's views corresponded with those held by Dundas.[10]

When Elphinstone learned that he was to be commander-in-chief "on a particular Service including all the Indian Seas," he claimed that "I instantly declined the offered high [command]," but Spencer persuaded him to accept on certain conditions. He could return home at the time of his choosing; his pay was set at an extraordinary £8,000 per annum; and he received control of all patronage.[11] Officers rarely rejected independent commands, but there were several reasons for Elphinstone's maneuverings. His chronic digestive complaint had been contracted in this region, so it was an unappealing destination, and serving there was also especially costly, which accounted for his pursuit of higher pay. As for the patronage powers, they were expected on foreign stations, and were necessary to assist his protégés.[12]

To expedite the operation, the British government ordered the invasion force to sail in several detachments. An advance squadron under Commodore John Blankett consisting of the *America* (64), *Ruby* (64), *Stately* (64), and *Echo* (16), with a battalion of the 78th Regiment under Major General James Henry Craig embarked, proceeded to sea on 27 February.[13] Meanwhile, at Portsmouth, Elphinstone assembled the rest of his fleet. For the first time he was the absolute commander, answering only to the Admiralty. This required some adjustment. He complained that he had not received men. In a terse reply, the secretary of the Admiralty explained that he could not dispatch sailors until he had returns detailing the current state of his ships. Overzealous, Elphinstone also wrote Vice Admiral William Cornwallis "in high style" about false muster books. Cornwallis retorted, "The Captains of your squadron are answerable to you. . . . The service you are going to perform may not be the only one for which seamen may be wanted."[14] These problems were soon settled, and eventually his squadron consisted of the *Monarch* (74), *Arrogant* (74), *Victorious* (74), *Sphynx* (24), *Rattlesnake* (16), and *Arniston* (Indiaman). Elphinstone originally had orders to escort the main invasion force under Major General Alured Clarke sailing aboard East India ships. This contingent was not ready in time, and Elphinstone's squadron proceeded to sea on 3 April; Clarke did not sail until 15 May.[15]

Trade winds afforded Elphinstone's squadron a pleasant journey, and of the *Monarch* he claimed, "I seem to have got good people with me which is pleasant at least." On 10 June his squadron reached the Cape Colony, where the lookouts sighted Blankett's squadron. The advance squadron had had worse luck with the weather and had arrived only three days earlier. On the twelfth the two squadrons finally worked into Simon's Bay near Cape Town.

The unannounced arrival of six ships-of-the-line and several smaller vessels in such a remote part of the world rightly occasioned fear. An officer of a Dutch frigate anchored in the bay sounded a general alarm, and a large body of militia converged on Cape Town. Once they learned that it was a British and not a French squadron, tensions decreased.[16] Since the Dutch had last received news from Holland on 22 December 1794, Elphinstone and Craig hoped to provide an edited version of recent events. This was in keeping with their instructions to obtain a negotiated settlement and treat the Dutch as allies; if this failed, the British were to use force. Craig and Elphinstone presented a letter to the governor from the Prince of Orange sanctioning the British to take charge of the colony's defenses, but some at the Cape considered their former ruler a fugitive since he had fled to Britain. Craig recorded that "nothing could well exceed the degree of inattention with which it [the letter] was received, indeed I could almost wish his name had not been made use of." The Dutch did not waver, and Craig lamented that the British had not brought a series of newspapers to substantiate the evidence they had presented to the governor and the council.[17]

The British faced several problems. As usual, Elphinstone had not enjoyed his voyage, having "been much indisposed, even confined to bed."[18] He was not the only one ill; many of the seamen, marines, and soldiers were bedridden with scurvy. Furthermore, all the field pieces, artillerymen, engineers, and entrenching tools were loaded aboard Clarke's ships, which had not yet arrived. All of this made it imperative to pursue negotiations. While these proceeded, the Dutch unwittingly solved several of the British problems by allowing the conveyance of fresh provisions to the ships and even providing for a hospital ashore at Simonstown.[19] Such consideration did not last. In late June the Dutch stopped sending provisions to the fleet and temporarily sent the sick back to their ships. Then on 28 June the *Columbia*, an American ship,

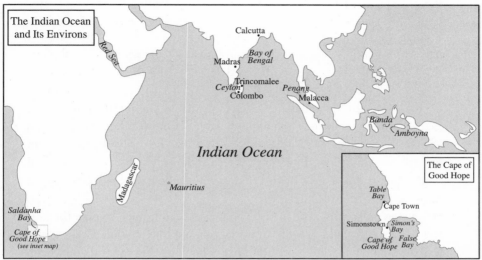

The Indian Ocean and Its Environs

Calcutta

Bay of Bengal
Madras

Trincomalee
Ceylon
Colombo
Penang
Malacca

Banda
Amboyna

Indian Ocean

Mauritius

The Cape of Good Hope

Table Bay
Cape Town
Simonstown *Simon's Bay*
Cape of Good Hope *False Bay*

Saldanha Bay
Cape of Good Hope
(see inset map)

Red Sea

Madagascar

Map by Sara McCranie, 2004

Map 4. The Indian Ocean and Its Environs.

arrived in Simon's Bay carrying dispatches from Holland. Elphinstone and Craig attempted to seize all newspapers, claiming that "we know the Truth cannot be published in Holland," but one newspaper reached the Dutch. In it there was a proclamation stating that the Prince of Orange was no longer their rightful ruler and that the French were treating Holland as an independent country. In response, the Dutch evacuated Simonstown.[20]

Without a steady influx of supplies, the sailors rapidly consumed the last of their victuals. It was a great distance to the closest British-controlled port, so on 1 July Elphinstone placed his men on two-thirds rations. Their situation became increasingly grim, but neither side resorted to open hostility.[21] The British remained aboard their ships, only maintaining a hospital ashore. On 11 July a surgeon's mate saw several horsemen in Simonstown, and he signaled the alarm. Elphinstone landed armed sailors and marines, but they soon withdrew. As tensions increased, the 78th Foot landed on 14 July, and a week later the admiral sent his marines ashore. In early August, after the Dutch militia near Simonstown fired on British patrols, Elphinstone and Craig contemplated initiating hostilities. The admiral continued to assist Craig by landing almost 1,000 sailors and having them train as infantry.[22]

These sailors were training for an attack on the Dutch camp at Muizenberg. Garrisoned by more than 600 men, this strong natural defensive position on a narrow part of the coastal plain was the major obstacle on the only road between the British position at Simon's Bay and Cape Town. At Muizenberg the Dutch right rested on a steep hill, and the ocean protected the left. Although they constructed a strong battery to sweep the coastal plain, the Dutch failed to erect significant defenses facing the sea, believing the water too shallow for large ships. Craig presented a plan to Elphinstone calling for his squadron to take the Dutch in the flank. The admiral pointed out that the water was shallow and unpredictable.[23] On the other hand, he said, "We have a raw enemy to deal with, so they may be easily alarmed." With provisions running low, the attack was seen as the only viable alternative to an evacuation, and perhaps a British victory would allow the English to reopen negotiations with the Dutch.[24]

Relying on surprise, the British commanders continued to plan their attack. The navy would provide an initial bombardment, while Craig would lead the infantry, marines, and sailors in a column up the road and overwhelm the Dutch. For the naval part of the operation, the weather needed to be calm, but high surf delayed the attack for several days. On 7 August the water was smooth with a gentle breeze from the northwest. Elphinstone's flagship, the *Monarch*, drew too much water and remained anchored in Simon's Bay; instead he delegated two sixty-fours for the operation. At 11:45 a.m. the *America* weighed anchor with both Blankett and Elphinstone aboard. The bombardment squadron approached Muizenberg with the *Echo* in the lead, followed by the *America*, then the *Stately*, and finally the *Rattlesnake*. The *America* opened fire at 2:00 p.m.; an hour later the two sixty-four-gun ships-of-the-line anchored and continued to bombard the Dutch camp. At 4:15 the order was given to cease fire. Return fire had proved light, since the Dutch soldiers had panicked and retreated in considerable disorder, abandoning all their baggage and several guns. Craig's column then occupied the position. However, the Dutch tenaciously defended the ridge beyond the camp, and it took the light company of the 78th Foot the remainder of the day to clear it. The Dutch tried to recapture Muizenberg the next day but failed.[25]

The Dutch then constructed another camp at Wynberg. They refused to parlay and vowed to defend the colony to the end. Although the *Arniston* arrived from St. Helena with nine artillery pieces and four hundred reinforcements, Craig maintained that his force was still too weak to assail Cape Town, so he decided to await the arrival of General Clarke's soldiers. In the

Figure 1. *Lord Keith at Muizenberg*, engraving after a painting formerly at Tullyallan, from Allardyce, *Memoir*.

meantime, supplies dwindled, and the British commanders determined that they would soon have to evacuate if reinforcements did not arrive.[26]

On 3 September, fourteen ships carrying Clarke's soldiers and a great quantity of supplies anchored at Simon's Bay. The admiral was still worried because the convoy did not bring bread and spirits.[27] Clarke moved slowly, and his soldiers did not advance against Wynberg until 14 September. After a short fight, the Dutch force again retreated in confusion. On the following day Elphinstone ordered Blankett to make a demonstration against Cape Town by sailing into Table Bay with the *America, Echo, Rattlesnake*, and *Bombay Castle* (Indiaman). These events proved too much, and the Dutch surrendered on the sixteenth.[28]

Elphinstone's first independent command had been stressful. Communications with Dundas and the Admiralty took months; he had essentially acted on his own. The Dutch had been suspicious from the beginning, though Craig and Elphinstone had worked diligently to obtain a negotiated settlement. After a month the British commanders were looking for an excuse to force hostilities, since provisions had become scarce, forcing Elphinstone to place his men on shortened rations. He later reflected that "had we failed, God knows how or where we must have gone for food."[29] On the bright side, cooperation between the two services had been excellent, attesting to joint planning and mutual respect. Craig reported, "I accordingly proposed it [the attack on Muizenberg] to Sir George Elphinstone, who immediately agreed to it, with that readiness which has so strongly attended all the instances of assistance."[30] Describing Elphinstone, Clarke wrote, "I should do injustice to my own feelings if I did not express the obligations I am under for the ready cooperation and assistance that he afforded upon every Occasion which so eminently contributed to the successfull issue of our joint endeavours."[31]

For two months after the surrender, the admiral remained in Cape Town. He had time to visit with the Dutch ladies, who admired his daughter's painting, but Elphinstone was not well. He related, "We have had great deal of sickness here. . . . All my house has been ill—one of my cooks dead."[32] In another letter he continued, "I do not like this climate, it is too frequent the changes from heat to cold."[33] During the period he remained at the Cape, the British began to dismantle a century and a half of Dutch East India Company rule. Craig became the governor, but Elphinstone and Clarke assisted him during his first months. Although the Dutch at Cape Town had agreed to surrender, many living in the interior had not, and the English were very careful how they handled these conquered people. Elphinstone claimed that "things go remarkably well and will do if they are gently treated." The admiral may have had a wrong opinion. Two years later a British subject claimed that Elphinstone "is sadly detested here for his extortionary practices." Two factors account for this reaction. The government was totally restructured during his brief stay at Cape Town. While Craig remained behind to smooth over the problems, Elphinstone left without understanding the dislocation he had caused. The second cause of resentment was prize money, for the British Crown considered all Dutch public and some private property to be legitimate prizes. As usual, the avaricious Elphinstone was very thorough, and this definitely alienated the Dutch.[34]

After the break in the monsoon occurred in October, Elphinstone sailed to India to carry out the second part of the assignment he had received in London. In addition to his command at the Cape, he was also to take charge of all British naval operations in the Indian Ocean. In "profound ignorance of the state of either country," England or India, he left Commodore Blankett in command at the Cape and sailed to Madras in mid-November with the *Monarch*, *Arrogant*, *Echo*, *Rattlesnake*, and *Prince of Wales* (armed transport).[35]

In the Indian Ocean, Elphinstone encountered a very different situation than at the Cape, for the British already had a naval presence in the region under Rear Admiral Peter Rainier. When Rainier learned that the French had conquered the United Provinces, he immediately organized several expeditions to destroy the Dutch maritime empire in Asia. In August 1795 Trincomalee, the best anchorage on Ceylon, surrendered, and Malacca capitulated without firing a shot. Given the slowness of communications, Rainier did not learn until 27 September that Elphinstone had superseded him as commander in chief, effective 10 June. This was particularly disagreeable because Rainier had planned and executed several operations against the Dutch. Since Elphinstone was technically the supreme commander, he would receive the commander in chief's share of the prize money even though he had taken no part in the operations.[36] Perhaps in spite, Rainier hastily sailed with several warships to capture the Dutch possessions of Amboyna and Banda in the Moluccas, which further scattered the limited British naval force.[37] When Elphinstone arrived at Madras in January 1796, he found the East India Squadron dispersed and Rainier more than a thousand miles to the east. Once Elphinstone ascertained the situation, he remained at Madras and sent the bulk of his available ships to capture Colombo, the last Dutch stronghold on Ceylon. After a brief operation, this port surrendered on 15 February. Off to the east, Rainier's squadron arrived at Amboyna on 16 February and took possession of it; he then sailed to Banda and captured it on 8 March. The conquests were of little strategic military value, but the capture of these places, known as the Spice Islands, disrupted Dutch trade and garnered pecuniary advantages for the British. In the meantime, French cruisers from their colony on the island of Mauritius in the Indian Ocean raided the Malabar Coast and the Bay of Bengal capturing ships and disrupting British commerce.[38] When the Indiaman *Triton* was seized, the Governor General of India, Sir John Shore, declared, "Although the presence of Commodore [*sic*] Rainier could not have prevented the accident, it might have deterred the French from appearing in the Bay."[39] Without reinforcements, Elphinstone maintained there was little he could do. The Admiralty had provided insufficient forces, yet it had ordered his ships to capture the Dutch colonies.

In Madras, Elphinstone received unwelcome reports that the Dutch and French were assembling naval squadrons to reinforce their presence in the Indian Ocean or even recapture the Cape. He realized that Blankett's squadron at Simon's Bay, with only the *America*, *Ruby*, *Princess*, and *Hope*, was too weak to meet this threat. He hastily sailed from Madras on 23 March with his two available warships, the *Monarch* and the *Sphynx*, leaving urgent orders for additional ships to follow. Elphinstone's instincts proved correct: a Dutch squadron had departed the United Provinces in January destined for the Cape. But the British almost uncannily followed their slow progress, and everything seemed to go awry for the Dutch. Royal Navy ships sighted them in the North Sea and again in the Atlantic between Madeira and the Canaries. The *Carysfort* (28), sent from Britain to warn Blankett, arrived at the Cape on 25 April and immediately received orders to alert Elphinstone at Madras. To Blankett's relief, Elphinstone arrived at the Cape on 23 May, having unknowingly passed the *Carysfort* at sea. Five days after Elphinstone's return, six transports escorted by the *Sceptre* (64) and the *Crescent* (36) anchored at the Cape. Several weeks passed, and the *Tremendous* (74) sailed into Simon's Bay on 21 June flying Rear Admiral Thomas Pringle's flag; on the same day, the *Jupiter* (50) made landfall escorting a convoy, and the *Moselle* (24) brought intelligence that she had sighted the Dutch squadron off Madeira. Finally, on 31 July the *Trident* (64) arrived with three ships of a convoy destined for India.[40] In a little over two months, the size of the British naval squadron at the Cape had tripled. Now Elphinstone's squadron had to intercept the Dutch. If they did not, the Dutch squadron could sail on to Batavia on the island of Java, then perhaps wreak havoc on the British China convoys. Likewise, they could cooperate with the French at Mauritius. The latter was of great concern, for the French already had seven large frigates in the Indian Ocean. Four of these had recently arrived from Rochefort under the command of Rear Admiral Pierre-César-Charles-Guillaume de Sercey, having passed the Cape in May prior to Elphinstone's return from Madras.[41]

While the French naval force and the imminent arrival of the Dutch squadron had to be dealt with, disconcerting news arrived at the Cape in late June. The members of the Admiralty had divided Elphinstone's command, since they believed it to be too unwieldy. Elphinstone would retain the British squadron at the Cape, but Rainier would now control operations in the Indian Ocean. Elphinstone objected vehemently to the decision and reiterated this in letters to Dundas and Spencer. He made a valid case, contending that a united command would more effectively utilize British naval forces. Elphinstone argued that until French-controlled Mauritius, located between India and the Cape, was captured, a split command would necessitate the maintenance of two squadrons to screen the island. A single fleet would allow for greater flexibility in responding to the French threat. The appeal failed. For the remainder of the Revolutionary Era, the Cape and India were two separate commands, and the only officer to hold both positions simultaneously was Elphinstone. The changeover in command went slowly given the extended area of operations. As late as October 1796, officers in the Indian Ocean addressed their dispatches to Elphinstone, and Rainier did not return to Madras from Amboyna and Banda until 13 February 1797. Furthermore, as long as the Dutch squadron remained a threat, Elphinstone vowed to follow it as far as necessary into the Indian Ocean regardless of the Admiralty's order to split his command.[42]

The primary threat to the Cape remained the Dutch squadron, and Elphinstone was worried that these ships would elude him. On 3 August he received intelligence through the army that several unknown ships were seen near Saldanha Bay. This was substantiated on the fifth, but poor weather forced Elphinstone to remain in Simon's Bay, and his squadron finally sailed on the sixth. Since an officer had brought news that unknown ships had been sighted the previous evening off Table Bay, Elphinstone sailed south and west searching for the Dutch. While his ships plied the stormy waters off the Cape, the *Stately*, *Rattlesnake*, and *Echo* finally arrived from India. Elphinstone's reinforced but battered squadron returned to Simon's Bay on the twelfth after sailing in what the Admiral called "the most tempestuous weather I have ever experienced."[43] On his return he finally learned that the Dutch had anchored in Saldanha Bay on 6 August, and the next day Craig dispatched 2,500 men to prevent them from landing. These soldiers were delayed by the lack of roads and habitation, and it took nine days to march the ninety miles to Saldanha. Because of the poor weather, Elphinstone's ships did not sail from Simon's Bay until the fifteenth. On the following day, they arrived off Saldanha Bay and sighted the Dutch squadron under Rear Admiral Engelbertus Lucas, consisting of two ships-of-the-line, one fifty-gun ship, two large frigates, two small frigates, a sloop, and a storeship. Meanwhile, ashore, Craig's advance guard finally arrived. One Dutch frigate exchanged cannon fire with the soldiers until they brought several guns and a howitzer into action. By this time it was late afternoon, and Elphinstone's squadron had begun to enter the bay. Craig ordered his guns to cease fire, since the Dutch ships were trapped. Elphinstone asked the outnumbered Dutch admiral to surrender. Lucas was receptive, but desired a truce so he could hold a council of war with his captains. The British admiral agreed. The next morning, when Lucas presented his terms, Elphinstone demanded an almost unconditional surrender, which the Dutch admiral accepted.[44] The triumph was complete, and Elphinstone sent a message to his daughter that "I bring her the Admiral's Dutch flag without a shot."[45]

The British were extremely fortunate. Decisiveness and flexibility rested with them. Their ships had spotted the Dutch squadron early. The Admiralty had reacted with vigor by sending reinforcements, and Elphinstone had acted indomitably. The British had assembled a superior force at the Cape and the admiral developed contingency plans to follow the Dutch into the Indian Ocean. Moreover, relations with the army remained excellent; in fact, Craig's men had located the Dutch. Unknown to Elphinstone, low morale aboard Lucas's ships proved critical. The Dutch admiral claimed that to his own crews "more than the great superiority of your ships I must ascribe the necessity of our reddition; for of this your Excellency may rest assured, that if they had been in order I should have tried the fate of war."[46] Craig echoed these sentiments describing the sailors: "at least three fourths of them are Austrians, or Soldiers of some of the other German powers, who were prisoners in France, and being marched to Holland, were put on board the Ships against their consent."[47]

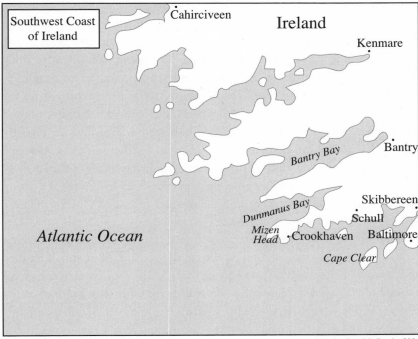

Map by Sara McCranie, 2004

Map 5. Southwest Coast of Ireland.

Meanwhile, Elphinstone planned his next move. Although British leaders in India wished for him to return to Madras, he decided in October to proceed to England.[48] One reason was his health, which had suffered while he was in India. When he returned to the Cape, his flag captain wrote, "I rejoice that you allow that you are rather better because I have hopes that you are better than you think." By July, however, Elphinstone again lamented, "Ah! my bad stomach and head."[49]

According to his original orders and those brought by Pringle, Elphinstone could return to England at the time of his choosing, and he was now prepared to exercise this option, for several reasons. The division of Elphinstone's command was not to his liking; he had accomplished most of the tasks in his original instructions; and he had taken an entire Dutch squadron. Only Batavia and Mauritius remained in the hands of Britain's enemies. While Elphinstone prepared to have Pringle assume command, intelligence arrived on 6 October that five ships had been seen in the offing near Simon's Bay. Elphinstone sailed on the following morning with the *Monarch, Tremendous, Trident, Fox* (32), and *Daphne* (24) to intercept the unknown squadron. Once at sea, the admiral learned that these were some of his own ships returning from patrol. Since the winds were favorable, he ordered his flagship, the *Monarch*, along with the *Daphne* to part company from the rest and make sail for Britain.[50]

The voyage proved arduous. The *Monarch* had been constantly at sea for eighteen months and had sailed from the Cape with only half her normal complement. The remainder of her men had been drafted into the recently captured Dutch ships, particularly the *Daphne*. Furthermore, the *Monarch* transported a hundred Dutch prisoners and an equal number of British invalids. The voyage became more grueling when the ships encountered a strong easterly wind on 16 November, and the weather remained foul for the next month. With no respite, the *Monarch* encountered a severe gale on 21 December off the Scilly Isles. The tempest forced the ships to sail west, making landfall at Crookhaven, Ireland, on the twenty-second. Even at half rations, the *Monarch* held provisions for only eight days. The shorthanded crew were exhausted, having sailed through poor weather for more than a month on little food and less sleep. They were too tired even to secure their sails when they anchored, and the gale quickly blew the canvas from the *Monarch*'s yards. The unrelenting storm continued to build, and it began to snow. Worse, a leak had developed that could not be fixed without a dry dock.[51]

In Crookhaven, Elphinstone learned that a large French fleet had put into Bantry Bay, about fifteen miles to the north, but the weather had prevented the French from landing their soldiers. Elphinstone was in a difficult position. The wind continued to blow furiously, and French ships were nearby. Not until the entire affair was nearly at an end did the admiral learn specific details about the French force in Bantry Bay. It comprised the remnants of a fleet that had sailed from Brest on 16 December, originally consisting of seventeen ships-of-the-line, thirteen frigates, and several smaller vessels carrying 14,000 soldiers. Mishaps had plagued the French from the beginning. While sailing from Brest at night, a ship-of-the-line had foundered. A British frigate had harassed the fleet, causing unimaginable confusion and the dispersal of the French ships. On the twenty-first, the bulk of the fleet, but minus their flagship, sighted the Irish coast. Finally, during the morning of the twenty-third, ten ships-of-the-line and six smaller vessels anchored in Bantry Bay while twenty others remained in the offing. During the night, the storm that had blown the *Monarch* into Crookhaven forced the French ships in the offing back out to sea, leaving a much depleted invasion force in Bantry Bay.[52]

Between the proximity of the French and the parlous state of his command, Elphinstone spent several very stressful days in Crookhaven. There was little he could do, but on 23 December he sent his flag captain, John Elphinstone, with telescopes to reconnoiter the French fleet. Ten or eleven ships were spotted in Bantry Bay and twenty in the offing. On the following day, a snowstorm reduced visibility to nearly zero. The storm continued to blow on Christmas, but visibility improved.[53] Elphinstone jokingly remarked, "All is ice here."[54] The French ships in the offing had again been forced out to sea, and several additional ships, unbeknownst to Elphinstone, had sailed from the bay. All the while, the storm continued to prevent a French landing. Although the French remained unaware of Elphinstone's presence, captured Irish fishermen told them that six British frigates had anchored at Cork. The senior French naval officer in Bantry Bay placed great credence in this report and feared that these frigates would disrupt any landing, so when the weather finally improved on the twenty-seventh, he ordered his remaining ships to sail from Bantry Bay.[55]

The *Monarch* remained at anchor in Crookhaven because of poor weather. To his sister Elphinstone commented that "the winds seem for once to take our side," as they prevented the French from landing their invasion force.[56] Nevertheless, a portion of the French squadron remained in Irish waters, and on the thirtieth the French frigate *Impatiente* (44) wrecked near Crookhaven. Out of six hundred aboard, only five lived. From the survivors, Elphinstone finally determined the purpose and composition of the invasion force; however, he learned these things only after the invasion had failed. On the day after the French frigate foundered, the weather improved, and the *Monarch* sailed from Crookhaven. Elphinstone had been both a victim of circumstance and extremely fortunate. First, his ill-manned and battered ships had survived the storms on their voyage from the Cape. When seeking an anchorage, he could have sailed into Bantry Bay and been captured or sunk. Moreover, the Admiralty commended Elphinstone's service, for the admiral did nearly all he could in ascertaining the strength and location of the French fleet. If the British Channel Fleet had arrived, this information could have been used to great advantage. In the end, Elphinstone's actions were overshadowed by problems in the Channel Fleet, which had failed in several of its principal tasks, including the blockade of Brest and preventing the arrival of a French invasion fleet on the Irish coast.[57] Indicative of these failings, the Channel Fleet, because of the weather, did not sail from St. Helens until 3 January 1797. Elphinstone easily relayed his intelligence to the fleet's commander, Admiral Alexander Hood, Lord Bridport, because the *Monarch* arrived off St. Helens on the very day that the Channel Fleet proceeded to sea. After telling Bridport all he knew, Elphinstone had the *Monarch* proceed to Spithead, where his battered ship anchored and he struck his flag.[58]

Upon his return to Britain after an absence of nearly two years, Elphinstone sought to utilize his newfound fame from his successes at the Cape and in the Indian Ocean. Moreover, he had secured a fortune in prize money totaling more than £60,000.[59] Although he looked to several individuals for support, Henry Dundas's patronage proved the most important. A loyal supporter of Pitt and the Crown, he was an influential cabinet minister and a high-ranking officer in the East India Company with extensive political connections in Scotland. Dundas was thus a powerful patron, and Elphinstone seemed a worthy target of his patronage.[60] Elphinstone received the first of Dundas's rewards while still at the Cape. In the 1796 general election, the incumbent of the Stirlingshire seat in the House of Commons had decided to forgo reelection, and Sir George Elphinstone was presented in absentia as the only candidate. Besides Dundas, his backers were his brother William, his nephew John, who was the current Lord Elphinstone, and James, 3rd Duke of Montrose, who had a controlling interest in the county. On 16 June 1796, Elphinstone won election by unanimous consent, but controversy soon erupted. A local squire, Robert Belsches, claimed that several freeholders had cast doubt on Elphinstone's eligibility but had had their protests ignored. Belsches successfully petitioned the House of Commons to study the election. When the petitioner died in December 1796, however, the appeal was dropped, allowing Elphinstone to again serve in Parliament.[61]

Dundas did more. At his request, the king agreed to create a barony for Elphinstone in the Irish peerage. This was part of two larger trends. First, many of the peers created in the 1790s were, like Elphinstone, connected with the existing aristocracy and had been in the Opposition prior to the 1793 declaration of war against France.[62] Second, Dundas again assisted one of his followers. However, when Dundas claimed that he was "at a perfect loss how to proceed further, as you give me no hint what title you would wish to take," Elphinstone settled upon Baron Keith of Stonehaven Marischal in recognition of his granduncle and namesake George Keith, 9th Earl Marischal. On 8 February 1797 the king bestowed the honor, and Elphinstone kissed his hands as a mark of subservience and respect.[63] No longer would he be called Sir George Elphinstone; now he would be known as Lord Keith.

Although Dundas's patronage had been pivotal in advancing Keith's career, the admiral maintained his fifteen-year friendship with the Prince of Wales, and only days after being created a peer, he became involved in the heir's attempt to attain high office in the Irish government. This was the result of the prince's concern over renewed tensions between the Protestants and Catholics. To add credence to his case, the prince had written a memorandum on the state of Ireland. The document called for an end to the coercive measures of the Dublin Government and the repeal of all restrictions against Ireland's Roman Catholics. If these things occurred, the prince claimed, "I should express my wish and readiness to undertake the Government in Ireland."[64] Although Keith was now a baron in the Irish peerage, he did not have extensive ties to Ireland, but he shared the prince's belief in reform and Catholic emancipation.[65] In addition, Keith's two-year absence from Britain meant that his political image was untarnished, and he had recently developed ties to Pitt's government through his dealings with Dundas. Keith attempted to use this connection to obtain an interview with Pitt and his leading cabinet ministers. Dundas was not enthusiastic, and responded, "In a private capacity I feel my reluctance to the interview you propose equally forcible. . . . I am satisfied it cannot lead to any good consequence." Still, Dundas conveyed the prince's memorandum on the state of Ireland to Pitt, who in turn presented it to George III. However, the king dismissed it and voiced disappointment with the prince's involvement in the affair since it "was not likely to be productive of any beneficial effect." Realizing the volatility of the situation, Keith beseeched the prince to "exert an extream degree of temper at so very delicate a moment."[66] The prince followed this advice and drafted a letter of apology to Pitt wherein he humbly maintained that "the only inducement the Prince of Wales could have for coming forward at the present moment, was the hopes of the possibility of being useful to his Majesty's service." Keith delivered this letter and received Pitt's response that the king approved of the Prince of Wales's loyalty to the Crown.[67] Keith's actions in the affair demonstrated temperance and political acumen; he attempted to restrain the prince when the proceedings went awry; wisely, he never forced his own views upon the king, Dundas, or Pitt.

The Prince of Wales maintained his relationship with Keith, who in late February told his sister, "Everything is extremely uncomfortable among the R[oyal] F[amily], they give me much concern and take much of my time."[68] In March, at Keith's residence, the prince spoke with Dundas about commanding a regiment, but this also proved unsuccessful. Keith had again acted as the agent, to whom Dundas replied that "he had only to lament that the Prince of Wales should be induced so repeatedly to urge a point on which he had every ground to know his [the king's] determination was unalterably taken."[69] The prince was bored and felt ignored, yet George III remained content to leave his oldest son without an appointment.[70] This placed Keith in a difficult position because of his friendship with the prince. As long as the admiral remained unemployed and in close proximity to London, it seemed that his involvement with the prince would continue.

To Keith's relief, the Admiralty ordered him to active duty in the midst of the great naval mutinies of 1797, which for a time crippled the British navy in home waters. The first mutiny occurred on 15 April at Spithead among the ships of the Channel Fleet. The majority of the grievances were not political; rather, the sailors demanded higher pay, improved provisions, and better medical attention. Their arguments, even to contemporaries, were legitimate. For example, inflation during the second half of the eighteenth century had reduced the sailors' wages, and their last raise had occurred in 1653. The Admiralty bowed to all their demands, and the ships put to sea on 16 May, a month after the mutiny had begun.[71] Even before the official termination of the Spithead mutiny, the sailors at Sheerness and the Nore had rebelled on 12 May. When Vice Admiral Charles Buckner, their commander, learned of it, he meekly went ashore and he did not attempt to crush the mutiny. Although the mutineers refused to obey their officers, they preserved a semblance of discipline by choosing one Richard Parker, a baker's son who had previously served as a midshipman, as president of their self-proclaimed Floating Republic. They wanted the concessions granted at Spithead, along with a more equal distribution of prize money and the payment of enlistment bounties to impressed seamen. Finally, they demanded that officers be allowed to reassume command only with the consent of their men.[72]

Like Buckner, the government moved slowly to suppress the mutiny. The mutineers bargained more effectively than the sailors had at Spithead, since Sheerness and the Nore were on the Thames below London, and the mutineers could stop traffic on the river. A writer published in the *London Chron-*

icle editorialized, "The mutiny at Sheerness grows more and more serious, and unless some very severe measures are taken against the offenders, there is not only an end to discipline, but the well-being of the State is in danger."[73] Negotiations ensued. The government refused "to make any further concessions," but the mutineers soon received welcome reinforcements when part of Admiral Adam Duncan's rebellious North Sea Fleet anchored at the Nore at the end of May.[74]

Harsher measures had to be taken, and the Admiralty dispatched Keith to Sheerness. Although he was technically second in command under Admiral Buckner, Keith was to report directly to Spencer, First Lord of the Admiralty, and to Dundas, bypassing Buckner.[75] Again there was a definite link between Keith and Dundas, and the admiral continued to form an alliance with Spencer by regular correspondence. Keith carefully obtained intelligence about the mutiny from sailors caught ashore. In response, the leaders of the mutiny attempted to destroy Keith's credibility by claiming that he and his officers, but not his sailors, had received prize money from their captures at the Cape. To trifle with the distribution of prize money was viewed harshly by the sailors, so Keith immediately wrote an open letter declaring, "I assure you . . . I have never received one farthing of prize-money . . . nor am I a man who would do so until the just demands of those who served with me are satisfied."[76] Keith maintained his credibility and successfully defused this situation.

Meanwhile, Parliament passed stricter measures against mutinous activity in early June, and Parker responded by blockading the Thames. This concerned Keith, who reported that they "had effectively stopped the Navigation of the River Thames and Medway and might have starved the capital."[77] Even as fear gripped London, the mutiny entered its final phase. Parker lifted the blockade on 5 June because of the confusion it caused, and some of the mutineers lost their enthusiasm. By 10 June several ships had sailed from Parker's Floating Republic under a hail of cannon fire, and the mutiny collapsed with the last ship surrendering on 15 June. Keith now assisted in the hunt for the leading mutineers by interviewing prisoners taken from the ships. Overall, his conduct was moderate, and most of the sailors involved were not punished. However, this mutiny had proved far more serious than the one at Spithead and examples had to be made. Several of the mutineers, including Parker, were tried and hanged for their activities. This led a troubled Keith to write his sister, "I hope this is all necessary it is unpleasant too." In addition to punishments, Keith told the officers to extract oaths of loyalty from their men. He was not above coercion and darkly told the officers to threaten the men by informing them that the Admiralty had the names of those most active in the mutiny.[78] Keith also realized that the officers were not without fault, and he issued orders to enhance their professionalism. In one memo he reminded officers not to go ashore except when necessary, and then always in uniform.[79] Even before the hanging of Parker, the president of the Floating Republic, Keith was ordered to Portsmouth to take command of a squadron of the Channel Fleet.[80] However, the Admiralty redirected him to Plymouth to defuse a new crisis.

In late June and early July, several ships mutinied at Plymouth. Although this was a relatively small affair, with much of the discontent centered on the *Saturn* (74), these mutineers demanded peace. On 5 July the commander at Portsmouth, Admiral Sir Richard King, ordered Keith to board the *Saturn* and detain the ringleaders. King also provided Keith with a list of suspects.[81] Aboard the ship, Keith found "a greater degree of gloom and taciturnity than I had hitherto observed in other ships." When asked to hand over their leaders, the crew remained silent, so the Admiral arrested the twelve on the list, but at that instant two experienced sailors "came forward and said they would tell me a great deal, notwithstanding their lives would answer for it, as there were many around them who were prepared to stab them with their knives."[82] That night, Keith sounded relieved: "I thank God all is subdued and thirteen of the worst I sent off in irons. At a moment I thought there would have been resistence but a good face had its effect and it went off."[83] Still, he lamented, "I am sorry to add the crew does not appear to me sufficiently sensible of their error or the gentle treatment they have met with."[84] The *Saturn* had belonged to the Channel Fleet of Alexander Hood, Lord Bridport, and after Keith had suppressed the mutiny, he continued to serve in the fleet with his flag aboard the *Queen Charlotte* (100).

The period from 1793 to 1797 solidified Elphinstone's position in the Royal Navy, and he proved himself in several capacities. While serving in the Eastern Seas, he faced extreme hardships, but he accomplished, often with the assistance of Admiral Rainier, nearly all the tasks assigned by Dundas and the Admiralty. The capture of the Dutch squadron at Saldanha Bay provided the capstone to a very successful command. Although much credit needs to be given to the army and the Admiralty, Elphinstone's actions pulled all the disparate elements together, enabling the capture of the Dutch squadron. Upon his return to European waters, he inadvertently became involved in the Bantry Bay fiasco. Although many were criticized by Parliament, the Admiralty, and the British people, Elphinstone emerged with his reputation intact. In fact, he was created a baron in the Irish peerage and easily won a seat in the Commons. Affairs with the Prince of Wales proved irksome, but Keith avoided censure while maintaining a potentially useful friendship with the heir to the throne. When the Admiralty needed a capable officer to crush the mutiny at the Nore, Keith was chosen. He acted judiciously both there and at Plymouth to defuse these volatile situations. Afterwards, Keith did not return to unemployment; instead, he received orders to join Lord Bridport's Channel Fleet as a subordinate flag officer.

4

"Reflecting on human events and their uncertainty"

Escaping the Stigma of an Affront (1797–99)

Keith continued to ride the wave of success with his role in the mutinies. In the two years prior to mid-1797, he had been created a baron in the Irish peerage, been elected to the Commons, made a fortune in prize money, and held two successful naval commands, most recently in bringing the mutinies both at the Nore and Plymouth to an acceptable conclusion. These accomplishments inflated Keith's ego, and he wrote to Spencer, the First Lord of the Admiralty, about being created a peer of Britain. Spencer responded, "I am not prepared at present to give a decided opinion. You have so lately been distinguished by the mark of His Majesty's favour which you now hold that it just now perhaps appears a little premature to think of the other step you mention."[1]

Smarting from the First Lord's rebuff, Keith raised his flag in the Channel Fleet during late 1797 as a subordinate admiral. Keith joined this fleet during a period of transition. The mutinies had bared severe social problems, and Bantry Bay had illustrated inadequate deployments. Bridport as fleet commander worked to overcome these failings, and the fleet, including Keith's ship, the *Queen Charlotte* (100), remained at sea exercising greater vigilance in the blockade of Brest than in the past.[2] Keith recounted one incident to his sister: "We are as usual idle, only our good Admiral conducted us so near rocks in the last night as made all my line not a little uneasy, & whereof I do not advise a repetition." Several weeks later, he bitterly added, "I have little to say . . . but that we are not all drowned." In October he railed, "It is absurd to keep us here [off Brest] any longer, for we have nothing to watch." The next month he declared, "I am tired here, 17 weeks on board." Another element factored into his discontent: his wife had been dead for almost a decade, and he questioned his sister in November, "Is Mrs. Bal^n. all alone at that place? I wish I were with her."[3] The identity of the woman remains unknown, but her absence contributed to his unhappiness. Furthermore, at the Cape he had held an independent command, answering only to the Admiralty. Now he served under the orders of another admiral, which curtailed his independence. He became weary, disgruntled, and not the ideal subordinate. Keith should not have been surprised when information reached him in early November that a disagreement had supposedly occurred between himself and Bridport. He responded to his sister that "it is impossible to live better than we do."[4]

Such was Keith's wishful thinking, but in reality his obstinate behavior had become noticeable. Given the past failures of the Channel Fleet, both Bridport and the Admiralty had a great deal to lose if their disgruntled subordinate let his views interfere with his duties. Accordingly, Keith was ordered in mid-November to return to England.[5] When he arrived at Spithead on 18 November, he believed that he had been superseded by Vice Admiral Sir Charles Thompson. As instructed by the Admiralty, he traveled to London to meet with Spencer. The summons led Keith to write a feisty and not especially coherent letter to Bridport, maintaining, "I was told I *was* to exercise the command of a division in the Channel Fleet where I cannot return without some explanation which I expect this day but if it ends in my resignation I beg your Lordship to accept my sincere thanks for your attention." Spencer's explanation did little to soothe Keith's anger, so he struck his flag on the twenty-eighth. He was furious, and to Dundas he claimed that this had occurred "without the least previous intimation or without any cause being assigned."[6] Here Keith lied, since he had heard of alleged differences with Bridport.[7] However, at the time of his dismissal, he maintained that no satisfactory reason existed for his removal. He claimed an affront, and he was "compelled to retire from service rather than to sacrifice the honor of the rank he holds or his own feelings." The next day Keith learned the supposed reason for his dismissal and explained it to Dundas: "Yesterday Lord Spencer *informed* me that He had *informed* you that I had requested to retire from the service without assigning any reason." Keith determined that the First Lord of the Admiralty's short involvement with the naval service prevented him from being entirely versed in related matters, and he had misunderstood Keith's request.[8] Keith had wished to consult a doctor ashore about deafness in his right ear; also, his chronic digestive ailment continued to plague him.[9] Instead, Keith's superiors apparently decided to use this requested absence as the pretext to have him permanently removed from the Channel Fleet.

Once Keith received an explanation for his dismissal, he withdrew his request to retire and sought a new post "as I really feel exceedingly displeased and mortified to be out of employment at a time like the present." Rather, Keith needed another command to rebuild his reputation. During the first half of 1798 he called on every available source of patronage, but his problems while serving in the Channel Fleet had cost him the support of the Admiralty. Keith turned to Dundas, claiming, "I have this instant heard of the Death of Rear Admiral Thomas Frederick at Lisbon which of course makes an opening for a flag in the squadron under St. Vincent who in his letters expresses a desire to have me with him as he had been my first captain in the Service." He wanted Dundas to influence Spencer.[10] The First Lord responded to Keith with a stinging retort: "Your Lordship being out of service at this time was entirely your own act and not at all in consequence of any desire of mine." Several days later Spencer continued, "Whenever your Lordship shall think fit to make an offer of your services generally, without any stipulations or restrictions, if the dispositions and arrangements of the naval force at the time shall be such as to admit of it I shall be very glad to avail myself of your offer."[11] Still needing employment, Keith asked Dundas in June if he might serve under the new Lord Lieutenant of Ireland.[12] This attempt also failed.

In late November, having been unemployed for nearly a year, Keith received orders to join the Earl of St. Vincent's Mediterranean Fleet. Keith had secured this command without Spencer's direct support. As late as February 1799 he recounted, "Circumstanced as I am with the Admiralty, I ask nothing."[13] Instead he had obtained St. Vincent's assistance. Neither Keith nor St. Vincent forgot that when young Keith Elphinstone had entered the navy thirty-six years before, it was aboard the *Gosport* (44) under the command of Captain John Jervis, now lately created an earl for his 1797 victory over the Spanish at Cape St. Vincent. The earl had followed Keith's career, describing him as "my *élève*, Elphinstone" during the American Revolution.[14] Later, in a backhanded compliment, St. Vincent added, "You will never find an officer native of that country [Scotland], figure in supreme command, they are only fit for drudgery, Lord Keith is by far the best I ever met with by land or by sea."[15] St. Vincent in late 1798 looked to Keith as his temporary replacement, so he could take a leave of absence to regain his health. Thus Keith immediately sailed for the Mediterranean, and after "the most turbulent passage I ever had" he anchored at Gibraltar on 19 December.[16] Keith immediately met with St. Vincent, who explained that he had decided to remain in command of the fleet. This exasperated Keith, who complained to his sister, "The Earl hinted at dinner his intention of *dying* on this *rock*."[17]

The Mediterranean was an extremely active theater of operations for the Royal Navy critical to the war against Revolutionary France. Spain, England's onetime ally, had in 1795 switched sides, and during the following year the French conquered much of the Italian Peninsula. In 1798 Napoleon Bonaparte led an expedition that captured both Malta and Egypt. Although Rear Admiral Horatio Nelson's stunning victory at Aboukir Bay had virtually destroyed the French Mediterranean Fleet, isolated units survived, and Bonaparte remained in Egypt. To combat Britain's enemies, St. Vincent scattered his naval forces from Egypt to Spain. West of Gibraltar, the Royal Navy blockaded the Spanish fleet at Cádiz. Within the Mediterranean, Britain's only naval base was Minorca, and Rear Admiral John Thomas Duckworth had orders to defend it from the Spanish. Elsewhere the British had to rely on allies for safe anchorages. Nelson commanded a squadron operating around Sicily and Naples. To the east, another detachment blockaded the French on Malta. In the eastern Mediterranean, a small squadron patrolled the waters off Alexandria, the principal French port in Egypt. Keith concluded, "I think there seems more to be done in the Mediterranean than those who are to do it."[18]

Several weeks passed, and Keith wrote his sister: "I hear Lord Duncan [commander of the North Sea Fleet] has resigned unwell, if so I am sorry, but I wish our chief had known his own mind for I would rather have been first there than second here."[19]

Disgruntled and thwarted, Keith felt his good fortune had turned against him. His personal correspondence was pervaded by gloom and depression, only made worse by the death of his mother one month shy of her eightieth birthday. To his sister he wrote, "I read the death of our good old mother. Although it was an event to be looked for one cannot help being affected by it, and reflecting on human events and their uncertainty."[20] Death was something Keith had dealt with since a young age. Several of his siblings had died as children; he had lost his father in 1781, his wife in 1789, and his eldest brother in 1794. And the "uncertainty" he mentioned had a second meaning—his naval career. This was a total change from July 1797 when he stood at the pinnacle of success following his role in the suppression of the mutinies.

Instead of controlling the entire Mediterranean Fleet as he was originally led to believe by St. Vincent, Keith was given command of the squadron blockading twenty-odd Spanish ships-of-the-line at Cádiz. To accomplish this, he raised his flag in the *Barfleur* (98) and commanded eleven to seventeen British warships. However, St. Vincent maintained that many were "in so crazy a state, they are obliged to come occasionally into the Mole [at Gibraltar] to be patched up." Despite his squadron's poor condition, Keith attempted to lure the Spanish out of Cádiz for an engagement. Yet even when adverse weather blew his ships off station, or when they had to victual, the Spanish did not sail. This led Keith to grumble, "As to blockading Cadiz we may as well be at Spithead."[21] During the first four months of 1799, St. Vincent remained at Gibraltar, confident that the blockade squadron was led by "the only man capable of commanding it."[22]

Meanwhile, the Directory government in Paris decided to undertake a major naval operation in the Mediterranean. France, however, lacked naval forces in the region following the virtual annihilation of the French fleet at the Battle of Aboukir Bay. The Directors instead ordered the powerful Brest fleet under Vice Admiral Eustache Bruix to sail to the Mediterranean, then locate and destroy St. Vincent's scattered fleet. At Cádiz, Bruix was if possible to take the Spanish squadron under his command and defeat Keith's blockade squadron. He was to seek the safety of Toulon only if he sustained damage or if a superior British naval force pursued him. Otherwise, the Directors instructed Bruix to support their army in Italy and then reinforce Corfu, Malta, and Alexandria. With these lofty objectives, the Directors ordered that Bruix "never forget that the conservation of the French fleet on one hand and the honor of the Republican flag on the other" were the twin pillars that should guide the operation.[23] On the night of 25 April 1799, Bruix slipped out of Brest with twenty-five French ships-of-the-line and five frigates. Although the Channel Fleet under Lord Bridport blockaded the port, the entire French fleet eluded them and sailed south. Not until the next morning did Bridport learn of Bruix's departure; he then immediately sent word to both London and the Mediterranean. After intercepting a dispatch stating that Ireland was the French objective, Bridport arrayed his fleet to protect the island. But these dispatches were a ruse designed to mislead the Channel Fleet and allow Bruix to sail for the Mediterranean.[24]

Under "moderate breezes and clear weather," Keith on the morning of 3 May counted fifteen ships-of-the-line in his squadron off Cádiz when the

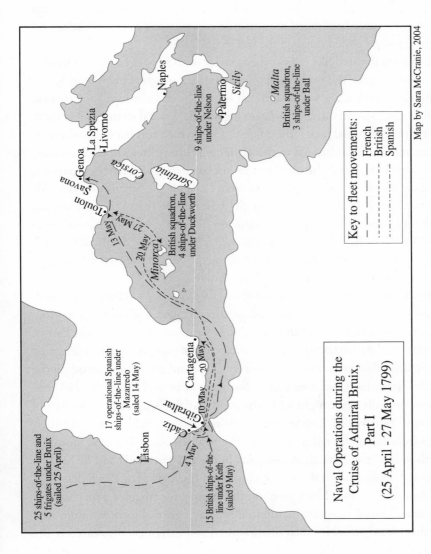

Key to fleet movements:

– – – – French
----------- British
– · – · – · Spanish

25 ships-of-the-line and
5 frigates under Bruix
(sailed 25 April)

17 operational Spanish
ships-of-the-line under
Mazarredo
(sailed 14 May)

Lisbon

Cadiz

Gibraltar

Cartagena

4 May

15 British ships-of-the-
line under Keith
(sailed 9 May)

10 May

20 May

20 May

Minorca

British squadron,
4 ships-of-the-line
under Duckworth

13 May

20 May

27 May

Toulon

Savona

Genoa

La Spezia

Livorno

Corsica

Sardinia

Naples

Palermo

Sicily

9 ships-of-the-line
under Nelson

Malta
British squadron,
3 ships-of-the-line
under Ball

Naval Operations during the
Cruise of Admiral Bruix,
Part I
(25 April - 27 May 1799)

Map by Sara McCranie, 2004

Map 6. Naval Operations during the Cruise of Admiral Bruix, Part I (25 April–27 May 1799).

Childers (14) brought news that Bruix had sailed from Brest. Later that day, the *Success* (32) arrived after sighting a French fleet off Oporto. Not a moment was to be lost. Keith immediately dispatched the *Childers* to warn St. Vincent at Gibraltar, then he ordered his squadron to weigh and clear for battle.[25] All night the ships glided through the waters off Cádiz.

Morning dawned like many others, but it would prove far from a normal day on blockade. The previous day's intelligence weighed heavily on Keith. With clear skies and a west-southwest breeze, he did not have long to wait. At 8:30 a.m., an entry in the *Barfleur's* log noted, "Several strange sail in sight, west on the larboard tack." The *Majestic* (74), which had been placed out to sea to provide an additional warning, sighted thirty-three sail at 10:00 a.m., and Keith ordered his ships to form line of battle.[26] As the first lieutenant of the *Barfleur* described it, "There we were . . . with the Spanish on one side and the French on the other . . . though [we were] less than a third in number of the enemies."[27] Another of the *Barfleur's* lieutenants noted, "According to Lord Keith's pithily expressed opinion, we lay between 'the devil and the deep sea,'"[28] and of the French, Keith later claimed, "Now if they want to go into Cadiz, it must be through the Barfleur's entering port."[29]

By noon the French fleet stood about fifteen miles southwest of Keith's squadron. Early in the afternoon the weather changed, and the *Barfleur's* logbook recorded "Fresh gales and dark cloudy weather." At 1:30 p.m. the French became shrouded in the haze. The weather cleared that evening, revealing that the Spanish fleet remained at anchor in Cádiz and the French stood on the southwest horizon, but Keith again lost sight of both fleets in the darkness. The storm built in the night with "the winds variable with a heavy swell from the west, northwest." This tested the British, who sought to prevent their ships from being dashed to pieces on the Spanish coast. The next morning, Keith found "the Fleet all in company but much scattered" and he became furious.[30] Even though the men had suffered through what Keith described as "the worst weather I have seen" on this station, his enemies were powerful and near.[31] His displeasure manifested itself as a general memorandum stating that "Lord Keith is much disappointed and extremely displeased at the want of attention of the respective commanders by not preserving their stations during the Night."[32] As the daylight on the morning of the fifth broadened the line of sight to the horizon, Keith's lookouts sighted only four of the French ships. The British admiral concluded, "I am apt to believe they passed to the Straits by force of weather or by some other motive." Around noon the last of these stragglers disappeared into the haze.[33]

For the British, several factors multiplied the stress and misery of all involved and particularly of their commanding officer. For three days Keith kept his ships cleared for action. The men had little warm food or sleep, and they were wet and cold from the storm.[34] From the weather conditions Keith correctly concluded, "The enemy had the power to have engaged the British Fleet who could not engage them."[35] On reflection, he attacked the competence of the French and Spanish admirals, saying that "they ought all to be hanged."[36] Afterwards both St. Vincent and Spencer, the First Lord of the Admiralty, praised Keith's conduct, and one British cabinet minister gave tacit approval when he stated that there was "no reason to be dissatisfied with the naval news" since he had been correctly informed that the French and Spanish fleets had planned to unite.[37]

During the night of 5 May, the French fleet passed Gibraltar and entered the Mediterranean. Keith remained off Cádiz, wracked by indecision: "I feel my mind much distressed in this difficult situation, and am at a loss how to decide. If I remain they [the French] may go into the Mediterranean and do infinite mischief—If I leave this, the Spaniards will certainly sail."[38] Keith chose to blockade Cádiz, reasoning that the Spaniards would attempt to sail or the French would return. Meanwhile at Gibraltar, St. Vincent learned that Bruix had entered the Mediterranean. He ordered the British squadron at Cádiz to make for Gibraltar, but contrary winds prevented Keith from receiving this order, and not until the tenth did his squadron anchor at Gibraltar.[39]

Upon Keith's arrival, St. Vincent assumed command and shifted his flag to the *Ville de Paris* (100). Since the ships had suffered terribly off Cádiz, several required repairs and were in no condition to follow Bruix. The adverse weather continued: "in the *Gibraltar*, 50 men struck by lightning, all our sails blown to atoms."[40] It took a whole day to reset the rigging and water the ships. The fleet finally sailed from Gibraltar on 11 May in pursuit of Bruix. This left the area from Lisbon to Gibraltar exposed, but the risk was deemed necessary. Although St. Vincent now exercised direct control over the fleet, his health still suffered, and he ordered Keith to oversee the administration of the entire fleet; Keith considered this "enough to do."[41]

From Gibraltar the ships steered for Port Mahon on Minorca, but on the seventeenth they encountered "strong gales and . . . a heavy sea" which caused extensive damage to the masts and rigging of several ships. The squadron arrived off Minorca on the twentieth and united with Duckworth's four ships-of-the-line charged with patrolling the waters around the island. St. Vincent learned that the French fleet, in great disarray, had passed between Majorca and the Spanish mainland on 10 May, and Duckworth had dispatched the *Santa Theresa* (30) to "dog" the French fleet. Reports from the frigate captain indicated that the French had sailed for Toulon.[42] Armed with this intelligence, St. Vincent on 22 May ordered his fleet to proceed to Toulon. However, as the ships sailed, the cutter *Sandwich* arrived from Gibraltar with news that Vice Admiral José de Mazarredo's Spanish fleet, consisting of seventeen ships-of-the-line, had sailed from Cádiz. St. Vincent deduced that they were attempting to combine with the French fleet. To prevent this juncture, he ordered his ships to sail for Cape Creus to intercept Mazarredo. However, the Spaniards had encountered the same adverse weather that St. Vincent's ships had met on their way to Minorca. Whereas the British quickly repaired the damage caused by the storm, it dismasted nine of the seventeen Spanish ships-of-the-line. It was not until the twenty-seventh that St. Vincent learned of the crippled state of Mazarredo's fleet. He looked for them in the Bay of Rosas but found nothing, for the Spanish had anchored at Cartagena on the twentieth.[43]

St. Vincent could not find his elusive opponents and claimed, "I am so much reduced and my facilities impaired in proportion" that he could not actively engage in the pursuit.[44] He sailed back to Minorca on 2 June. Keith was placed in command of the squadron engaged in the pursuit of the Spanish and French fleets. However, St. Vincent retained overall command for the next two weeks, hindering naval operations with out-of-date orders. St. Vincent remained particularly preoccupied with Minorca's safety, since the Spaniards had assembled naval and military units to retake the island.[45] These Spanish invasion preparations wreaked havoc on British operations. Keith's squadron, by St. Vincent's orders, divided its attention between two disparate objectives—the defense of Minorca and the destruction of the French fleet. When forced to choose, St. Vincent chose Minorca.

In addition to defending Minorca, the British fleet operated under another disadvantage. There were too many admirals. Nelson commanded a growing squadron off Sicily, Keith commanded another squadron, and St.

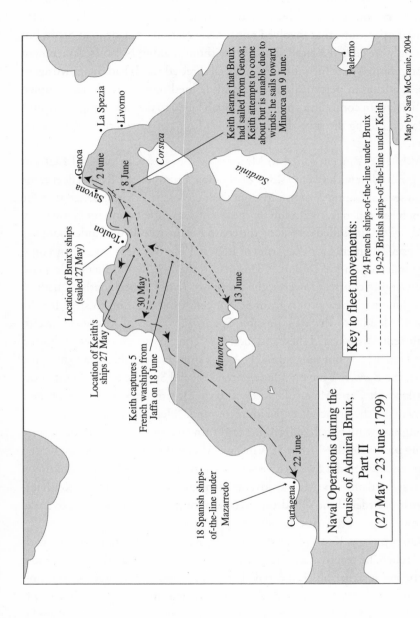

• La Spezia
• Livorno

Corsica

Genoa •
1/2 June

Savona •
8 June

Keith learns that Bruix had sailed from Genoa; Keith attempts to come about but is unable due to winds; he sails toward Minorca on 9 June.

Location of Bruix's ships (sailed 27 May)

• Toulon

Location of Keith's ships 27 May

30 May

13 June

Keith captures 5 French warships from Jaffa on 18 June

Minorca

Sardinia

• Palermo

Map by Sara McCranie, 2004

Key to fleet movements:

— · — · — 24 French ships-of-the-line under Bruix
· · · · · · · · 19-25 British ships-of-the-line under Keith

Naval Operations during the Cruise of Admiral Bruix, Part II (27 May - 23 June 1799)

18 Spanish ships-of-the-line under Mazarredo

Cartagena •
22 June

Map 7. Naval Operations during the Cruise of Admiral Bruix, Part II (27 May–23 June 1799).

Vincent, who retained overall command, tried to control the movements of both squadrons from Minorca. To do this, he devised an extremely complex plan of operations that involved reinforcing Nelson's squadron at Sicily, but this only weakened Keith's squadron without making Nelson's detachment strong enough to confront Bruix. Also, all three admirals had their own agendas, resulting in petty jealousies and ill-defined objectives. When coupled with delays in communications, the British failed to take advantage of Bruix's isolation during the time that the Spanish fleet remained crippled at Cartagena.

While St. Vincent sailed to Minorca to convalesce, he ordered Keith to sail for Toulon with twenty ships-of-the-line. En route, the British fleet came upon several fishing vessels, and from their crews the British learned that the French had sailed from Toulon on the twenty-seventh, bound for Genoa. Accordingly, Keith sailed east along the coast. Meanwhile, Bruix landed supplies and reinforcements for the Army of Italy at Vado Bay near Savona and on 6 June sailed again for Toulon.[46] This placed the British and French fleets on a converging course. However, the transport *Triton* joined Keith's squadron on 6 June with new orders from St. Vincent directing him to steer for the Bay of Alcudia to thwart a possible Spanish invasion of Minorca.[47] Keith admittedly disregarded these instructions: "contrary to my orders I followed [the French] . . . but met calms."[48] As his ships clawed their way along the coast, the *Barfleur*'s log on 8 June noted "Several Strange Sail in Sight" near an island off Cape Mele.[49] Unknown to the British, these were the advance elements of the French fleet. Keith recounted, "Here we were overtaken by a strong east wind which obliged me to return to cover Minorca in obedience to my positive orders" from St. Vincent. After sailing twenty leagues, Keith's ships encountered a Swedish vessel whose captain identified the unknown ships sighted off Cape Mele as advance elements of the French fleet. Keith immediately ordered the squadron to come about, but his ships failed to make headway against the easterly wind.[50]

On 9 June, as Keith's fleet struggled against contrary winds to close with the French, he received another order from St. Vincent dated 3 June.[51] These confusing instructions indicated that Keith should reinforce Nelson and return to protect Minorca as "the Spaniards will make an attempt on this island the moment they are ready."[52] Since this was the second order from St. Vincent ordering him to defend Minorca, Keith determined that the island had to be in imminent danger. He summoned his captains to his flagship and

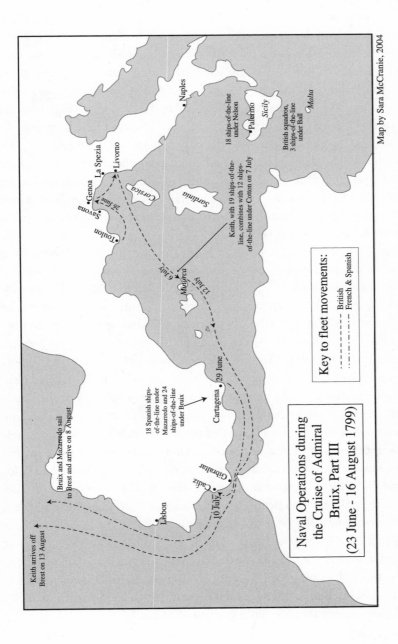

Map 8. Naval Operations during the Cruise of Admiral Bruix, Part III (23 June–16 August 1799).

Within the map:

Naval Operations during the Cruise of Admiral Bruix, Part III (23 June - 16 August 1799)

Key to fleet movements:
- - - - - British
- · - · - French & Spanish

Naples

18 ships-of-the-line under Nelson

Palermo

Sicily

British squadron, 3 ships-of-the-line under Ball

Malta

La Spezia

Livorno

Genoa

Savona

26 June

Toulon

Corsica

Sardinia

Keith, with 19 ships-of-the-line, combines with 12 ships-of-the-line under Cotton on 7 July

6 July

Mallorca

13 July

Cartagena

29 June

18 Spanish ships-of-the-line under Mazarredo and 24 ships-of-the-line under Bruix

Gibraltar

Cadiz

Lisbon

10 July

Bruix and Mazarredo sail to Brest and arrive on 8 August

Keith arrives off Brest on 13 August

Map by Sara McCranie, 2004

told them that it was St. Vincent's decision that they curtail the chase. After the meeting, one of the *Barfleur*'s lieutenants heard Keith venting his frustrations at length on the quarterdeck. "I never saw a man more irritated. When annoyed, his lordship had a habit of talking aloud to himself." The lieutenant reported that Keith's dialogue contained "some very strong expressions, imputing jealousy on the part of Lord St. Vincent as constituting the motive for recalling him."[53] Later, when Keith calmed down, he accurately wrote his sister, "You may prepare to hear me abused because I have been unlucky . . . after having missed destroying the only remains of the French Navy. Although I shall be blamed I have no fault, but having gone farther than I ought strictly speaking."[54] Rear Admiral Cuthbert Collingwood, then on his way to join the Mediterranean Fleet, likewise stated that St. Vincent "wou'd have ill brooked the laurels which presented themselves to us, being gathered by another hand under his nose."[55]

Keith arrived off Minorca on 13 June. The next day, he shifted his flag from the *Barfleur* to the *Queen Charlotte* (100) and assumed command of the Mediterranean Fleet. St. Vincent had decided that his health possibly hindered British naval operations. Moreover, the situation was not fair to Keith, and St. Vincent explained his decision to Nelson as being for "the public good."[56] With the entire fleet now under his orders, Keith again pursued Bruix. On 18 June, about fifty-five miles southwest of Cape Sicié and Toulon, the squadron located "5 strange sail in sight to the NW." Keith ordered Captain John Markham of the *Centaur* (74) with three other ships-of-the-line to ascertain their identity. During the evening, the British came up on the ships, found them to be French, and captured them without a fight. However, these ships were not part of Bruix's fleet. Rather, they consisted of three frigates and a pair of sloops under Rear Admiral Jean-Baptiste Perrée that had sailed from Jaffa in May.[57] After taking the five ships, Keith's fleet cruised off Toulon before sailing east to Bruix's last known location off Cape Mele and then south toward Corsica. Near this island he learned that the French had been sighted around Cartagena. Since Mazarredo's Spanish fleet was completing its repairs at this port, Keith concluded that the French and Spanish fleets had combined. Fearing for the safety of Minorca, Keith's nineteen ships-of-the-line returned to the island, and he sent orders to Nelson, then off Sicily, to dispatch all the ships he could spare to Minorca.[58]

On 7 July, while Keith's fleet sailed toward Port Mahon, they fell in with twelve ships-of-the-line from the Channel Fleet under Rear Admiral Sir

Charles Cotton. The British now had thirty-one ships-of-the-line and six frigates to confront the combined fleet of forty-two ships-of-the-line and a dozen frigates. On 8 July the fleet anchored at Port Mahon, and Keith claimed, "I have had a hard life these last two months," for the constant failures had taken their toll. He was sanguine about how others would perceive his actions. He declared, "Ill fortune is always guilty in the eyes of the ignorant, and I am prepared to be abused by all my old friends at least, and most new ones, if it will serve their turn. Such is friendship in politics."[59]

With the British fleet at Minorca, a spy from Barcelona arrived to report that the Franco-Spanish fleet had sailed for the Straits of Gibraltar on 29 June.[60] Keith feared that "it might be a blind to lead me below them whilst they doubled back to the southward and came upon this island."[61] Rather than immediately commit his force, Keith sent his six frigates to search for Bruix, while he partially watered his fleet and then sailed on 12 July for Cartagena. In the meantime, he prepared for Minorca's defense during his fleet's absence, for the Spanish still had several serviceable warships in the area, even after Mazarredo had sailed with the Combined Fleet. First, Keith commissioned the recently captured French ships of Perrée's squadron and sent Nelson another order to dispatch the majority of his eighteen ships-of-the-line to Minorca.[62]

Off Naples, Nelson received Keith's first letter ordering him to reinforce Minorca, but he failed to comply, believing that if the British were to risk either Minorca or Naples, it should be Minorca. Nelson also claimed that he needed his entire squadron to destroy the last vestiges of a Jacobin rebellion in Naples. He did, however, agree to dispatch several ships when he had concluded the sieges of Capua and Gaeta. Even after receiving Keith's second appeal, Nelson temporized by maintaining that he needed "to drive the French scoundrels out of the Kingdom."[63] It was the twenty-third before Nelson detached Duckworth to Minorca with only four of his fifteen British ships-of-the-line.[64] St. Vincent too remained concerned about the island, and on 7 July he had suggested that Keith have Nelson send several of his ships to Minorca. However, Nelson continued to believe that he should protect Naples. Not until ten days after the first of Nelson's ships had sailed did he send two more ships-of-the-line to Minorca. To his wife Nelson complained, "As to myself he [Keith] has so pushed me with orders that had I obeyed them literally the Kingdom of Naples would certainly at this moment have been in the hands of the French and this country in a state of confusion."[65]

Meanwhile St. Vincent, on his way to convalesce in Britain, arrived at Gibraltar, and on 7 July he learned that the Franco-Spanish fleet was attempting to pass through the straits. He at once dispatched Captain Andrew Todd aboard a small privateer to warn Keith. It proved an arduous passage, and "Todd passed through the [Franco-Spanish] fleet at two o'clock on the morning of the 8th, becalmed about forty miles to the Eastward of Gibraltar." On the fourteenth he fell in with Keith's ships near Cartagena. The admiral immediately steered for the straits, lamenting that he had failed to rendezvous with any of his six frigates, for without these ships he lost much of his reconnaissance capability.[66] Still, Keith claimed, "Together this squadron is equal to combat them, notwithstanding their apparent superiority."[67] It seemed probable that Keith would leave the Mediterranean in pursuit of Bruix, so on 15 July he ordered Nelson to assume temporary command of His Majesty's ships in the Mediterranean. By the time Keith approached Gibraltar on the twenty-first, five of the six British frigates had rejoined the fleet. On the following day the *Impétueux* (74) brought news from Gibraltar that the Franco-Spanish Fleet had sailed from Cádiz. Even so, Keith ordered his ships to stand toward Tetuan Bay on the North African coast for desperately needed provisions. On the twenty-third the ships weathered a hard west gale as they lay at anchor, and Keith learned that the Combined Fleet had sailed toward Cape St. Vincent. A combination of adverse weather and the lack of provisions delayed the British fleet until the night of the twenty-sixth, when the wind shifted to the west, but on the twenty-seventh a gale developed, dispersing the fleet. The next day, the ships "worked around Europa Point" at the southern tip of Gibraltar before anchoring in Algeciras Bay. They finally passed through the straits on the thirtieth, pushed by a northeasterly wind.[68] The pursuit then continued past Cádiz, and Keith feared that the Combined Fleet had sailed for either the West Indies or Ireland. Not until 8 August when the British fleet approached Cape Finisterre did Keith receive positive intelligence about the Franco-Spanish fleet. His ships stopped a Danish vessel whose captain reported that he had sighted the Combined Fleet on the sixth. From this information Keith determined that Bruix had in fact sailed for Brest, and he continued the pursuit.[69]

Keith left a curious situation in the Mediterranean. Nelson, the ranking officer in the region, refused to follow orders for the defense of Minorca. However, delays in communication prevented Keith from realizing the extent of the insubordination, and Nelson's seniority meant that command devolved to him when Keith's ships sailed through the straits. When the Admiralty learned of the problems relating to the defense of Minorca, the Lords Commissioners indicated to Nelson that they did "not therefore see any sufficient reason to justify your having disobeyed the orders you had received from your commanding officer." These views were echoed by St. Vincent, who declared that "under all circumstances, it appears that Lord Nelson had more force with him than could be spared with England and Ireland at stake."[70] Even with these statements censuring his conduct, the Lords of the Admiralty sent another dispatch to Nelson giving him temporary command of the Mediterranean Fleet during Keith's absence.[71] This indicated that the Admiralty did not view Nelson's insubordination as a severe breach of orders that would necessitate his recall.

With the movements of Franco-Spanish fleet uncertain, the Admiralty prepared for all contingencies. Spencer hoped that Keith would fight Bruix wherever possible. If this did not happen, and if the Combined Fleet reached English waters, Bridport had twenty-seven or twenty-eight ships-of-the-line, exclusive of Admiral Lord Duncan's squadron off the Texel, to confront Bruix.[72] Even with these British preparations, the Franco-Spanish fleet slipped into Brest on 7 August. A week later Keith received confirmation when he ordered Captain Sir Edward Pellew of the *Impétueux* to look into the harbor. Pellew also interrogated a French pilot found aboard a Prussian vessel near Brest, who indicated that there were forty-four ships-of-the-line in the French port but some were in urgent need of repair.[73]

After learning of the Combined Fleet's arrival at Brest, Keith anchored on 16 August at Torbay, where he obtained much-needed supplies. Many of the ships that had blockaded Cádiz in early May were in poor condition even before Bruix made his appearance. These ships had thereafter been constantly at sea for more than three months, and the remainder of Keith's ships had been at sea for at least two. Many urgently needed repairs, and others lacked stores such as sails, cordage, canvas, twine hammocks, and small spars, since sustained operations by a reinforced Mediterranean Fleet had nearly exhausted supplies at Port Mahon and Gibraltar. However, the Admiralty was hard pressed for ships, and only those in the worst state underwent repairs. Moreover, Keith received orders on the nineteenth placing his fleet under Bridport's command. Spencer hoped that the arrival of Keith's ships would allow for the formation of a large fleet out of the Mediterranean and Channel commands to combat the Franco-Spanish fleet in Brest.[74]

The voyage of Admiral Bruix had come to a conclusion. Although the British leaders would have preferred a decisive naval engagement, the entire affair could have gone much worse. Upon entering the Mediterranean, Bruix could have destroyed the scattered British fleet. Instead, the French plan had continuously evolved from the one envisioned by the French government. The original orders directed Bruix to destroy the dispersed British squadrons in the Mediterranean and then resupply and reinforce Corfu, Malta, and Egypt, but there was a caveat to his orders. If his ships received damage, then Bruix was to anchor at a French port for repairs. Several of his ships did sustain weather damage, so he sailed for Toulon. There he learned that Corfu had surrendered, so he abandoned plans to resupply that island as well as Malta and Egypt. He was instead to support the French army in Italy. Additional orders and sometimes faulty intelligence confused the situation, and Bruix received little support from his grudging Spanish ally. Bruix's return to the Atlantic and his eventual passage to Brest were duly approved by the Directors, and the Spanish were forced to comply.[75] As Keith stated after the near engagement at Cádiz, "The French have a great game before them if they play it well, but their late conduct leads me to doubt it."[76] Did the French play it well? They survived, yet they could have achieved far more than they did with such a concentration of naval forces.

During the pursuit of Bruix, Keith had an unenviable job. He began as a subordinate closely watched by St. Vincent, whose illness impeded the British quest as he attempted to direct the fleet's movements from Minorca, hundreds of miles away from the battle fleet. More damning, several of Keith's contemporaries argued that St. Vincent did his best to interfere with operations so as to make a naval engagement between Keith and Bruix an elusive quest.[77] Then, during a very intense period of naval activity, Keith took command of the entire fleet. Although he had been in the Mediterranean for six months, he had to assume these additional responsibilities while continuing the pursuit.

This was Keith's most important command to date, and the outcome of the operation had a profound influence on the naval war until the Peace of Amiens and possibly beyond. When the combined French and Spanish fleets had anchored at Brest, no naval force remained in the Mediterranean capable of defeating the Royal Navy. At the same time, the concentration of French and Spanish forces at Brest posed a direct threat to England. If Keith had defeated Bruix, he would have eliminated the most serious remaining challenge to British sea power. On the other hand, if Keith's fleet had been destroyed, this would have been the largest naval engagement of the Napoleonic Wars, and the losses sustained by Keith's force, numbering thirty-one ships-of-the-line, could possibly have threatened Britain's naval dominance. It was under these weighty conditions that Keith attempted to resurrect the career he had almost destroyed in late 1797 while serving in the Channel Fleet. Although he retained his cynicism, Keith demonstrated that he was a capable but cautious leader despite St. Vincent's interference and Nelson's insubordination. In the end, the pursuit of Bruix reestablished Keith's reputation and restored Spencer's faith in him, and instead of the Admiralty replacing him upon his return to England, they appointed Nelson as temporary commander in the Mediterranean with the object of having Keith return in the near future.[78]

5

"I am a great loser"

Keith in the Western Mediterranean (1800)

With Bruix's powerful Franco-Spanish fleet anchored in Brest, the Admiralty decided to amalgamate the ships Keith brought from the Mediterranean with Lord Bridport's Channel Fleet. However, animosity still existed between Bridport and Keith following the November 1797 altercation that had resulted in the latter being removed from the Channel Fleet. Serving again in this fleet worried Keith, who speculated, "I think it is likely they will order me to Plymouth or Torbay so that I may not interfere with the Lord Bridport or Gardiner [second in command]."[1] This concern proved accurate, since Bridport attempted to reignite the controversy by claiming that Keith had altered the deployments of two Channel Fleet ships while pursuing Bruix. Later the Admiralty approved of Keith's decision, but Bridport declared that they were "strictly under my command" and these movements were "unnecessary, if not altogether unprecedented."[2]

Keith disliked serving in the Channel Fleet, and to his sister voiced his dissatisfaction: "I [am] of no more use here than you would be; the ship may, but not me as third in command."[3] Yet Keith demonstrated maturity by not antagonizing Bridport. Instead, he looked to the patronage of Dundas and Spencer. At an interview with Spencer, Keith learned that he would take command of the Channel Fleet if a pretext could be found for dismissing Bridport. On 10 September, however, Keith claimed, "I only languish to get back to the Mediterranean where I feel my responsibility independent." Spencer decided that if Bridport remained in the Channel, he would return Keith to the Mediterranean. Although support from the Admiralty was important, Dundas's influence also helped, and on 15 November the Admiralty ordered Keith to raise his flag in the *Queen Charlotte* (100) and sail to the Mediterranean to supersede Nelson as commander of the fleet, which then numbered seventeen ships-of-the-line, ten frigates, eight sloops, and several other vessels. To Dundas, Keith rejoiced, "I beg to return to you my most sincere thanks for the Handsome and manly support you have given me on this and former occasions."[4]

The *Queen Charlotte* sailed from Britain on 20 November, and in early December Keith encountered Rear Admiral John Thomas Duckworth with five ships-of-the-line blockading several Spanish warships in Cádiz. Keith then sailed into the Mediterranean and received a situation report from Nelson. A British squadron still sailed off the Egyptian coast under the command of Captain Sir Sidney Smith. Nelson's last reports from him were dated 7 September. One notable event relating to France and Egypt had occurred during Keith's absence—Napoleon Bonaparte had sailed to France, abandoning his army. In addition, Nelson wanted to station ships off Genoa to assist the Austrians, but he maintained that he did not have the resources to extend the British commitment. At Malta, Nelson explained that Captain Sir Thomas Troubridge's squadron continued to blockade Valletta, the last French stronghold on the island, but the British and the Maltese were too weak to end the siege.[5] Disappointed, Keith realized that little had changed in the Mediterranean in the five months he had been absent. To his sister he sarcastically wrote, "Lord Nelson is arrived. I am much employed. Of course he brings no news."[6]

To remedy some of Britain's deficiencies in the Mediterranean, Keith appealed directly to the king and queen of Naples for soldiers to serve on Malta and ships to blockade Genoa. This led Nelson and Keith to visit the Neapolitan royals at Palermo on 9 February. Afterwards a disgusted Keith complained, "The King, Queen and the family have passed the day with me and seemed content—so am I that they are gone." Overall, he claimed, "the whole was a Scene of fulsome Vanity and Absurdity all the *long* eight days I was at Palermo." He added, "Notwithstanding every attention this life does not suit me. Business and pleasure go ill together."[7] Still, the stay at Palermo yielded several tangible results. By treaty, the Neapolitans were to furnish the British Mediterranean Fleet with several ships-of-the-line; since they no longer possessed any ships of this type, they decided to send in their place two frigates and several other vessels to reinforce the British and Austrians off Genoa. The Neapolitans also promised 1,200 newly raised soldiers for service on Malta, albeit "those troops were by no means good, being newly raised and badly officered." On 11 February, Nelson and Keith sailed from Palermo with the Neapolitan soldiers destined for Malta embarked aboard their ships.[8]

While Keith remained at Malta, a French squadron under Rear Admiral Jean-Baptiste Perrée sailed from Toulon on 7 February with supplies and reinforcements for Valletta. His Majesty's frigate *Success* (32), while patrolling off the southwest coast of Sicily, discovered the French squadron on the twelfth and sailed to warn the British ships off Malta. The arrival of Nelson and Keith near Malta meant that Perrée faced a reinforced squadron numbering six ships-of-the-line and several frigates. The French squadron consisted of the flagship *Généreux* (74), three corvettes, and a storeship. With the wind blowing from the northwest, Keith ordered Nelson in his flagship the *Foudroyant* (80), along with the *Audacious* (74) and the *Northumberland* (74), to sail off Valletta to windward. The *Lion* (64) patrolled the waters between Malta and Gozo, while the *Alexander* (74) and the *Success* sailed southeast of Malta. Keith, aboard the *Queen Charlotte*, anchored in the mouth of Valletta harbor in case the French eluded the blockade.[9]

The *Alexander* and the *Success* intercepted Perrée's squadron at 8:00 a.m. on 18 February and immediately forced the French storeship to strike her colors. The British then continued the pursuit. Being to windward, Nelson ordered his ships to run down on the French. As his squadron closed, he ordered the *Audacious* and the *Corso* (18) to secure the storeship, while he chased the *Généreux* with his remaining ships. Around 1:30 p.m. the *Success* and the *Alexander* closed with the French squadron. The three corvettes tacked to windward and escaped, but the British ships prevented the *Généreux* from following. The *Success* then raked the French ship-of-the-line with several broadsides. Meanwhile Nelson in the *Foudroyant* closed with the *Généreux*. At 4:30 p.m. he came up on the French ship, and after a very short engagement Perrée surrendered.[10]

Several days after the capture of the *Généreux*, Keith returned to the western Mediterranean but lamented, "I am plagued with fools about me."[11] Nelson was left in command of the blockade squadron off Malta, since several French warships remained at Valletta. Nelson pleaded illness and asked for time to recuperate at Palermo. Keith countered by ordering him to stay away from Lady Hamilton in Palermo and direct the blockade from Syracuse, Messina, or Augusta.[12] Instead of repairing to one of these Sicilian ports, Nelson grudgingly remained off Malta in response to intelligence indicating that several French warships anchored at Valletta were preparing to sail. Even so, Nelson placed Captain Troubridge in temporary command on 10 March and sailed for Palermo. Although an extremely capable officer, Troubridge was also ailing, and this worried Keith; however, important occurrences elsewhere in the Mediterranean kept him from Malta.[13] British intelligence about the ships at Valletta proved correct, and the *Guillaume Tell* (84), the last vestige of the French fleet that Nelson had virtually destroyed at Aboukir Bay, sailed on the night of 29 March. Troubridge's ships intercepted her, and after fighting off three British warships for three and a half hours, the *Guillaume Tell*, nearly dismasted and little more than a hulk, surrendered.[14]

Nelson was never Keith's ideal subordinate, and several of his actions after Keith's return to the Mediterranean smack of insubordination. Admiral William Young, a member of the Admiralty, contended, "Nelson must have been sadly mortified at not having been present when she [*Guillaume Tell*] was taken; that will be a sort of crisis to his disgrace, and will certainly make him ill enough to come home, and perhaps for his sake it is much better that he should."[15] While Nelson remained in Palermo, Keith readily granted him permission to convalesce in England, but a defiant Nelson returned to the waters off Malta on 4 May to assume command of the blockade squadron, and Keith could not guess his intentions. In May the Lords of the Admiralty gave official sanction for Nelson's departure, but he remained with his command until 11 July, when he accepted an invitation to accompany the queen of Naples and the Hamiltons on a tour across Europe.[16] Nelson, who had hitherto functioned as one of Lord Keith's chief subordinates and who had commanded the Mediterranean Fleet during Keith's absence in late 1799, resented having his authority superseded upon Keith's return to the Mediterranean. Since he had garnered much fame, particularly for his actions at Aboukir Bay, he sought to exercise greater independence than his position warranted, and he also used a legitimate illness to excuse the pursuit of his own interests with Lady Hamilton. Overall, his departure from the Mediterranean enhanced the effectiveness of the fleet and left Keith's authority unquestioned.

While Keith dealt with Nelson and Malta, he determined that he must blockade Genoa. With an excellent harbor, it had once been a great maritime power, but it had fallen into decline, and in the wars of the Revolutionary Era the French had occupied the city along with much of Italy. However, French control of the region was shattered in 1799 by a combined Russian and Austrian offensive which ground to a halt that winter only a dozen miles east of Genoa. Keith decided that an effectual blockade of the city would hinder French efforts to supply their army in Italy. In January he sent Captain Thomas Louis to blockade Genoa with the *Minotaur* (74), two frigates, and three smaller vessels. The Austrian army commander, General Michael

Frederick Melas, suggested to Louis and ultimately to Keith that cooperation should increase between the Austrian army and the British navy for the reduction of the city.[17] After departing Malta, Keith sailed for Livorno and immediately met with Colonel de Best of the Austrian army to discuss joint operations. The conference laid the groundwork for cooperation between Britain and Austria in the upcoming campaign against Genoa.[18]

In an attempt to act in concert with the Austrians, Keith along with several members of his personal staff landed at Livorno on 16 March. While he and his party remained ashore, the *Queen Charlotte* slipped out of port on the morning of the seventeenth under the command of Captain Andrew Todd to reconnoiter the nearby island of Capraia, which served as a base for ten to twenty privateers that attacked merchant ships in the area. While still in the offing, the *Queen Charlotte* burst into flames. At 7:30 a.m. Keith received information that his flagship had caught fire some ten miles outside the mole. He quickly dispatched his flag lieutenant and a master's mate to mount a rescue operation. At about the same time, the British consul, the health officer, the Chamber of Commerce, and the Austrian commander in Livorno sent tartans and other small vessels to assist the *Queen Charlotte*. Keith watched his flagship burn all morning. The fire quickly spread; soon Keith could see the sails and masts engulfed in flames. As the men tried to escape, he watched the bowsprit snap under the weight of men desperately clinging to it for safety. Once the vessels sent out of the harbor reached the *Queen Charlotte*, most did not close with the burning ship, fearing that her magazines would explode and destroy them as well. By 9:00 a.m. the fire had weakened several of the beams, causing some of the middle-deck guns to fall through to the lower deck. From the forecastle the sailors tried to stem the fire for another hour before abandoning ship. Later the burning hull sank, and then the magazine exploded underwater, shooting the mainmast some distance into the air and killing many of the sailors as it landed in the water.[19] Small merchant vessels and harbor boats sought to rescue the struggling survivors, but an offshore wind delayed their return to Livorno. Not knowing the human cost of the disaster and with many friends' and protégés' lives in the balance, Keith waited "with the utmost impatience to hear the fate of those who were of late so comfortable on board the first of ships."[20] The losses were staggering. Over the next day and a half, eight vessels arrived at Livorno with the almost naked and often injured survivors. At most, 11 officers and 159 were saved out of a crew of 790.[21]

Keith took the loss of his ship personally, explaining, "My late blow has been a hard one."[22] Among those lost were several acquaintances brought aboard the *Queen Charlotte* so Keith could exercise his considerable patronage powers in securing their promotions. As fleet commander he lamented, "I am for the second time this war left oppressed with affairs Naked without orders, instructions, papers, maps or Instruments, Flags or Signals to conduct a squadron."[23] Since he lost all his personal effects as well, he wrote to Mary, his sister, instructing her to ask Admiral Young, a member of the Admiralty Board and Keith's personal friend, to ship him new furniture, plate, and linen. Keith also complained, "I am a great loser; besides all my things I had a considerable sum of money on the ship."[24] Finally, this disaster deprived Keith of the most powerful ship and the only three-decked ship-of-the-line in his command. Given the space requirements of an admiral and his staff, most flag officers and especially fleet commanders preferred three-decked ships, since these allowed for tolerable accommodations for both the ship's captain and the admiral. Besides, three-decked ships-of-the-line were more imposing and prestigious than ships of two gun decks. For these reasons, Keith appealed to the Admiralty for a new ship, but the concentration of the French and Spanish fleets at Brest prevented the Admiralty from dispatching a replacement.[25] Even without his assigned flagship, Keith remained busy at Livorno during the rest of March cooperating with the Austrians as they formulated their plan of operations against Genoa.

In early April, 60,000 Austrian soldiers commenced attacking on a broad front. The French army numbering 29,500 men under the command of General of Division André Masséna attempted to halt the offensive. However, the Austrians penetrated to the coast at Vado, seized Savona, and severed Masséna's lines of communication with France. Then, on 11 April, British gunboats and cutters sailed close to the shore, firing in support of the advancing Austrian columns. Similar operations continued the next day when British gunboats assisted their ally in capturing the port of Veruggio. English gunfire prevented the French from withdrawing along the coastal road on the thirteenth, forcing them to retreat through the mountains. At the same time, the Royal Navy landed munitions and evacuated Austrian wounded. Despite a calm coupled with a strong current that carried all the larger vessels twenty miles out to sea on the eighteenth, the Austrians continued their attack with the effective support of a few cutters and launches. Keith exulted that the smaller vessels "compensated for our absence by tearing the enemy to pieces and to use Melas's words they filled the Streets with blood and decided the fate of the day."[26]

Besides providing naval gunfire to support the Austrian advance, the Royal Navy ferried troops and supplies, leading Keith to claim, "They declare they cannot take Genoa without me, nor feed their army on the coast."[27] In addition, the Royal Navy effectively maintained the blockade, as was evidenced by captured dispatches indicating that the French had begun to run short of grain. Twenty ships had sailed from Marseilles to revictual the city, but several British ships turned them back, and during the first week of May, Keith's ships captured an entire convoy of vessels laden with provisions for Genoa, adding to the dearth of food in the city.[28]

While operations continued at Genoa, the fortress of Savona with its small French garrison also resisted. Although surrounded by the Austrians on land and Keith's ships at sea, the fortress proved a difficult position to assail, and the allies starved the French into submission after a forty-one-day siege. The Austrians under General St. Julien accepted the French surrender at sundown on 15 May without the concurrence of any British naval officer. This violated the agreement made by Keith and Melas prior to the campaign: in any negotiation dealing with fortresses and towns located on the coast, the British and Austrians were both to be parties to all discussions and decisions. Whereas the Austrians had total control over civil, military, and political arrangements, the two nations shared in the prizes garnered in the capitulation of any seaside town or fortress. When Keith learned that the Austrians and French had finalized the surrender arrangements for Savona, contrary to his previous agreement with Melas, he believed that the Austrians had infringed upon the honor of Britain and upon the possibility of additional prize money. Keith explained that the navy had played a critical role in preventing supplies from entering Savona during the siege and yet had no voice in negotiations for its surrender. On 23 May, Keith received an apology from Melas stating that St. Julien had acted inappropriately and that the Austrians wished to deal fairly with the British in the future.[29] Following this event, Melas upheld his promise until the French forced the Austrian army to cease hostilities.

The Austrians continued to tighten their perimeter around Genoa, and by the last week of April they had driven the French back to the walls of the city. Several days later the British shelled Genoa and exchanged gunfire with French shore batteries. This caused unrest among the civilian population, and some of the city's residents attempted to escape by sea. Since the city was under a notice of blockade, Keith refused to allow civilians to sail from the harbor. This resulted in many deaths, but Keith understood that the city would surrender earlier if the French had more mouths to feed. In a letter to Masséna, Keith threatened to fire on anyone fleeing the city.[30]

The British ships remained in the offing, and Keith's bomb vessels fired on the city during nights when the weather remained favorable. However, storms caused the suspension of operations for several days in mid-May. This respite allowed the French to assemble a small flotilla consisting of a galley and several smaller vessels. About noon on 20 May they ventured out of Genoa and exchanged shots with Keith's squadron; before dark, they withdrew and anchored under the protection of their shore batteries on the mole. That evening Keith dispatched Captain Philip Beaver of the *Aurora* (28) with several vessels to bombard the city. Beaver drew fire from the French flotilla and resolved to eliminate it. In a daring nighttime raid, he led ten launches and ships' boats into the harbor and captured the *Prima*, a galley of fifty oars. Afterwards the 115 galley slaves joined the British sailors in rowing her out of the harbor. These slaves comprised some of the worst criminals in Genoa, and Keith did not know what to do with them. If he freed them, they would ravage the Italian countryside, so he offered them to Masséna. Surprisingly, the French general responded that members of the local government agreed to take back the convicts. At this point Keith appears to have returned most of them to Genoa.[31] Captain Beaver's operation on the night of 21 May was a complete success. The remainder of the French flotilla did not venture again from the harbor.

While Masséna grimly held Genoa, Napoleon Bonaparte attempted to force the Austrians from northern Italy. With the French Army of the Reserve, Napoleon crossed the Alps and entered Milan by the end of May. This maneuver placed the Army of the Reserve on the left rear of the Austrian army. To confront this threat, Melas had to transfer soldiers away from his operations at Genoa, and thus he began to raise the siege. Meanwhile, Masséna had all but exhausted his provisions, leading Keith to claim, "In Genoa things is very bad and if I could get *Men* to be honest it must yield in a day or two but alas this is not the Age of Honest men."[32] Ignorant of Bonaparte's maneuver, Masséna, with only three days' rations left, decided on 1 June to enter negotiations with the Austrians and British. Although little resulted from the first two days of talks, Masséna sent word that he wished to meet directly with Keith and the Austrian commander on the fourth. However, this was the day that the Austrians had planned to raise the siege, but Keith claimed that he persuaded the Austrian commander to delay his army's departure. They all met at 8:00 a.m. on the fourth, and a bitter interview ensued, lasting until 7:00 p.m.[33] Keith later referred to Masséna as both "the greatest Brute in Christendom"[34] and "the most brutal fellow I ever met,"[35] but in the end the French general announced that he would evacuate the city. At the conclusion of the meeting, Masséna later claimed, Keith took his hand and said, "General, if only England and France could get together, they would rule the world." With an air of superiority, Masséna responded that "France was sufficient."[36] Later Keith's arrogance or his overly inflated ego led him to claim, "I beged *one* day and in that time got Genoa."[37] This was hardly the case; it was the Austrians who had won Genoa after fighting the battles and suffering the great majority of the losses in the campaign. This is just one instance where Keith attempted to magnify his personal role and demonstrate the importance of the navy. Indeed, his actions at Genoa over the following weeks would make these actions seem mild.

Following the French evacuation agreement, a convoy loaded with food entered Genoa, and before midnight the French soldiers received provisions. In addition, Keith ordered a captured French vessel loaded with biscuits to anchor at Genoa. These provisions were sold at a low price to the city's poor. By 8 June, 20,000 sacks of grain plus vegetables had arrived in Genoa for the inhabitants. While Keith attempted to alleviate the suffering, his men took possession of the port facilities on 5 June. On the following day many of Masséna's men sailed from the harbor, and Keith detailed several English ships to assist in the operation, while those French who were healthy enough to march moved out of the city toward Nice.[38]

During the nine-week siege, coalition warfare had proved remarkably successful. The British dealt exclusively with nautical matters while the Austrians controlled the land forces, providing a clear division of authority. At sea, Keith's ships had successfully halted French supplies destined for the city; only one vessel containing a cargo of chestnuts and 600 sacks of flour successfully ran the blockade. As for relations with the Austrians, Spencer, the First Lord of the Admiralty, felt that Keith had performed admirably to facilitate cooperation between the two nations, while Keith wrote, "It is fortunate the Austrians are enchanted with the services the ships yield there, which is so far good."[39] Yet all was not well. Even before the French army crossed the Alps and threatened the Austrian rear, Keith complained, "Good God what a pity these Austrians were not more Active, had Genoa fallen when it ought we might have been at Grenoble if not Lyons."[40] Nor did Austrian customs appeal to Keith, who groused, "I live the life of an Anchorite against my will and never see the face of woman, but I am duly kissed by the men it is a vile Austrian custom."[41] Still, Keith refrained from making complaints to the Austrians in an effort to maintain cordial relations.

As Genoa changed hands, Keith expressed doubts about the city's security—correctly, for events elsewhere in Italy soon would dramatically change the situation for the British squadron anchored at Genoa.[42] The French Army of the Reserve had crossed the Alps, and the Austrians, many of whom had withdrawn from around Genoa, fought several engagements with the advancing French army. On 14 June 1800, at the village of Marengo between Milan and Genoa, the decisive battle of the campaign was fought. The Austrians lost, and the following day at nearby Alessandria, Bonaparte forced Melas to accept a convention that stipulated the return of Genoa and Savona to the French. As the proceedings did not include the British, Keith was left unaware of the Convention of Alessandria until the seventeenth. The incredulous admiral wrote to his sister, "The transactions of the 14th and 15th [Marengo and Alessandria] are of so extraordinary a nature as to exceed my comprehension."[43]

Since Keith had no appropriate instructions from the Admiralty, he was forced to take the initiative. He knew his ships could not remain at Genoa. He also knew that General Sir Ralph Abercromby and a detachment of the British army would soon be arriving in the Mediterranean. These soldiers were to act in concert with the British fleet to strike at targets of opportunity in support of Melas. When the Austrians had begun to waver after the French army appeared in Milan, Keith hoped to employ Abercromby's reinforcements to defend Genoa. Since the new British commander was still in transit, Keith had appealed for soldiers to General Henry Fox, who commanded the British soldiers in the Mediterranean. Yet Abercromby was slated to replace Fox, who refused to dispatch any soldiers until the new commander arrived. When Keith learned of the Convention of Alessandria, he abandoned his plans to use British soldiers to hold the city.[44] Spencer supported Keith's actions, believing that there was little to gain from holding the city "as it most probably would become another Toulon without the Recommendation of a Fleet to destroy."[45] Even so, Keith lamented the intransigence of General Fox: "I shall not soon forget nor that there are 14,000 men on Minorca which cannot be used by reason there is no General, and Fox has not Nerves to send a man on I had determined to defend Genoa for ourselves but alas it is too late."[46]

In keeping with the Convention of Alessandria, the Austrians prepared to deliver Genoa to the French, but this agreement made no mention of the British, and Keith's squadron remained in the harbor. The admiral ordered his sailors to render the port useless by seizing the ships and loading military stores, including cannons, aboard his own ships. When Bonaparte learned of Keith's actions, he ordered Masséna to urge the admiral to comply with the terms agreed upon at Alessandria.[47] But Keith, who had not signed the convention, insisted, "I was in no shape implicated in these transactions."[48] Another British official in Italy declared, "The Austrians are to evacuate . . . , but it is by no means understood that the English are to do so also."[49] The ships in the harbor remained Keith's most pressing concern. Before the convention, he had decided to confiscate only the armed French and Spanish ships along with any that had run the blockade, allowing most of the vessels to be retained by their owners. The British ambassador in Vienna explained how the situation changed following the Convention: "The Austrians restored to the Enemy Genoa and all that was in possession of the Army within the Fortress. They could not surrender the shipping because it was in the actual occupation of the British Admiral who was not party to that convention. Whatever was not restored by the Convention of Alessandria remained a separate and distinct conquest of the British Fleet."[50] Until Keith sailed from the harbor on 22 June, he controlled all affairs relating to the ships in the harbor. First, he directed any merchant ships that had arrived since the capitulation to sail from Genoa to prevent them from trading with the French when they reoccupied the city.[51] For the remaining ships in the harbor, "the merchants of Genoa made a separate agreement with Lord Keith for the ransom of their shipping."[52] Although the Austrians believed Keith's activities to be contrary to their agreement with the French, the merchants of Genoa paid the British approximately £25,000. According to the law of nations, the ransoming of merchant vessels was an acceptable option in lieu of seizing or burning the ships.[53] This was especially true at Genoa because Keith lacked sailors to take possession of the hundreds of vessels in the harbor, and the ransom provided compensation to the officers and sailors through the eventual distribution of prize money.

On 22 June the British sailed from the harbor, since the Austrians had to deliver Genoa to the French the next day. Keith in the *Minotaur* wrote, "The wind blew hard into Genoa which we quitted with great risk. . . . The *Généreux* and this ship did not clear the point of the harbour by more than 10 yards."[54] As the British squadron proceeded to sea, Keith had dealt with the immediate and local results of the Battle of Marengo. As commander on the scene, he had, on his own authority, switched the emphasis of British operations after the Convention of Alessandria. Although he no longer cooperated with the Austrians, he did not resort to open hostility. However, the French contrived to create a disagreement between the British and the Austrians regarding Keith's conduct after the convention. This led the British ambassador in Vienna to write to Keith: "I do not understand Hohenzollern's letters that are published in all the French newspapers and give an impression of a serious quarrel, and almost open contest with you."[55] Keith categorically denied these allegations, and on the day after sailing from Genoa he claimed, "In connection with Austria no dispute or difference has arisen."[56] Following the convention, the admiral did pursue a policy in keeping with Britain's national interests by seizing additional ships in the harbor and ensuring the safety of his squadron in Genoa.

Between January and June 1800, operations around Genoa involved a significant proportion of British naval force in the Mediterranean. Although the operation began in an unfortunate manner with the burning of the *Queen Charlotte*, Keith effectively blockaded Genoa and supported the Austrian army. Whereas the British and Austrians effectively cooperated for several months, the situation changed after the Battle of Marengo and the Convention of Alessandria. This led Keith to bitterly rant, "A battle certainly not lost has rendered all Italy and 11 garrisons (which they had not the means to have taken any one) into the French power."[57] While the fracture in the coalition resulted in the British pursuing their own policies, it should be remembered that Keith and the British expected to deal with the Austrians on an equal footing even though the Austrians had fought all the major engagements and suffered the majority of the casualties, while British losses were very light in comparison.[58] In the end, the British and Austrians had captured Genoa after several months of intensive operations only to let the French reoccupy the city nineteen days later when Keith sailed from Genoa under circumstances beyond his control. One British official mused, "What a fury he must be in, and with what just reason."[59]

On the morning of 22 June, around the time Keith's squadron cleared the harbor at Genoa, Abercromby finally arrived at Minorca. Learning of the situation from Keith's urgent letters, he immediately sailed for Genoa with eight battalions. Meanwhile, Keith's squadron made for Livorno, while Abercromby, unaware of the British evacuation, pressed onward to Genoa, hampered by calms. When he finally reached the city on the thirtieth, he sighted a British naval vessel outside the harbor and learned that the French again controlled Genoa. The transports accordingly changed course and sailed to join Keith at Livorno, where they anchored on 1 July.[60]

Here Abercromby and Keith met for the first time to discuss operations. Delays in communications as well as a cabinet dispute in London involving the modification of Britain's wartime strategy in the aftermath of the Austrian defeat led Abercromby and Keith throughout July and August to exercise substantial latitude in the employment of Britain's naval and military units in the Mediterranean. They were aided by Abercromby's original instructions allowing them to use their "professional judgment" to take into account local changes.[61] Even with this considerable authority, the two were hindered by what Keith called "numerous and contradictory" intelligence reports respecting the state of affairs in Italy.[62] Confusion resulted, and one naval officer confided, "In fact, it appears to me, our commanders in chief, are perfectly at a loss of what steps to pursue in consequence to the Armistice, or the supposed one, with the Austrians and French in Italy."[63] Even so, Britain's allies, including Austria, Tuscany, and Naples, inundated Abercromby and Keith with requests for the use of English soldiers.[64] Keith thought that a resumption of hostilities was probable and declared, "I have no great dependance *on french faith*—I think it is probable the Quiet will not last long." Abercromby refused all the requests, claiming he did not have the authority to act until he received orders from London. Although his original instructions provided enough latitude to intervene, he did not wish to commit to an operation until the situation had clarified. Personally, Keith thought it would be prudent to defend Naples, but he maintained, "I am but one of two Voices and on Military affairs it is reasonable I should be much inclined to the opinion of an officer like my Coleague [Abercromby]."[65] British relations with Austria continued to deteriorate, and on 15 July the Austrians supplemented their armistice in Italy with one concluded at Parsdorf in southern Germany. Keith realized nothing was to be gained by his continued presence at Livorno, and he sailed for Minorca on 7 August. When new instructions finally reached the commanders in the Mediterranean on the twenty-fifth, the British government confirmed the policies begun by Abercromby and Keith that abandoned the states on the Italian peninsula to the French.[66]

Instead of continued operations in the central Mediterranean, the center of gravity shifted toward Gibraltar, where Keith's ships and Abercromby's soldiers were ordered to combine with another amphibious group commanded by Lieutenant General Sir James Pulteney. The force would then make an amphibious landing at Cádiz to destroy the Spanish naval arsenal. The operation started off well. Keith's fleet, transporting Abercromby's soldiers, arrived at Gibraltar in mid-September. Owing to the size of the fleet and the limited port facilities at Gibraltar, many of the ships anchored in Tetuan Bay on the African side of the straits. On the nineteenth, 84 ships of Pulteney's detachment arrived, and the British invasion force now comprised 192 ships transporting approximately 24,000 soldiers.[67]

Unlike most aspects of Keith's career, the Cádiz operation has excited a great deal of scholarly controversy. One point that all the authors agree upon supports A. B. Rodger's conclusion that during the operation cooperation between the army and the navy deteriorated to an alarming degree.[68] Much of this had to do with interservice rivalry. Also, Keith's instructions from the Admiralty contributed to the problems between the army and navy. When compared with similar instructions that Keith received for other operations, his orders respecting Cádiz were terse and placed the fleet in a subordinate role to *assist* the army. However, Richard Harding has aptly pointed out that the two services during the Age of Sail usually operated as separate entities with no overall commander.[69] The government in London seemed, whether consciously or unconsciously, to appoint Abercromby the supreme commander for the landing at Cádiz. This caused great confusion, and neither commander remedied the problem.

With the units massed at Gibraltar and Tetuan Bay, the commanders planned the operation. Immediately Keith appealed to Rear Admiral Sir Richard Bickerton, who commanded the blockade squadron off Cádiz. He responded that locations existed along the coast where a landing could take place. As for the weather, he could promise nothing in this season, but the ships could ride out a storm while anchored on the coast. With this mixed response, planning continued. Keith, from his prior knowledge of the area and from local intelligence, determined that a landing site near Rota was the most feasible, since it protected the fleet from west and northwest winds. Abercromby agreed that this site was close enough to Cádiz for his soldiers to attack the arsenal. In addition, Keith and Abercromby interviewed a harbor pilot who confirmed that the anchorage was acceptable and protected from all but southwesterly winds.[70]

Another problem was a yellow fever epidemic that raged at Cádiz. While still at Gibraltar, Keith was told that 4,343 people had died within the walls of Cádiz between 27 August and 11 September. Keith questioned the accuracy of this intelligence, but he "observed, that, if on our arrival before Cadiz, we should find by the accounts of Sir Richard Bickerton that the sickness prevailed to the extent reported, it would induce me to object to the disembarkation at all."[71] Information circulating through the fleet indicated that "the Plague or Yellow Fever is carrying off great numbers at that place [Cádiz] daily, but it is much better." Bickerton believed that with proper precautions and treatment, the yellow fever posed little threat.[72]

Although Keith expressed some reservations to Abercromby about the safety of the anchorage and the yellow fever, he presented a more realistic and distressing summation on 22 September to Spencer, the First Lord of the Admiralty. Keith contended, "All this would have been easy a month ago, but this season the weather is so precarious that it is impossible to promise co-operation for an hour without the ships finding an anchoring place for the transports, many of whom are very bad." The admiral continued, "I have serious apprehensions for so numerous and ungovernable a mass of ships in that cul-de-sac, at this critical season of the year." From these statements the Lords of the Admiralty concluded that Keith would call off the operation, and one member later claimed, "I had no notion of a landing being attempted."[73]

While Keith had convinced the Admiralty of the inherent dangers, he did not convey these fully to Abercromby, and he decided to proceed with the mission. Rather than sailing to Cádiz with the object of landing the army, Keith considered this merely a possibility, because he wanted to have "a look at Cadiz." By Abercromby's own admission, Keith reserved "his final determination till such time as he should have seen Sir Richard Bickerton, who commanded the squadron cruising off Cadiz." Finally, Keith realized that his ships must sail from Gibraltar, "where there is not room for one third of the fleet."[74] If his ships did not sail for Cádiz, his instructions were to wait at Gibraltar for new orders, but Keith did not consider this an option, given the constricted nature of the anchorage and the inevitability of damage to the ships if a gale tore through the region. For his part, Abercromby did not understand the admiral's reasoning and believed that the possibility of landing the army was high; otherwise, he later claimed, he would never have sailed from Gibraltar.[75]

With the two commanders pursuing two different courses of action, 192 ships and vessels sailed from Gibraltar and Tetuan on 2 October and arrived within sight of Cádiz on the evening of the fourth.[76] During the next two days, the British prepared for the landing, and Keith met with Bickerton, Abercromby, Captains John Elphinstone and James Morris, and several senior army officers to finalize the arrangements. Keith outlined the plan and discussed the anchorage north of Rota. The naval officers protested that this anchorage was unsafe during the present season. In a strong southwest wind, the warships would have to put to sea, and many of the transports would be dashed to pieces against the shore, since their poor condition and their smaller crews would prevent them from riding out the storm. Keith then declared that he could not guarantee communications between the fleet and the shore. Still, Keith's behavior mirrored sentiments expressed at Gibraltar about the difficulty of the anchorage in a southwest wind.[77]

At the conclusion of the meeting, Keith's behavior became negligent. Given the difficulties voiced by the naval officers, Abercromby wanted a definitive answer.[78] For the general, who did not have a lifetime of experience at sea, this was only natural. However, Keith was under considerable stress, and Abercromby's appeal, perhaps irrationally, irritated the admiral. Several reasons account for Keith's response. First, a number of previous joint operations during the Revolutionary Era had failed, so there was considerable pressure in Britain to avoid another fiasco. Keith later explained, "The undertaking is important; our force is great; the Nation will expect something; the difficulties are numerous; and success is doubtful; But it is our duty to the country, and to those who employ us, to make the attempt."[79] Second, this operation had been advocated by one of Keith's patrons, Henry Dundas. If Keith disappointed him, he would jeopardize his powerful support. Third, the admiral likely felt insulted by the subordinate status of the navy in this operation. A copy of Abercromby's instructions included in Keith's orders stated: "it is His Majesty's pleasure that you should consider in concert with Vice Admiral Lord Keith . . . to assist in your operations in the practicability and mode of making an attack upon Cadiz"[80]—that is, Keith had orders to "assist" Abercromby. During the operation, the general conferred with the admiral as an equal, yet Keith functioned as an assistant, giving information to Abercromby and then letting him make the final determination. A more resolute commander might have taken the responsibility, but Keith, although well qualified for command, lacked this aggressiveness.

On the other hand, Abercromby failed to realize an important aspect of naval operations. There were few places on earth where a fleet commander could guarantee an anchorage—too many factors such as adverse winds and lee shores prevented this. In a letter to Spencer, Keith remarked that "in truth the military seem to think they are so perfectly master of our profession, it is not easy to give them satisfaction however much it has been my study."[81] He touched a sensitive issue. In the army, maneuvering units seldom depended on the weather, but in the navy, weather conditions could spell success or failure. Keith could make no meteorological promises even though the general wanted a definite answer. Finally, Keith felt misled by Abercromby and claimed, "I never heard that 14 days was as short a period as the fleet must have continued at anchor, till we had passed the Straits." Keith maintained that this was too long, given the season. Still, the admiral agreed to attempt the operation and risk the unsafe anchorage, "but could not, with truth, say that it was a safe one."[82]

Abercromby wanted a more definite response and spoke about this with the admiral in his cabin at 2:00 a.m. on 6 October.[83] Again Abercromby did not receive a positive assurance, but he decided to continue with the operation. At 10:00 a.m. orders were given "to prepare to land." Soldiers soon boarded their flatboats, which then assembled near Captain the Honourable Alexander Cochrane's ship, the *Ajax* (74), since he had been charged by Keith with directing the landing. At the same time, the *Phaeton* (38) with Abercromby aboard anchored near the landing site. Problems soon emerged. The number of troops aboard the flatboats fell far short of the number expected. When Cochrane recognized this problem, he went to see Keith. In the opinion of one of Abercromby's subordinates, General Sir John Moore, Keith gave Cochrane little encouragement.[84] Here the admiral and his captain were both at fault. Communications between the two officers had failed. Cochrane, moreover, had not carried out his assigned task. Still, Keith was the naval commander in chief, and the ultimate responsibility rested with him.

At this point Keith's behavior became negligent, for he refused to take the initiative. Moore, commanding some of the soldiers in the first wave, took a boat to Keith's flagship to discuss the lack of men in the first wave and the excessive distance of seven or eight miles between the fleet and the shore. He recounted, "I found him all confusion blaming everybody and everything, but attempting to remedy nothing." Later that day Moore met with the admiral again, and recalled, "He went on repeating much more incoherent nonsense. It was with difficulty I persuaded him to make the signal to the troops to re-embark."[85]

Much had gone awry during the day. Keith's behavior, by all accounts, was despicable, and as the highest ranking naval officer, the failure was his. How-ever, this conclusion might be skewed, since the sources detailing what trans-pired on 6 October originate almost completely with the army. Particularly, historian A. B. Rodger points out that Moore harbored animosity for the navy, and no available naval sources substantiate the confusion indicated by Moore. In addition, Cochrane, who had been ordered to oversee the landing, had created a plan utilizing the ships' boats to put the army ashore, but he had failed to assemble the landing craft in appropriate numbers.[86] Finally, the two commanders were separated at a critical juncture. Abercromby remained on the frigate anchored near the shore, and Keith was aboard his flagship. There was no unity of command.

After calling off the operation on the sixth, Keith decided to attempt a landing on the following day. This time the entire process of embarking the men would begin at 4:00 a.m., and Keith planned to have the troops ashore by 8:00 a.m.[87] Abercromby did not want a repeat of the events of the sixth, so he wrote the admiral, "I shall follow your opinion, because I must consider it in this case as better than my own." Keith replied that "it is impossible for me to promise an assurance to the question you put at this advanced season. . . . Therefore, under these circumstances, I cannot advise your Excellency to land troops consistent with the spirit of the instructions."[88] With this answer, the two commanders decided to call off the expedition, and at 3:00 a.m. on the seventh, the fleet was hit by the very storm Keith most feared, a southwest gale.[89]

As the fleet weathered the storm off Cádiz, Keith faced the first of many allegations about his conduct when Abercromby claimed, "We certainly sailed from Gibraltar convinced of the practicability of this measure, and de-termined to put it into execution. . . . I did not sail from Gibraltar without having fixed on a plan." Keith responded with his own lengthy account al-leging that Abercromby had operated under certain misconceptions. While this can be viewed as an attempt to distort the truth, Keith's appraisal did not contradict other sources, although there were glaring omissions in the admiral's account. The description made no mention of Keith's activities on 6 October when the soldiers almost landed, and the admiral did not mention the many appeals made for his assurance that the anchorage was safe.[90]

Although he was not nearly as culpable as Keith, a portion of the blame should be also ascribed to Abercromby. The following instances demonstrate a breakdown in communications between the two services: both officers failed to specify what they expected of the other in the operation, and Abercromby remained separated from Keith during the aborted landing. In the planning stages, the general did not address the duration of the proposed operation. Only after the fleet had sailed from Gibraltar did he indicate that it would take two weeks. In addition, Abercromby's failure to understand the intricacies of naval operations should be mentioned, for he did not comprehend that the navy could not, with the season and the weather, guarantee the anchorage.

When Keith wrote the Admiralty explaining the operation's failure, he did not mention his indecision or Abercromby's efforts to obtain his opinion. One scholar, Piers Mackesy, contends that this was part of "a smokescreen to conceal his role." Yet, his letter to the Admiralty contained legitimate points of contention, many of which had been mentioned since the early planning stages at Gibraltar. These included the yellow fever, the lateness of the season, the fourteen days needed for the operation, the unpredictability of the winds, and the difficulty in taking the city.[91] This satisfied Spencer, who responded, "I believe I ought also to congratulate you on escaping the danger you would have incurred had you effected a descent in the neighbourhood of Cadiz; the season was far advanced, and the horrible distemper that raged there made the attempt too hazardous to be ventured." Another member of the Admiralty echoed this conclusion: "It was a most happy escape."[92] To his sister, Keith affirmed that it was "entirely a resolution of prudence" that the operation had been called off. Mackesy contends nonetheless that "Anticipation of blame figures in his correspondence." This is true. In a letter to his sister on 7 October, the day the fleet withdrew from Cádiz, Keith wrote that "we did not [think the] object equal to the risk and gave up the attack . . . of course we shall be abused."[93] Keith was savvy enough to understand that anyone in a command as important as his would be open to attack by opportunists, and although the Admiralty approved, other naval officers did not think as highly of Keith's actions.[94] At least one officer under his orders expressed his concern: "I trust future operations will be planned more conducive to the honour and benefit of our country."[95] Still, Keith had impressed the right people. With the support of the Admiralty, he remained in his command; the opinions of other officers did not carry the same weight.

Even though Keith successfully convinced the Admiralty that he had performed adequately, problems emerged with Henry Dundas. At the end of December, he received information detailing supposed troubles between Abercromby and Keith. The only concrete evidence of any problem was that the commanders sailed in different ships. Since the fleet was conveying Abercromby's soldiers to Egypt at that moment, Spencer, Young, and the Admiralty Board drafted separate letters suggesting that Keith might wish to hand over command of the Egyptian operation to Bickerton since the situation in Italy might demand Keith's personal attention.[96] Yet Dundas questioned the propriety of this suggestion, as "it will be impossible for Lord Keith not to suppose that we had concealed some of the topics we urge."[97]

The supposed differences between the commanders placed Dundas in an awkward position. Both officers were Scottish, and he had used his patronage to advance both careers. As secretary of state for war, Dundas was Abercromby's superior. Furthermore, Abercromby's mother's maiden name was Dundas, and through one of his sons, Abercromby was Henry Dundas's in-law.[98] When forced to choose between the two officers, Dundas supported Abercromby, and to Keith he sent a veiled warning: "I have never had the most remote communication from Sir Ralph Abercromby either in his public or private correspondence to lead me to such a suspicion, and I shall therefore continue to contradict it as an idle and ill-intentioned report." Dundas then suggested that Keith immediately fix any problems.[99] Although correspondence between the two had diminished over the preceding months, this incident forced a major shift in Keith's choice of patrons; he increasingly looked to Spencer and the Admiralty for support instead of Dundas.

Given the slowness in communications, it was mid-February 1801 before Keith received letters from Spencer, Young, and Dundas detailing the supposed animosity with Abercromby. Keith claimed that he had no knowledge of the rumors but learned that Abercromby was aware of them. Keith informed Spencer that if the Admiralty or any of the king's ministers believed that he was incapable of doing his duty, then they should remove him from command of the Mediterranean Fleet.[100]

In the end, Keith escaped from Cádiz with a questionable blot on his record. The admiral later claimed, "It is surprising how little men consider the difficulty of landing and supporting an army in an enemy's country," but who was he describing when he reflected that "every obstacle was magnified to an impossibility, as Cadiz . . . can bear witness"?[101] As in most failed operations, no one person was at fault. Some part of the failure should rest with Cochrane, while Abercromby should accept a portion of the blame. Still, the majority lay with Keith. He failed to assume a decisive and positive role, and his conduct at Cádiz, resting on a lack of understanding with the army, was in many ways the nadir of his career.

The Cádiz operation mirrored Britain's overall position in the Mediterranean during 1800. The only bright spot occurred on 4 September when Malta finally surrendered to the British after a siege lasting nearly two years. Otherwise, numerous blemishes marred the navy's record in the region. Keith lamented in late July that "the Brest fleet seems so intirely to occupy the Admiralty that we are forgotten and there is so much to do here and so little comfort in those who are to do it that I have asked Lord Spencer to let me go home."[102] A frustrated Keith complained of complex political pressures and considerations. In addition, he commanded a fleet much smaller than before Bruix's cruise, yet his responsibilities were not reduced proportionately. Despite the use of a large proportion of his fleet, the siege of Genoa ended in failure, and later the arrival Abercromby's troops posed added strains on Keith's command. When he asked the Admiralty to replace him, one of its members indicated that "one more equal to the task will not be easily found."[103] Keith remained in command of the Mediterranean Fleet. And even as it came under increased French pressure, the British government provided the overstretched fleet with a new objective—Egypt.

"An arduous task to perform"

Keith and the Egyptian Campaign (1801)

Following the failure at Cádiz, Egypt, a province of the Ottoman Empire under French occupation, became the target of Keith's and Abercromby's amphibious force. The British government had come to this decision only after an arduous debate. The importance of Egypt in Britain's world strategy was extremely difficult for the political leadership in London to conceptualize. Between 1798 and 1800 the British had constructed a continental strategy based upon alliances with Russia and Austria, but French military victories had caused both countries to seek peace. Without allies on the Continent, Henry Dundas, the secretary of state for war, advocated the use of British naval and military forces to secure Egypt, but several cabinet members vehemently objected. Dundas perceived the French occupation of Egypt as a threat to Britain's position in India. Moreover, an operation against Egypt would allow the British to take the offensive and strike at France without relying on a continental ally such as Austria. The British would still have the support of the Ottoman Empire. With these thoughts, Dundas in early October 1800 secured the cabinet's reticent support, and instructions were immediately addressed to Abercromby and Keith.[1]

On 24 October these dispatches arrived at Gibraltar, and Abercromby—not wishing for a repeat of Cádiz—outlined exactly what he expected of the navy. The prospect of extended cooperation with the navy failed to enthuse the general, who "saw his situation in the most unpromising light."[2] Abercromby consequently demanded the following: that the Mediterranean Fleet would convey the army to Egypt; the navy would land the soldiers; and the fleet would provision the army. These requirements compelled Keith to make several changes in his staff by assigning Captain Philip Beaver to command the *Foudroyant* (80), with Captain William Young, formerly Principal Agent for Transport, as assistant captain. The latter was of particular importance, since Young knew a great deal about the loading of transports, the movement of soldiers, and the landing of an army—operations that, Keith suggested, "my age now prohibits me from attending to personally." These two appointments were designed to remedy a deficiency observed by Collingwood, who claimed that Keith "always has about him a set of very dull men, very incompetent to the aid of a Comm[ander]-in-Chief needs." Probably the changes were the result of his performance at Cádiz, which demonstrated Keith's inability to simultaneously command the fleet and oversee the landing of soldiers.[3] The complexity of the subsequent naval operation and the alacrity with which the tasks were carried out illustrate that Keith overcame his critics and formed an excellent staff. Although he had critics, Captain Young indicated, "I am very comfortable with Lord Keith, who is really a worthy good man, and zealous for the good of his country, he has an arduous task to perform, and I think he is, all things considered, as capable of performing it, as any man I know—he has wonderful information, in most points—He has generally stood high in estimation, as an officer."[4]

The fleet sailed from Gibraltar by division toward Malta, while Keith's flagship, the *Foudroyant*, sailed alone, affording the admiral the independence to go where his presence would be most useful. Keith's first stop was at Port Mahon on 16 November. The exertions of the last months had taken their toll, and for several days in late November, illness confined him to bed. He was also "oppressed by the weight of business and complaints from others." On 2 December he sailed from Port Mahon toward Malta, where he arrived on 8 December. Inside the harbor Keith found nearly all of his ships riding at anchor. The fleet finally sailed from Valletta on 20 and 21 December; there were too many ships to exit the harbor in a single day. Again Keith traveled ahead in his flagship, to arrange Ottoman assistance.[5]

On 28 December the *Foudroyant*, in company with the *Peterell* (16), fell in with part of the fleet. The weather deteriorated on the following day, and Captain Charles Inglis of the *Peterell* led the squadron into the Bay of Macri on the coast of Asia Minor, searching for the protected harbor of Marmaris. From out at sea, the mountainous coast looked like a solid black mass, making it difficult to find the harbor's narrow entrance. To compound the difficulty, visibility was only half a mile, and the fleet sailed toward a lee shore. The *Peterell*, to the horror of many, headed straight for the rugged coast, followed by the *Foudroyant* and the rest of the fleet. As the ships neared land, the narrow mouth of the channel became visible, and one by one they entered a harbor approximately twenty miles in circumference. Several days later, on

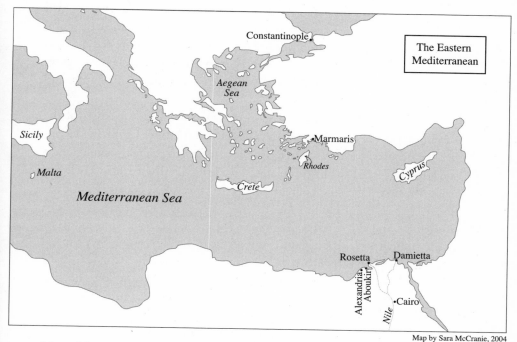

Map by Sara McCranie, 2004

Map 9. The Eastern Mediterranean.

1 January 1801, the remainder of the fleet arrived, having been delayed by the weather.[6]

While Keith sailed to Egypt, he retained command of all naval forces throughout the Mediterranean. Particularly, he worried about Britain's naval strength in the central Mediterranean, since he had almost stripped this part of his command to assemble the invasion force. With justification, he complained to the Admiralty that he needed more ships, but Admiral Young responded, "We cannot send you more large ships, . . . unless a superior force should be sent against you."[7] Denied reinforcements, Keith had commissioned the *Athenian* (64), which had been taken at the surrender of Valletta under the name *Athénienne*, to join the *Alexander* (74) and the *Généreux* (74) as the only ships-of-the-line deployed between Minorca, Malta, and the Italian Peninsula. Keith treated these ships as a fire brigade, ordering them to "go from place to place to cover the threats."[8] At one point he had even considered sending the expedition to Egypt without the ships-of-the-line, so he could maintain a stronger presence in the western and central Mediterranean.

He decided against this course of action because Abercromby "was decided in his opinion that the Expedition could not proceed without the large ships, and that he thought the number too few. And it must be confessed that it is the men from the ships of war who must man the flat boats, land the guns, manage them when on shore, and debark the daily consumption of water and provisions for the Troops."[9]

Napoleon Bonaparte, as First Consul, understood the weakness of the Royal Navy in the Mediterranean and decided to reinforce Egypt. In December, the Admiralty even warned Keith that the French probably would send a squadron to thwart the British plan to invade Egypt. These fears were legitimate. The first detachment of reinforcements sailed on 23 January from Brest under Rear Admiral Honoré Ganteaume with 4,000 soldiers, seven ships-of-the-line, and two frigates. Two more frigates sailed from Toulon on the twenty-fourth with supplies and reinforcements for Egypt, and they slipped into Alexandria in early February.[10] A third relief expedition, also consisting of two frigates, sailed from Rochefort on 13 February, but the ships became separated during a gale, and off Gibraltar a British frigate captured one of the ships on the nineteenth.[11] While the French sent reinforcements to Egypt, Keith attempted to maintain the secrecy of the expedition by prohibiting unauthorized letters or individuals from leaving the fleet after it had sailed from Valletta; he also refused to disclose his destination to anyone without a need to know. These efforts prevented Bonaparte from obtaining intelligence about the expedition for several months, but on 2 March he received a letter from Constantinople indicating that Keith had anchored at Marmaris, and he determined that there was only one legitimate destination for the British—Egypt.[12]

As the French attempted to counter the threat posed by the British in the eastern Mediterranean, Abercromby and Keith continued their preparations. The navy oversaw the logistics of the operation, and it quickly became a nightmare securing sufficient supplies for 15,000 soldiers and more than 10,000 sailors hundreds of miles from the nearest British naval facility. Keith required Ottoman assistance. As his previous relations with the Austrians and the Spanish indicated, Keith dealt poorly with people of other cultures. To his sister he wrote, "I am surrounded with Turks of all ranks, I do not much like their company they are nasty." He continued, "I am constantly worried—pipes and tobacco, beards or whiskers, Turks, Arabs, Egyptians and such like, they all mean to be civil but are wearisome to a degree."[13] Perhaps his view of the Turks would have moderated if they had provided more assistance. The Grand Vizir, the Ottoman chief minister and second only in power to the sultan who ruled the empire, ordered his officials to assist Keith in every way possible, but by 1801 the central authority of the Ottoman Empire had become tenuous. The Grand Vizir's directives were either discarded or obeyed with reluctance. This proved disconcerting, especially since the Grand Vizir wrote Keith as if everything had been provided. The lack of Ottoman support delayed the operation, much to the disappointment of Abercromby and Keith. Yet Turkish assistance did trickle into Marmaris, and Keith received assurances that only the winter storms delayed the appearance of more Turkish gunboats. In mid-January the Kapudan Bey arrived with one ship-of-the-line, dismasted by lightning, and several corvettes. Although these reinforcements were small, the arrival of this contingent demonstrated Turkish resolve, and to help placate Keith, the Kapudan Bey instructed that all his ships and gunboats would sail under British orders.[14] Still, Keith anxiously awaited the remainder of the fleet and the Kapudan Pasha—the Ottoman grand admiral. Disenchanted with the prospect of Turkish assistance, an exasperated Keith complained of "Waiting here forty days for Vessels &c. and promises from the Turks which are of as little Value as those of the Christians[.] The Weather become Warm and I am anxious to quit this place."[15]

While awaiting Ottoman support, the navy and the army practiced all aspects of the amphibious operation to avoid a repeat of Cádiz, and the two services developed an effective command structure. Keith again placed Captain Cochrane in charge of the landing craft and the movement of the soldiers to the shore. On several occasions the British practiced coordinating the movements of the boats with the soldiers. The complexity of the amphibious assault was startling. According to the plan, 6,000 to 7,000 men and fourteen guns would be landed in the first wave. For this, 60 flatboats, 107 launches, and 156 cutters were to be utilized.[16]

Meanwhile, Abercromby had sent General Sir John Moore on a mission to the Grand Vizir's Ottoman army in Syria. Although this army had existed for several years by early 1801, Moore returned on 20 January with a gloomy prognosis detailing their combat ineffectiveness. Abercromby immediately chose Aboukir Bay as the preferred landing site, since it would allow the British to threaten Alexandria without relying on the support of the Ottomans. Abercromby then called a council of war to solicit the opinions of Keith,

Rear Admiral Sir Richard Bickerton, and Captains Benjamin Hallowell and Sir Sidney Smith. Although Keith had never served in the region, this time he was prepared. As early as October when his fleet was still anchored at Gibraltar, he had sent dispatches to Smith, the British commander in the eastern Mediterranean, asking about possible landing sites near Alexandria, and Keith had interviewed officers in the fleet who had served off Egypt, including Captain Hallowell. By the time of the 20 January meeting, Keith could say with confidence that Aboukir Bay was an acceptable anchorage for the fleet. It was protected from the weather and encompassed a large inlet between Alexandria and the mouth of the western branch of the Nile. If Aboukir Bay for any reason proved impractical, the council of war decided on an alternate site near Rosetta which would enable the British army to sever communications between the two major French-controlled cities of Cairo and Alexandria.[17]

Since Keith agreed to provide more support than Abercromby had received at Cádiz, extensive cooperation resulted. A battalion of 600 marines, taken from the detachments serving aboard the warships, received orders to land along with 350 seamen to assist in serving the artillery. In the absence of horses, the supply train would consist almost entirely of boats manned by the navy. The myriad of demands caused Keith misgivings, and he wrote Abercromby outlining the severe lack of sailors in his command. The poorly manned troopships could contribute little. The five ships-of-the-line at Marmaris should have contained 3,339 officers and men, but these ships were 356 short of full strength and 236 were sick. After subtracting those sailors and marines tasked with supporting the army, only 1,342 officers and men would remain aboard, or approximately 40 percent of their normal complement. Keith could rely on the support of only two additional ships-of-the-line which were off Alexandria, but they were in no better condition.[18] To the Admiralty, Keith explained that "the General has called on me for a very large detachment of Seaman and Marines being landed which I could ill afford, . . . but as the object was national I have complied as far as possible."[19] Effective cooperation with Abercromby resulted, and Keith summarized, "I have laid my shoulder to it, the army has . . . been refused nothing."[20] One factor contributing to the high level of assistance was that Keith received dispatches from London outlining the problems that had occurred off Cádiz. Clearly his actions would be subject to scrutiny. For the prestige of the navy and the future of his career, a similar failure could not occur in Egypt.

On 22 February the fleet sailed. Only nineteen of Keith's ships were warships; in addition, there were forty troopships—older warships with part of their armament removed. Keith also commanded sixty transports and fifty-seven Turkish vessels. The apparent weakness of the invasion force was deceptive, because eight additional British warships were blockading Alexandria and would join Keith off the coast of Egypt. Furthermore, the Kapudan Pasha had promised an Ottoman amphibious force for the operation, while the Grand Vizir, commanding the Ottoman army in Syria, stood poised to invade Egypt. Finally, at least five thousand soldiers from British India had orders to land on the Red Sea coast of Egypt.[21] Even with these detachments, the units directly under Abercromby and Keith provided the lion's share of the forces used in the operation.

The main body of Keith's fleet sighted Alexandria on 1 March, and by that afternoon when the fleet received orders to heave to, they were nine miles off the coast. During the night the fleet steered for Aboukir Bay, where they anchored on the second. The shallowness of the bay forced the ships to remain six to seven miles off the coast. Although Keith and Abercromby hoped to land the troops immediately, the weather had deteriorated and the surf had become rough. The storm continued until the seventh. Neither Keith nor Abercromby wished to hazard a landing until the weather cleared.[22]

While the fleet weathered the storm, pressing intelligence arrived on 3 March from the western Mediterranean. Ganteaume's French squadron, having sailed from Brest on 23 January, had slipped past Gibraltar on 9 February. The British squadron blockading Cádiz under Rear Admiral Sir John Borlase Warren, with five ships-of-the-line and several other warships, unsuccessfully pursued the French squadron into the Mediterranean. Keith worried that Ganteaume might appear off the coast of Egypt, especially since contradictory reports inflated his strength to ten ships-of-the-line. To oppose Ganteaume, the British had relatively few warships in Aboukir Bay. None of Keith's options seemed good. If his ships-of-the-line sailed off Alexandria, the army could not land, since sailors drawn from his ships were needed to man the assault craft. Furthermore, the absence of the ships-of-the-line would enable the French to attack the transports in Aboukir Bay. On the other hand, if the British warships remained in the bay to protect the transports, Ganteaume could disembark reinforcements almost unopposed at Alexandria—which would make the British conquest of Egypt militarily unfeasible. On 5 March, Keith met with Bickerton and Abercromby. The general maintained that the

Admiralty would send a squadron after Ganteaume. This was true, but the ships had sailed for the West Indies instead of the Mediterranean. Ultimately the ships-of-the-line, at Abercromby's request, remained in Aboukir Bay. If Keith learned that Ganteaume was in the vicinity, they would then take station off Alexandria. Until then, the largest British ships blockading the city were frigates.[23]

On 7 March the weather finally moderated, and the commanders decided to hazard a landing on the following morning. The delay had given the French commander at Alexandria time to assemble 1,300 infantry, 150 cavalry, and eleven guns on the beaches of Aboukir.[24] The British army would have to make an opposed landing, but they had practiced for this at Marmaris and were ready. At 2:00 a.m. on 8 March the *Foudroyant* sent up a rocket, the signal for the landing craft to load and steer for the assembly area. The weather was perfect—the storm had abated and the water in the bay was smooth. By 3:00 a.m. the first wave, under General Moore, had boarded their landing craft. With muffled oars the sailors slowly rowed the soldiers toward the assembly area, while Sir Sidney Smith directed the loading of the artillery aboard other landing craft. In all, the first wave consisted of approximately 7,000 soldiers plus the crews of more than three hundred landing craft. As several miles separated the transports from the assembly area, it took until 8:00 a.m. for the boats to rendezvous. Cochrane, with several captains from the other warships, marshaled the landing craft, while Keith and Abercromby waited aboard one of the bomb vessels to exercise some control.[25]

Around 9:00 a.m. Cochrane signaled the landing craft to advance. The sailors rowed quickly, while the bomb vessels, sloops, and gunboats, positioned close to the shore, fired at the French. Soon the French artillery responded with solid shot and shell, sinking three landing craft. As the British drew closer to the shore, the French gunners switched to grape and canister. When the boats were three hundred yards out, the French infantry fired, causing many casualties. Still, the boats pushed through the maelstrom before running ashore. The soldiers quickly disembarked and formed a line of battle while receiving artillery and small-arms fire. The British then pushed the French from the beach in a short but bitterly contested engagement. After disembarking their human cargoes and collecting the wounded, the sailors pulled their flatboats off the beach and rowed back to the ships to embark the next wave of soldiers.[26]

The landing was a great success. Abercromby congratulated Keith and his command, mentioning the work of Cochrane and the other officers involved in the landing. This duty came with a price, and to his sister Keith wrote, "A fine day—the landing made good but a considerable loss." The navy sustained 97 casualties, while the army lost 652 officers and men, or approximately 10 percent of the first wave.[27] Opposed amphibious landings during the Age of Sail were uncommon; they called for a high level of cooperation and a great deal of luck. The period spent at Marmaris had afforded both services time to prepare for the operation, and the training paid handsome dividends. The day before the landing, General of Division Abdullah Menou, the French commander in Egypt, evinced a degree of brazenness when describing the British and their inability to conduct joint operations. He cited several failures including the one at Cádiz, contending that British generals and admirals did not attain a high level of cooperation.[28] When reviewing joint operations over the previous years, few would have disagreed with Menou's assessment, but the landing at Aboukir demonstrated near perfect cooperation.

Although a British army had stormed ashore, a battle-hardened French army remained in Egypt, and Keith lamented, "I wish I could tell my good friend it was over[;] we are in great danger."[29] The endeavor had just begun. Over the next months, the navy supported the army, and Keith described his duties as an "agent of transports" rather than a fleet commander. The admiral commented, "It is a young army and has little resource, . . . I am convinced were I to refuse or withdraw a man the troops would re-embark and charge the failure to me."[30] Keith had a myriad of concerns about the operation. Although he realized that supporting the army was important, Ganteaume's French squadron remained Keith's most pressing concern and provoked a major disagreement with Abercromby. After the landing, the admiral wished to station most of his ships-of-the-line off Alexandria. Even poorly manned, he felt that "our appearance may intimidate the enemy from approaching."[31] Emphatically, Abercromby countered, "As far as I see at present I shall consider you withdrawing from Aboukir, as a [disgrace] to the public service. . . . Linked together as the two services are, they cannot be Separated." The general claimed that if Keith received intelligence that the French fleet was near, he would "be the last person to object to your sailing to meet them."[32] Taken aback by Abercromby's dictate, Keith contended, "I made the proposal of going off Alexandria with the squadron, in its present feeble state, knowing that if the Enemy can get in a succour, the Expedition must fail."[33] After this exchange, Keith remained in Aboukir Bay supporting the army and worrying about the arrival of the French. On the French side, Bonaparte incorrectly minimized the British reaction to the movements of Ganteaume's squadron. He overestimated Keith's strength and failed to realize that many sailors and marines were supporting the army, but Bonaparte correctly assumed that the British would abandon their expedition if the French in Egypt received a powerful reinforcement.[34] Thus a successful relief operation would be tantamount to a British failure. However, Ganteaume, upon arriving in the Mediterranean, had sailed to Toulon, and it would take time to ready his ships for a dash to Egypt.

Meanwhile, immense naval support allowed the British to move out of the beachhead toward Alexandria with the Mediterranean coast on their right flank and Lake Aboukir on their left. As the British approached Alexandria, the French attacked on the twenty-first. Although the British won a resounding victory, Abercromby was mortally wounded, and Major General John Hely-Hutchinson assumed command. The campaign was still far from over, and the French retained control of all of Egypt except for a narrow coastal strip between Aboukir and Alexandria. Keith continued to have his sailors defend the inland waterways and bring up supplies, while other sailors and marines served ashore directly supporting the army. In the wake of the victory on the twenty-first, Keith also obtained greater freedom of movement for his ships. Some sailed off Alexandria, while others engaged in resupply missions, sailing to Turkish-controlled lands for biscuits, cattle, lemons, wood, and water. These ships and others returned with much-needed supplies and intelligence. Furthermore, the Ottoman fleet under the Kapudan Pasha finally arrived at Aboukir Bay in late March, bringing additional warships and Turkish soldiers.[35]

In mid-April Keith received a letter detailing the fall of the Pitt government in London. The ostensible cause was the question of Catholic emancipation, but several factors contributed, including Pitt's poor health and divisions within the cabinet. The collapse of the ministry affected Keith directly. Dundas, the prime supporter of the Egyptian expedition, no longer held office, and a friend in London wrote, "Lord Spencer is also a great loss."[36] Keith's two greatest patrons were out of power and incapable of assisting him. The new First Lord of the Admiralty was John Jervis, the Earl of St. Vincent, who had a history of serving as Keith's superior. Most notably, in 1761, he had been the captain of Keith's first ship, and St. Vincent had commanded the Mediterranean Fleet when Keith flew his flag there as a subordinate admiral in 1798–99. Although the two officers knew each other, the new First Lord remained reticent in dealing with Keith's requests for reinforcements, for this was just one of many operations demanding the navy's limited resources.

The lack of support crippled Keith's ships. Most had been employed constantly for at least a year without a major dockyard refit. Among the troopships, many had been removed from the ordinary while awaiting extensive repairs, since it was thought that their service would be temporary. Similar problems afflicted several ships, including the *Swiftsure* (74), *Alexander* (74), and *Minotaur* (74), that had continuously operated in the Mediterranean since the Battle of Aboukir Bay on 1 August 1798. Among the crews, illness, accident, and service ashore resulted in attrition. Keith wrote to the Admiralty that he needed 400 seamen and 250 marines. St. Vincent had none to send. Thus the naval force in the Mediterranean remained stretched, and every ship was needed to maintain control of the sea while the French threat became stronger.[37]

Much of the threat came from Ganteaume's squadron, but Keith was finally able to secure permission from Hutchinson to station most of his warships off Alexandria. The British success in battle had solidified the army's position, making an immediate evacuation unlikely. Hutchinson asked only to retain the use of Keith's boats to supply the men ashore. Now Keith had the authority to conduct operations as he chose against Ganteaume. He deployed his frigates and sloops along the approaches to Egypt to provide as much of a warning as possible, and he placed his ships-of-the-line off Alexandria under Bickerton's orders. These deployments were necessary as long as Bonaparte still planned to send aid to Egypt, and with Ganteaume's squadron anchored at Toulon, the French were now better positioned.[38] Ganteaume sailed on 19 March. On the twenty-sixth, southeast of Sardinia, Warren's squadron sighted the French and gave chase but lost the quarry in the darkness. Noting Warren's failure, Keith contended, "I am not sorry for it—he was rather too weak—but the enemy fled from him." This was true, but Keith desired glory instead of allowing it to be garnered only by his subordinate, and to his sister he elaborated, "If I can lay hold of Gaunthame [*sic*] I shall not be a week longer here I hope." Meanwhile Ganteaume returned to Toulon, while Warren sailed for Alexandria, believing this to be the French destination.[39] On 21 April, Warren reached Egypt; Keith now controlled fifteen British ships-of-the-line. Not until 29 April did Keith learn that the French squadron had probably returned to Toulon. Warren remained off Alexandria until 11 May, then sailed toward the central Mediterranean with seven ships-of-the-line.[40]

On Ganteaume's return to Toulon, he received pressure to make another relief attempt. Menou in Egypt wrote, "But Ganteaume, Ganteaume, where is he?" He needed reinforcements to improve his army's morale. Bonaparte echoed these sentiments, and the squadron again sailed for the Levant in mid-May. This time it consisted of four ships-of-the-line, a frigate, a corvette, and four transports.[41] On 8 June, Keith learned that Ganteaume was near Alexandria. Keith immediately sent his sloops and frigates to the north and west, while the British and Turkish squadrons weighed anchor. On the ninth, Ganteaume's corvette slipped into Alexandria, having been mistaken for a British vessel. Given the strength of the British fleet, Ganteaume decided to follow Bonaparte's instructions: land the soldiers west of Alexandria and have them march across the desert to join Menou. As the French prepared to land, several strange sail were sighted on the horizon. Fearing that this was Keith's squadron, the French hastily cut their cables and withdrew, but Ganteaume ordered his transports to slip through Keith's blockade to resupply Alexandria. Over the next two days the British captured all of the transports, and Keith ordered Bickerton to search for the French with one Turkish and three British ships-of-the line. Bickerton, however, returned on 15 June without sighting Ganteaume. This experience left Keith shaken, and to his sister he explained, "But what a risk it is! had they got in we must have embarked, . . . I cannot expect to be always fortunate." Meanwhile, on 24 June, Ganteaume captured the *Swiftsure* while she was sailing west for repairs. The French admiral arrived at Toulon on 22 July with his prize, but received no further instructions to sail for Egypt.[42]

Operations continued ashore, but the British proved too weak to take Alexandria. Instead they began a siege operation. Since Hutchinson's soldiers only occupied a small strip of land by the sea, the French could receive supplies over the dry bed of Lake Mareotis, south of Alexandria. Cochrane suggested that the British refill the lake by cutting the dike holding back the water. Keith approved of the idea and explained the concept to Hutchinson, who eventually agreed. On 11 April the British effected four breaches in the dike, flooding the lake. This restricted communications between Alexandria and the interior. No longer could caravans resupply Alexandria; all goods had to arrive by boat, and the British controlled many of the inland water-ways.[43]

The initial British strategy had called for operations near Alexandria; a drive into the interior was seen as hazardous, especially given the prevalence of disease.[44] However, the French front lines before Alexandria were strong, so rather than attack the city, Hutchinson in early April sent an expedition to take Rosetta on the western branch of the Nile. To sustain the army, Keith sent additional boats to the area for the conveyance of supplies. These proved essential, but the number of boats employed on the river led to a major disagreement between Hutchinson and Keith. Even though Hutchinson had not been there to determine an actual lack of support, he asked Keith why he had not received adequate naval assistance for river operations.[45] The admiral questioned why this was the first he had heard of the problem and told Hutchinson in future to consult a naval officer on the river. Keith then provided the list of small craft on the Nile and said bluntly, "I believe the [naval] officers to be correct." He declared, "I cannot permit them to act under the orders of every Land officer in Civil or Military Departments." Hutchinson explained that he had received an account from Captain John Morrison, of the navy, which did not correspond with Keith's figures. Instead of 73 boats, Hutchinson claimed that only 26 operated on the river.[46] The discrepancy in the number of boats can be partially explained. Both commanders relied on secondhand information. There were two naval captains on the Nile, and Hutchinson spoke with only one of the officers. When Keith investigated, one of his officers answered that sustained operations ruined boats at an alarming rate. A recent gale had destroyed several, and the remaining boats were in constant need of repair. The captain contended, "I am very sensible the numbers fall apparently very short . . . , but I do positive assert, that what are left of them have been constantly employed."[47]

When the British finally advanced toward Cairo, horses and camels were still in very short supply. This meant that the army would have to operate along the Nile and the various canals so that the boats could serve as transports. Keith ordered Captain Thomas Stephenson to oversee the naval aspect of the Cairo expedition. Operations proceeded smoothly, but as the distance between Keith and Stephenson increased, communications became more difficult. The admiral was irritated with the lack of timely reports and no longer wished to receive information about Stephenson's operation by "hearsay." Stephenson responded that he had written either Keith or Captain Young every day. In this instance, both officers were probably correct, since many letters were lost in transit.[48]

As the army consolidated its position on the Nile north of Cairo, it left the navy completely uninformed. Even Stephenson, who was directly involved in the operation, remained at a loss, and in early June he claimed that "what is their intention God only knows." Two weeks later he continued, "Our Troops are so close to Cairo in every Direction, that something decisive must take place in a day or two."[49] This proved correct, for General of Division Augustin-Daniel Belliard surrendered the 13,754 men of the French army in Cairo to the British and Ottoman Turks on 27 June. No naval officer signed the agreement, even though Articles 2 and 8 guaranteed that all the French troops and baggage would be returned to one of their Mediterranean ports aboard British and Turkish ships within fifty days.[50] Stephenson finally got word of the surrender to Keith on 2 July, but even then the captain did not have a copy of the articles of capitulation to send. The Kapudan Pasha had sent Keith a copy, but the boat carrying it had sunk en route. On 5 July, Keith protested to Hutchinson, "It is impossible that I can form any arrangements for the transportation of the French and the effects they have to remove till I am officially informed of their number and destination, and the conditions to which they have been induced to subscribe." By this time the differences between Keith and Hutchinson had become increasingly pronounced. Hutchinson testily replied that "your Lordship can have nothing to complain of, because it must always have been your fate to have procured them a passage to France." The general was right; this corresponded to Keith's instructions at the start of the campaign.[51] However, the admiral still needed information so he could prepare the correct number of ships and have each supplied with food, water, and an adequate crew.

The French, carrying everything with them, moved slowly from Cairo to the coast. Keith later commented that they had "baggage so much they have stripped the wretched inhabitants to the skin."[52] The French army's slow movement proved beneficial for Keith, since it allowed him time to assemble transports for their voyage to France. Still, it took longer than intended to embark them aboard ships, considering the amount of baggage and the number of people involved. Altogether, the French sailed aboard fifty transports and six troopships, and the last vessels did not depart from Egypt until 17 August.[53]

Although the objectives of the campaign severely taxed Keith's command, internal dissention nearly crippled the navy. The problems involved a personal grudge against Keith by Cochrane, the senior captain in the fleet who had overseen the 8 March landing. His subsequent service ashore as commander of the naval forces supporting the army had been commended by Keith, and Cochrane received permission in late March to return to his ship, the *Ajax* (74). Relations appeared normal until late April when Warren's squadron joined the fleet, bringing its strength to fifteen ships-of-the-line. This reinforcement complicated the sailing order of battle, which specified the station for every ship-of-the-line when maneuvering at sea. When Cochrane read the list, he felt "aggrieved" since, he maintained, the senior captain traditionally commanded the lead ship. Keith explained that the sailing order of battle was complex with three admirals present, and for many years the senior captain had not led the fleet into battle; if anything, this officer assisted the commander in chief. Here Keith ignored the facts. In 1793, when he had served in the Mediterranean Fleet, the sailing order of battle called for Keith, then the senior captain, to command the lead ship in the line of battle.[54] Cochrane rightly felt affronted.

After the initial threat posed by Ganteaume subsided, the captains of the fleet met aboard the *Swiftsure* on 4 May for a court-martial. More important than the judicial question at hand was a conversation among the officers, who determined that Keith had not provided fresh food for the sick. The group chose three senior captains including Cochrane to express their discontent. They believed that the admiral could have obtained supplies from the Egyptians at Rosetta or from the British camp outside Alexandria.[55] Keith responded that their method of censure was irregular and inappropriate. This led eleven of the captains to justify their demand and declare that "our conduct in this business has been actuated *only* by zeal for His Majesty's service."[56]

Keith rebuffed their complaints, claiming that there was a difference between being unable to provide for the infirm and neglecting them. He adamantly insisted that he had never done the latter, but he would relate these events to the Admiralty. The captains again repeated their demands, but this time they focused on Cochrane, who had purchased eighty sheep for the sick while serving ashore. He had told Keith that he could send more but had never received an answer.[57] Keith attempted to refute these allegations, claiming that he had offered to reimburse Cochrane if he purchased two hundred sheep per week. After the captain returned to the *Ajax*, Keith sent another naval officer to procure the livestock, but he "was refused that indulgence by the Military Command." Furthermore, Keith had attempted to buy cattle and fresh provisions from the Turks, but they were either slow or unable to fulfill the requests.[58]

To complicate matters, on 9 May, Captain Benjamin Hallowell of the *Swiftsure* questioned Keith on the price of shoes for his sailors. Instead of being charged 4s.4d. per pair, Hallowell explained, sailors aboard the *Northumberland* (74) paid only 3s.11d. for the same pair of shoes, and he wanted Keith to look into this.[59] A discrepancy of fivepence per pair of shoes was less serious than the other allegation, and Hallowell addressed Keith personally. However, several factors make this more seditious and allow it to be construed as the second thrust of a concerted attack on Keith's character and his fitness to command. Hallowell was one of the captains who had charged the admiral with neglecting the sick and hurt. In addition, he sent Cochrane an exact copy of the letter to Keith dated 9 May. This linked Hallowell and Cochrane, making it more than an isolated query.[60] Keith later agreed, "I have many reasons to believe that Captain Hallowell was actuated by other motives than a conscientious regard to the Public good."[61] After studying the receipts for more than 20,000 pairs of shoes purchased in Sicily, Keith found no problems with the transactions, but this did not convince Hallowell.[62] All remained quiet until the end of May. Possibly in an attempt to break up the combination of captains, Keith sent away Hallowell's ship, which was in desperate need of a major overhaul. After his departure the admiral received a report, supposedly from the captains of the fleet, detailing further evidence of irregularities in the purchase. Keith wrote Nicholas Brown, his secretary, who responded that the agent who procured the shoes was away. Brown conceded it was possible that dishonesty had occurred, but he thought it very unlikely.[63]

Eventually Keith interviewed the purser of the *Northumberland*, who said that the ship was at Sicily when the shoes were purchased and thus avoided freight charges on them. Furthermore, he had procured the shoes in 1799, not in late 1800 as Hallowell contended. This proved extremely important, since the exchange rate in 1799 differed from the rate in 1800, causing the British to pay more for the shoes on the latter date.[64] Keith was correct in his summation: "none of the facts stated by him [Hallowell] being true except one, viz. the price that the Northumberland's shoes cost."[65] When the news reached the Admiralty, they demanded an interview as soon as Hallowell arrived in Britain, but Ganteaume captured him when his ship surrendered on 24 June. Even after he was released, he did not return immediately to Britain. Neither Hallowell nor Keith let the matter rest; both considered it an affront to their honor. Not until 1804 were Keith and his associates cleared of all wrongdoing.[66]

Meanwhile, problems with Cochrane intensified on 5 June 1801 when he sent a letter to Keith with malicious undertones designed to undermine the admiral's authority. Cochrane declared, "I found the united voice of the Fleet crying out against your Lordship's general conduct. As an officer you was spoken of with slight." He contended that the officers thought that their admiral had become engrossed with trivialities and neglected things of importance. Keith responded, "I declare to God I am unconscious of ever having said or done a thing calculated to offend . . . any officer in the fleet. . . . As to my capacity as an officer I will pass it over because I can be no judge. I only endeavour to do my best." Cochrane also repeated allegations that Brown and Keith's brother in London had interfered in the selection of prize agents and then delayed payments to the beneficiaries, so they could accrue interest from the temporary investment of the prize money. Cochrane even hinted that Keith knew of the irregularity and did nothing to stop it. The admiral declared that his "Brother is a man of strict honor" and that Brown was honest and controlled only Keith's portion of the prize money. Cochrane's letter further accused the admiral of building a private fortune by having Brown manipulate the rate of exchange and then run the navy's money through various channels for his own advantage. Keith denied that this was possible. Most transactions were made in Spanish dollars, and the British agent at Lisbon bought the currency at a fixed rate. Keith added that items purchased in the region were expensive but he did the best to minimize the costs "and can defy all mankind to say I ever touched a farthing of its [the government's] money." In one last attack, Cochrane concluded, "I can assure your Lordship that there is no necessity for your being on bad terms with the officers under your command, but your manner is such upon many occasions that no gentleman can put up with."[67]

For several weeks, problems continued to build. Cochrane continually complained of Keith's actions, and the more he protested, the more hostile and uncompromising the admiral became. The ill will finally exploded over a disabling collision between the *Hector* (74) and the *Diana* (38) on 20 July.

The force of the impact drove both ships into the *Ajax*. The damage was severe, requiring a court-martial. Officers from each of the involved ships were to be brought before the court. Cochrane, the commander of the *Ajax*, complained, saying the officers of his ship were clearly not at fault. Keith replied that the court-martial would allow the officers to vindicate their characters, but Cochrane demanded a "redress for the undeserving insult I have received, which I shall ever consider as *hasty, harsh* and unbecoming." He then told Keith that he was writing the Admiralty since "I have not been able to discover that my character was attacked by any other than Lord Keith himself." He also contended, "You thought it [the collision] afford Your Lordship a fair occasion to attack me in my official capacity."[68] Cochrane displayed dubious judgment in continuing to push Keith. He had nothing to gain, since the fleet commander held all the power. But by this time it had become a personal issue for Cochrane over honor and the truth.

With the court-martial still scheduled, Cochrane wrote to Captain John Elphinstone, who Keith had appointed captain of the fleet to preside over daily administrative duties, including courts-martial. Cochrane objected to the validity of the court-martial, pointing out that John Elphinstone had been appointed captain of the fleet not by the Admiralty but by Keith. This led Keith to suspend the proceedings.[69] The Admiralty, informed in November, determined that Cochrane's complaint about the captain of the fleet was well grounded and ordered a study to determine if Keith had the authority to appoint Elphinstone. Keith cited the delay in communications and the need for an experienced officer to assist him, especially since illness had forced Captain Young to sail for England. Keith's argument was legitimate. For squadrons with more than fifteen ships, the commanding admiral had discretionary power to utilize the services of a captain of the fleet.[70]

A considerable delay occurred between the allegations of supposed mistreatment of the sick and the response of the Admiralty. St. Vincent, the First Lord, wrote Keith, "We all disapprove of the mode which the Captains addressed you; anything like combination has a most dangerous tendency." Rather than being concerned with the condition of those unfit for service, the Admiralty looked to the broader picture. The First Lord believed that Keith had acted properly when dealing with the captains but refused to condemn any of them for their actions. Instead, more information was needed, and several of the captains received orders to communicate directly to the

Admiralty. Such correspondence between the Admiralty and captains on foreign stations was unusual, but so was this incident. The captains contended that the complaint was not issued out of disrespect for Keith, and they acted only for the good of the service. In the end, St. Vincent thought it best to conclude the debate, because he considered Keith "inattentive" to the sick and the officers had acted "improperly."[71]

The entire affair was carried forward on both sides in an unbecoming manner. What had begun in May as a complaint about the treatment of the unwell quickly escalated. The lack of fresh provisions was a legitimate concern that Keith had not resolved. He had tried to obtain provisions but did not tell the captains or the Admiralty of the problems he had encountered. A major contributing factor was the army's refusal to allow naval officers to purchase livestock ashore. In addition, Abercromby's demand that all British naval forces assist the army negatively affected Keith's ability to procure supplies, since it proved difficult to detach ships for resupply missions. Once Hutchinson allowed Keith more control over naval operations, the ships had been off the Egyptian coast for nearly a month, and the provisions and stores aboard his ships had fallen to dangerous levels. Still, Keith was the commander; ultimate responsibility for his men rested with him, and he had failed to provide for his sailors. Even with mitigating factors, Keith's conduct was unbecoming and deserved reproof.

Although numerous captains had signed the letters, Cochrane's name recurred both as author and as witness to the allegations. At nearly the same time, Hallowell made his accusation involving the price of shoes. The timing was too opportune, and Hallowell was certainly a collaborator with Cochrane. Keith realized this and sent Hallowell away. This excellent maneuver isolated Cochrane. Now alone, he repeatedly lashed out against Keith, attacking his competency and questioning the legality of the administration of his command. Cochrane belonged to a well-placed Scottish family with close, if not always cordial, connections to the Elphinstone family, and their fathers had often been involved in disputes. Of Captain Alexander Cochrane, Keith later commented, "He is a crackheaded, unsafe man."[72] Off Egypt in September 1801, Keith recounted to his sister, "I have had much trouble with Captain Cochrane, I believe he has lost his senses. I am really sorry but he abuses me on all occasions as I am told. . . . I respect his family and above all his wife. I fear he will ruin himself and them all." Later Keith wrote that "there is something very wrong there." Cochrane's father echoed these senti-ments, lamenting that the "unfortunate correspondence between our dear Alexander and Lord Keith vexes my soul."[73]

Cochrane's criticisms of Keith's conduct undermined the admiral's empa-thy for the captain, especially after his very hostile letter of 5 June. Moreover, any direct censure of a commander, like those made by Cochrane or the cap-tains of the fleet, could have led to further problems and at worst a mutiny. It was a period of great anxiety for Keith as he took each complaint, studied it, and informed the Navy Board or the Admiralty. Although Keith was cleared of overall negligence, the Admiralty did on several occasions censure his con-duct, most notably over the care of the sick.[74]

Between the problems with Cochrane, the fear of a French relief expedi-tion, and the support of the army ashore, Keith had become disgruntled by mid-June and claimed, "This expedition is a millstone about my neck; it is so spun out, and indeed I see no end to it. This fleet is in a wretched way for ships and men." Three weeks later Keith told Hutchinson that the condition of his troopships would prevent them from remaining in Aboukir Bay during the autumn and winter storms.[75] This necessitated rapid action, and in late July the commander of the British forces outside Alexandria, Major General Eyre Coote, asked Keith to consider a plan to land some of his soldiers on the isthmus west of the city. This would allow the army to attack Alexandria from both directions. Since this operation involved ferrying a large part of the army across Lake Mareotis, Keith and a member of Hutchinson's staff made a reconnaissance on 12 August to gauge the strength of the flotilla the French had placed on the lake and determine a suitable landing site. Using the information gathered, Captain Stephenson's gunboats neutralized the French flotilla on the sixteenth. During that night Captain Elphinstone as-sembled small craft loaded with British soldiers, and in the morning the sail-ors rowed and sailed across the lake, disembarking the soldiers to the west of Alexandria.[76] Over the next few days Coote established a beachhead and captured Fort Marabout, at the far western end of Alexandria's Grand Har-bor.

On the afternoon of the twenty-first Bickerton, who commanded the blockade squadron off Alexandria, sent four British and three Turkish sloops under Cochrane into the Grand Harbor. Although the operation was made dangerous by the shallowness of the harbor and the presence of uncharted rocks, these vessels successfully anchored near the shore and fired on the

French with considerable effect, allowing Coote to advance. If the French frigates in Alexandria attempted to engage the smaller British and Turkish vessels, Bickerton had several frigates ready to support Cochrane's detachment. Although this operation was accomplished without loss, Keith did not approve of it, since he believed that it needlessly endangered his vessels. Bickerton apologized for this action but insisted that only naval support had allowed Coote to advance.[77] However, Bickerton's note to Cochrane—"Everything which I propose His Lordship [Keith] disapproved even to giving you the direction of the force employed. I am therefore obliged to order you off, but *privately* I recommend you to stay till morning by which time his Lordship will probably be out, as he seems to be seriously alarmed, at our want of caution here"[78]—was inappropriate, since Keith was the overall commander. The admiral was understandably loath to risk his vessels in a difficult harbor. And he was already upset with Cochrane over his openly slanderous activities that challenged and undermined his authority. Keith did not wish to entrust Cochrane with such a task, given his insubordination, and Bickerton knew his commander's position on the subject.

On 26 August, Coote again attacked, supported on both flanks by naval gunfire. This led Menou to ask for a three-day armistice to discuss a capitulation. It took several days to reach acceptable terms, but Keith, Hutchinson, the Kapudan Pasha, and Menou signed the articles of capitulation on 30 August. The French could keep their small arms and baggage, but they had to surrender most of their cannons and stores. The allies would then transport the French to one of their Mediterranean ports. In addition, Keith made sure that the terms of the agreement allowed for the confiscation of the fifty-one merchant vessels and the ten warships in the harbor. Even though he divided these ships with the Kapudan Pasha, the remaining ships created a windfall of prize money.[79]

The surrender of 11,712 men at Alexandria caused new problems. Keith estimated that it would take until the end of October to embark the French, since the transports he planned to use were the same ones he had employed to evacuate the Cairo garrison, but contrary winds and quarantine had delayed their return.[80] Keith left detailed instructions with Bickerton to oversee the evacuation, and then weighed anchor on 13 September with seven ships-of-the-line and a frigate transporting 1,700 soldiers. This squadron sailed for Corfu, since intelligence indicated that the Russians were planning to hand that island over to the French. On the fourteenth, Keith's squadron fell in with a vessel carrying dispatches indicating that Tsar Paul had been assassinated and "the object of Corfu had been given up" since the new ruler, Alexander I, was friendlier to Britain.[81]

Meanwhile, the British and French governments signed peace preliminaries on 1 October 1801. Keith learned of the impending peace only in late October, from a French brig carrying the news to Malta.[82] The peace preliminaries ended hostilities in Europe for the first time in nearly a decade, but Keith remained in the Mediterranean while the diplomats agreed to a definitive treaty. To better supervise operations, Keith sailed for Gibraltar on 9 March 1802. In addition to his other tasks, he received orders to dispatch his best ships-of-the-line to the West Indies, since a large French fleet had sailed to the Caribbean. The Admiralty set the peacetime establishment of the Mediterranean Fleet at only five ships-of-the-line, eight frigates, and seven sloops. This was at less than one-third of its strength at the conclusion of hostilities.[83]

The definitive peace was signed at Amiens on 27 March 1802, and Keith received notification on 15 April. The treaty's articles provided for Malta, within three months, to be returned to the Knights of Saint John of Jerusalem. In addition, the British would vacate Minorca. While the British complied with this latter provision, the Admiralty informed Keith that Malta would probably not be turned over to the Knights as stipulated in the treaty. The reasons the British government reneged on the agreement involved the strategic importance of Malta and the fear that the French would regain it from the Knights of Saint John.[84]

By 1802 Keith was both tired and depressed, with a visitor describing him as "a damned sullen old Scotchman," and Keith told his sister, "I have written a public resignation upon account of ill health . . . but [it] need not alarm you. . . . there can be no use in keeping me here . . . as the [Admiralty] Board show little attention to my wishes; and as for business if they do any it is not here. I never get answers for my dispatches for months after they are sent."[85] In this, Keith did not exaggerate. During the time that Spencer was First Lord, Keith received handsome support, and the Admiralty quickly replied to his dispatches. Once St. Vincent became First Lord, it seemed that the government in London almost ignored him. Often it took five or more months to receive answers to dispatches, by which time the information was dated and even irrelevant. Furthermore, in August 1801, St. Vincent had indicated to Nelson that he would appoint him to command the Mediterranean Fleet when Keith vacated the post. The following April, Keith wrote to his sister, "Say nothing of this. I understand that Lord Nelson was coming here—the Admiralty say nothing of it, therefore I do not know in what capacity."[86]

The lack of support from the Admiralty resulted from two disparate factors. Keith was appointed by the preceding Admiralty Board, and the Mediterranean Fleet was one of the patronage plums that the new Lords of the Admiralty could dispense. Moreover, Keith's personality seemed to aggravate others, and his letters to Hutchinson, to his captains, and even to the Admiralty had at times been impertinent. Thus in mid-June 1802, when Keith requested a furlough to return to Britain, the Admiralty readily agreed. Placing Bickerton in command of the fleet, he sailed from Gibraltar on the sixteenth aboard the *Foudroyant*. After an uneventful voyage, Keith arrived at Plymouth on 3 July. Two days later the Admiralty gave him permission to haul down his flag and go ashore.[87]

The Egyptian campaign was the defining moment of Keith's Mediterranean command and perhaps of his naval career. It yielded important results for the security of the British Empire and in England's war against France. Although the Egyptian operation was long and tedious, Keith demonstrated that he was capable of handling the stresses. First, he was able to defend the navy's independent status while engaged in joint operations. Although Keith's conduct was acceptable, it was far from perfect. His major problem involved his lack of charisma and a personality that seemed to grate on others. Relations between Hutchinson and Keith fluctuated from amity to barely veiled hostility. Problems with his captains can be partially ascribed to Keith's abrasive character. Still, he kept a capable staff. This included Brown, his secretary, and Captains Beaver and Young. Later he utilized the services of Captain John Elphinstone. Although far from brilliant, Keith employed capable subordinates and maintained a fleet comprising nearly two hundred ships off the coast of Egypt for seven months. Given Egypt's geographical location and the lack of suitable harbors, this was an outstanding achievement, and it resulted in accolades. From the Ottomans, Keith received gifts worth approximately £10,000, and the sultan named the admiral to the Ottoman Order of the Crescent, First Class. In Britain, both houses of Parliament officially thanked him. Finally, Keith, already an Irish peer, was raised to the peerage of the United Kingdom on 15 December 1801 with the title Baron Keith of Stonehaven Marischal.[88]

"Such times require the ablest men that can be got"

Keith in the North Sea (1803–7)

With the Peace of Amiens, Keith stood little chance to obtain another command as Britain prepared for a long period of peace. Whereas many believed that Amiens would endure, it survived for little more than a year. By March 1803 the renewal of hostilities loomed. Both sides held grievances. Britain refused to relinquish control of Malta. Bonaparte tried to regain control of the French colonies; his actions in Europe caused alarm; he appeared to be rebuilding his fleet; more significant, he refused to open ports to British trade. Even as the Admiralty authorized the expansion of the navy, secret negotiations continued between the two countries. Everything appeared contradictory, and Keith wrote, "With peace one day, war the next, it is wearisome."[1]

In the midst of the uncertainty, the Admiralty ordered several prominent flag officers to expedite war preparations at Britain's naval facilities. Rear Admiral James R. Dacres, the port admiral at Plymouth, was superseded on 17 March when Keith arrived to superintend the fitting of the ships in the "ordinary" for active service by making sure that they received guns, stores, masts, and rigging.[2] Keith was a natural choice for this command. He was an experienced flag officer whose abilities were well known to St. Vincent. Moreover, St. Vincent had long supported Keith's career with his patronage, and this demonstrated to potential protégés the loyal assistance St. Vincent could provide. At Plymouth, work progressed at a rapid pace, leading St. Vincent to tell Keith, "I heartily wish we could raise men as fast as you equip ships."[3] The admiral did not disappoint the First Lord, demonstrating an aptitude, if not a liking, for naval administration.

Meanwhile Keith's attitude remained gloomy, and he confided to his sister, "However little the French may be prepared we are in a wretched state in every respect—they might burn this place with five ships and 5,000 men and go home without risk." Over the next few days, the defenses improved as guns were mounted in the coastal defense batteries. However, Keith correctly indicated that the navy was in a "wretched state." St. Vincent, expecting a long period of peace, had begun a series of reforms to eliminate corruption and streamline naval administration and the dockyard establishments. He had even cancelled contracts, sold supplies, and dismissed dockyard workers. Ultimately, he had left the navy unprepared for hostilities.[4] Keith saw at least some of these shortcomings and did not relish being a port admiral who would have to confront such problems daily. In any case, Keith asserted, "one hour after war is begun it will be impossible for me to remain at Plymouth as a Port Admiral, because it would be tacitly acknowledging my incapacity to serve." This was an accurate statement. Port admirals were generally undistinguished flag officers or physically incapable of holding an active command.[5] Keith, however, did not need to worry; the command at Plymouth was, in St. Vincent's words, "*pro tempore.*"[6] The First Lord merely wanted the presence of a distinguished, capable flag officer to oversee the chaotic initial phase of preparations.

Although Keith privately maneuvered for command in the Mediterranean, St. Vincent replied that Nelson would receive that position. Instead, the First Lord assured Keith that "the command in the North Sea will be an important one and I will do my best to place you in it." This failed to satisfy Keith, even though St. Vincent tried to soothe his feelings by claiming that he had "a sincere regard and esteem" for Keith and "shall endeavour to demonstrate [it] to the latest period of existence."[7] Meanwhile Keith prepared to resign at Plymouth, since he had fitted all the ships that could immediately proceed to sea and nothing more could be done without adequate crews. However, St. Vincent asked him to stay, saying that "coming away from Plymouth at this moment might have a very bad effect on the pending negotiation" with France.[8] The First Lord could not appoint Keith to the North Sea, because this would appear provocative. And if Keith resigned, it would make Britain appear weak and unprepared for hostilities. In early May, Keith complained to his sister, "I find all is war and Cornwallis in the Channel. What is to come of me I know not." Only a day later, he received orders from St. Vincent to turn Plymouth back over to Dacres and travel to London, where on 17 May he was given command of the North Sea Fleet. Keith immediately traveled to Sheerness armed with a directive to detain all French ships—war was declared the following day.[9]

Keith's new appointment was a hybrid of several commands from the previous war including the North Sea Squadron and the Downs Squadron. Before long the North Sea Fleet would be Britain's largest, numbering more than two hundred vessels. Even then, the totals would seem insufficient, given Keith's area of responsibility from the Frisian island of Texel in the north to Le Havre in the south. Further north, his ships eventually blockaded the Elbe and the Weser on the North German coast. In addition, Keith had to account for the defense of the British coast from Leith to Beachy Head. Between the British coast and the Continent, Keith's ships patrolled the waters and escorted convoys as far as the ports of Norway and Russia. At the same time, other cruisers patrolled against privateers. Initially Keith oversaw port duties as well, but St. Vincent considered this too much and divested him of the assignment in late June 1803. Still, the number and variety of operations were startling, and at one point he would have six subordinate flag officers.[10]

As the war continued, it quickly became obvious that Keith's command, serving as the direct deterrent to a French invasion of Britain, was of the first importance. While the main French and Spanish battle fleets were blockaded by Britain's Channel and Mediterranean Fleets, the North Sea Fleet opposed the invasion flotilla that Bonaparte planned to use for a cross-Channel attack. Unlike the Channel Fleet, which was composed principally of ships-of-the-line, Keith's had very few large ships. In January 1804 he had no first or second rates and only ten third rates, half of which were smaller, generally older sixty-four-gun ships. Rather, Keith seemed to receive preference in newly commissioned frigates and sloops, and in January 1804 he commanded twenty-one frigates and twenty-six sloops. Also, he had an unusually large proportion of smaller vessels, which were considered more useful to intercept hundreds and later more than a thousand of Bonaparte's flat-bottomed boats, brigs, and schooners.[11] Still, there were never enough British vessels, leading Keith to declare, "The want of sloops is a constant complaint."[12]

In addition, Keith found it difficult to obtain capable officers, given the rapid expansion of the navy. Although these laments could be construed as the ravings of an aging, jaded admiral looking to the "good old days," specific examples indicate that his complaints were well grounded. The Admiralty sent several difficult subordinates to the North Sea, including Captain Sir Sidney Smith, whom Keith described as "truly ridiculous," and Captain the Honourable Henry Blackwood after he had written disrespectful letters to the First Lord.[13] Problems with his officers proved discouraging, and Keith

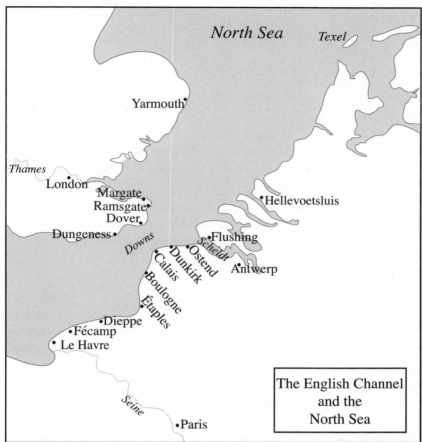

Map by Sara McCranie, 2004

Map 10. The English Channel and the North Sea.

complained, "A flag officer is certainly wanted, and . . . they are difficult to be found. . . . We, the old, wear out."[14] Worse still was the insubordination, as "it has for years past been the uniform system to abuse and find fault with every superior whenever any request was denied." Keith commented that his captains would hang or flog their men for the same offenses that his officers were guilty of every day.[15] Incompetence also proved troublesome, and Keith complained in October 1803 that his commanders relied too heavily on pilots: "This used not to be the case, . . . I can hardly get them to go from the Downs to Spithead without a pilot." Inattention by naval officers led St. Vincent to comment prophetically, "If this is not checked many of the ships

under Your Lordship's command will be thrown away." Three months later
Keith concurred: "It is quite ridiculous these frequent accidents and must
be want of common attention or from conceit." A month later, when Keith
described an officer who lost two anchors in a mere six fathoms of water, he
ranted, "What a damned set they are!"[16]

Even with inferior officers, the Admiralty expected Keith to accomplish
all the tasks assigned. Fortunately for Keith, the French invasion preparations were in the nascent stage. Thus it became a race to see if the French
could build an invasion flotilla before the British could assemble an effective
fleet. The British public believed that Bonaparte had too many troops assembled for an invasion not to occur. One affirmed, "I do not doubt for a moment, that the French will endeavour to invade this country."[17] Intelligence
reports correctly indicated that Bonaparte was assembling an invasion force.
To counter this threat, the British had to intercept the French vessels if they
sailed, but logistics exacerbated Keith's task, as his ships needed to come into
port occasionally to repair, water, and revictual.

Mid-1803 saw another crisis, occasioning an extension of the area that
Keith's ships had to patrol. The French invaded the Electorate of Hanover to
strike indirectly at Britain. On 25 July the Admiralty attempted to strengthen
their grip on the region with a declaration of blockade.[18] This caused resentment among British merchants, one of whom complained, "The blockade of
the Elbe and Weser interrupts all commerce."[19] The sharp reaction against the
blockade was echoes by neutral powers, preventing the Admiralty from ex-
tending the measure to include the entire French-controlled coast. Only the
Elbe and Weser along with Le Havre were under official notice of blockade
during 1803. This limited Britain's ability to stop and seize ships. Keith would
have preferred a strict blockade, but St. Vincent felt they must be "aware of
the offence we give to neutral maritime powers by placing ports in blockade."
The French thus continued to slip naval stores from the Baltic into their ports
to help build the invasion flotilla. Only in August 1804, after fifteen months
of the war, did the Admiralty, at Keith's request, blockade the coast from Le
Havre to Ostend.[20]

Unlike Keith's previous commands, the North Sea was close to the government in London, and the Admiralty severely restricted his independence.
In the past it had often taken months to receive replies from London, and
Keith accordingly had to take the initiative, hoping his decisions would correspond with the government's desires. In the North Sea, information could

reach London in hours; at most, Keith received replies to his messages in several days. This resulted in a daunting increase in correspondence with the Admiralty, though most was about minutiae. For example, Keith dispatched sixteen letters to the Admiralty on 27 May 1803 and twelve more on the following day. Between 27 May and 4 June he posted an average of nearly seven letters per day. Most of these were short and attested to a high level of Admiralty oversight and even micromanagement. This is particularly true of the myriad of notes that dealt with minor problems with single ships and complaints lodged by individual sailors.[21]

Although in close proximity to London, Keith was not stationed there. At the height of the invasion scare, he had to be careful to travel to the city only when the weather became so foul as to preclude a French landing. If not, his being seen would have caused public alarm—the people of England worried that his mere presence in London had left the coast exposed to invasion.[22] Unlike his previous commands, the North Sea Fleet dealt directly with the defense of Britain, and the public watched Keith's every move. This could be irksome, since many armchair admirals believed that the fleet's deployments were wrong or inadequate. However, disparaging remarks from one caused a chuckling Keith to recount, "There is a foolish paragraph-maker hereabouts who has made me converse with people I never saw, give balls and dinners to those whose names are unknown to me, and provided me a Lady Keith without my consent."[23]

Just as Keith rarely traveled to London, he seldom put to sea. Instead he attempted to oversee operations from a central location near the Thames. In late 1803, his flagship anchored at Ramsgate, and Keith purchased a house at East Cliff near Ramsgate. He claimed that the residence was "nearer the Downs, and from which I see over the Thames at the same time, and I keep a boat constantly ready in Ramsgate and Margate." Being ashore helped Keith to remain healthy until early spring 1804, when he suffered a stomach disorder, but he claimed that "a blister has done me good," and he quickly recovered. Moreover, he could surround himself with his family. His unmarried sister, Mary, lived at East Cliff, and he was able to spend a considerable amount of time with his teenage daughter, Margaret Mercer Elphinstone. On the negative side, living at East Cliff prevented him from personally influencing events. However, an argument could be made that a stationary headquarters was more effective, given the extended nature of the North Sea command. It allowed his subordinates and the Admiralty to always know Keith's location. To improve communications, a coastal signal station was maintained at Ramsgate—a necessity since Keith could not sail at short notice.[24] Rather than personally leading a battle fleet, the admiral mostly dealt with the administration of a fleet composed of a myriad of detached squadrons. In many respects, Keith's success in the North Sea rested on meticulous records and sound paperwork.

The North Sea Fleet began to take the war to the French during September 1803. As the Admiralty and Keith envisioned it, the French invasion flotillas would have to cross the English Channel or the North Sea under incessant attack by the Royal Navy. The importance of an active defense was exemplified between 14 and 20 September as the British attacked Dieppe, St. Valery, and Fécamp with bomb vessels. At Dieppe, Keith's ships fired numerous shells at the harbor with disappointing results—one fishing boat damaged, several buildings hit but only one burnt to the ground, and two or three French soldiers lightly wounded. This was followed on the twenty-seventh by an attack on Calais.[25] In each case, the bomb vessels were under sail and received fire from French shore batteries. Both factors reduced the effectiveness of their bombardment. The Admiralty concluded that Keith should suspend these operations until he had more bomb vessels and a stronger flotilla. On 1 October the members of the Admiralty changed their tack and ordered Keith to personally determine the feasibility of bombarding Boulogne. Keith responded that the strength of the French batteries and the small size of the targets precluded an attack, which would result in more damage to the British than the French. His opinion convinced the Admiralty, and they temporarily abandoned the undertaking.[26]

As Keith suspended operations against the French ports, the Admiralty presented a plan to blockade the harbors where the French were massing the small craft of their invasion flotilla. Keith agreed with the basic premise of the Admiralty's plan and made only minor modifications. The result was a working system that would remain in effect for the next three years. Off Le Havre, on the western extremity of Keith's command, he positioned three frigates and three sloops, with an additional two sloops and two cutters anchored in the Seine estuary. Further east, operating out of Dungeness, another squadron with a two-decked ship, four frigates, three sloops, a bomb vessel, three gun brigs, and two cutters was deployed to blockade Boulogne, Fécamp, and Dieppe. Of these ports, Boulogne would assume the greatest significance over the next months. A third squadron, based at the Downs and ordered to blockade Ostend, Calais, and Dunkirk, consisted of two third rates, one being Keith's flagship, plus three frigates, five sloops, two bomb vessels, and ten to twelve gun brigs and cutters. Keith concluded, "Ostend to Dunkirk is difficult, the sea is narrow and dangerous in long nights." At Flushing and the Scheldt, Keith deployed one fifty-gun ship, three frigates, three sloops, and two cutters. For the blockade of Hellevoetsluis, he positioned three frigates and two sloops along with several smaller vessels. The Texel—a shorthand term encompassing the port of Den Helder and the Marsdiep, a channel that separated Den Helder from the island of Texel and gave access to the Zuider Zee—was blockaded with three third rates and a pair each of frigates, sloops, gun brigs, and cutters. This was the largest concentration of ships-of-the-line in the North Sea Fleet, and the only port where France or one of its allies had a squadron of ships-of-the-line. Finally, the Elbe and Weser were watched by three frigates, a sloop, and several smaller vessels. These forces were completely independent of the coastal defense forces in the Humber, the Firth of Forth, and the Thames. Although the Admiralty devised this deployment in October 1803, Keith complained the following March that only the squadrons at the Texel and Dungeness were at full strength, and he had no effective reserve.[27] The deployment of these squadrons remained constant, but their sizes fluctuated with changes in local conditions. Increasingly they mirrored Keith's concern that Boulogne and the Texel posed the greatest threats.

Although intelligence indicated that the Dutch had made few preparations at the Texel as of October 1803, Keith learned the following January that the Dutch had three ships-of-the-line, a frigate, and two brigs ready to sail. A fourth ship-of-the-line was nearing completion, and the Dutch had also assembled some fifty merchant ships. Keith predicted, "Our wear and tear is and must be excessive, and that armament in the Texel will become vexatious in the spring." He was right. By May 1804 their strength had increased, especially among the merchant ships and other transports. Keith feared that the Dutch warships would sail from the Texel to cover the invasion flotilla as it departed either Boulogne or Flushing. Reflecting the importance he placed on the Texel, Keith ordered Rear Admiral Sir Edward Thornbrough, his most trusted subordinate, to command the squadron.[28]

Beginning in the late autumn of 1803, the Dutch and French began sailing their invasion craft from Flushing toward Ostend, Dunkirk, Calais, and eventually Boulogne. Even with the British navy operating along the littorals, the French and Dutch were able to transfer their forces along the coast almost at will because the French had deployed a series of batteries to cover their movement toward Boulogne, where Bonaparte planned to mass his invasion flotilla. At Boulogne, however, there were serious problems with the anchorage.[29] In November Keith even speculated that "they are going to give up Boulogne; it is too easy to watch it for their purpose," and in January he argued that the British "must see them embarking, for it cannot be done in one tide."[30] Keith's point was important: the tides were a real hindrance given the shallow harbor. However, public opinion differed, as the *Naval Chronicle* reported: "One thing, however, seems generally believed by most intelligent persons, that a much greater number of their flotilla can get out on one tide than was heretofore supposed."[31]

Since Boulogne was the location where the French massed their invasion flotilla, it also became the center of British schemes to annoy and retard their preparations. The Admiralty began these forays by looking into the practicability of bombarding Boulogne. Several months later, Keith presented his own plan to send launches filled with combustible material into the harbor in the night. He claimed, "The risk is nothing if well managed, the effect is chance."[32] However, Keith's idea receded in the wake of the "stone ship expedition," which involved sending three vessels filled with stones into the harbor mouth and then scuttling them to prevent the French invasion flotilla from sailing until the obstacle was cleared. This entire affair was misconceived from the beginning. The plan did not originate with the Admiralty, and the people readying the stone ships proved incompetent. Several naval officers challenged the plan's feasibility, including Captain E.W.C.R. Owen, commanding the squadron off Boulogne, who declared, "I am of opinion that the attempt would be worse than ridiculous." He believed that it would be difficult to scuttle the ships in the harbor channel since it was nearly dry at low tide, and this factor would allow French workmen to clear the obstacle quickly.[33]

In the meantime, St. Vincent received pressure from other cabinet ministers to go forward with the attack. The First Lord even considered replacing Owen with someone who believed in the plan.[34] Keith sided with Owen, claiming, "My whole time is taken up by this Boulogne business, which shall not stop with us, despicable as it is."[35] However, Keith demonstrated his savvy by neither wholeheartedly supporting the expedition nor opposing it. If it succeeded, it could not appear that Keith had objected to it, and if it failed, he did not wish to be heavily implicated. "Although I confess that I am not sanguine though to anticipate compleat success," he said, he was "little disposed that either His Majesty's Ministers or agents should experience the mortification of a failure." He concluded, "I think that the object is of sufficient importance to justify the attempt."[36] Preparations continued, but a plethora of factors retarded its implementation. When the British finally appeared off Boulogne in April 1804, the French estimated the British strength at thirty-five warships, and the defenders prepared for an attack, but the British never attempted to use the stone ships, since a gale blew the squadron away from Boulogne.[37]

While Keith grudgingly became involved in schemes against Boulogne, he also faced the responsibility of protecting trade. In June 1803 he lamented that his patrols were weak and ineffective, and French privateers interrupted trade. The public echoed the sentiment that "our whole coast is infested with privateers."[38] In mid-June the Admiralty ordered Keith to see that Baltic convoys received appropriate escorts. These convoys were extremely important, since this region supplied tremendous quantities of naval stores needed by the navy, and an average of ten to twelve escorts were required during 1803. For example, in late June the Russia Company's ships sailed, escorted by a cutter and a frigate, and in mid-August a Baltic convoy of 382 merchant ships sailed under the escort of only eight British warships. During the winter the Baltic ports froze, but operations resumed in late March 1804. Keith contended that during the winter months the French had had time to fit more privateers for service, which resulted in a greater problems than the previous year, and he needed more convoy escorts to ensure the safety of commerce. During 1804 the Admiralty wished for a convoy to sail from Britain every two weeks, but Keith correctly questioned the feasibility of the plan, given the lack of escorts.[39]

The Baltic was not the only area where privateers threatened trade. Closer to home, Keith contended with privateers on the English coast who targeted fishing boats and particularly the coastal trade. Although these were not very lucrative prizes, Bonaparte desired intelligence from their crews about British defensive preparations.[40] In the wake of these French actions, Keith received numerous appeals for protection. In each instance, Keith replied that he had ships patrolling the area affected by privateers. On the other hand, protecting the coastal trade often took a backseat to assigning escorts to foreign convoys. For example, in April 1804 he had five gun brigs and two cutters assigned to patrol the coast from Newcastle to Oxfordness, but two brigs and one cutter had been detached to serve as convoy escorts. This left this area open to attack.[41]

As the first year of the war drew to a close in the spring of 1804, frustration among the British populace increased, and Addington's majorities in Parliament slowly eroded. William Pitt, who claimed that the current ministry had mismanaged the war effort, was widely regarded as an acceptable alternative. Keith saw that the Addington government was doomed. This deduction came with mixed feelings. St. Vincent had supported Keith, while John Markham and Sir Thomas Troubridge, two naval members of the board, proved staunch and extremely loyal allies. However, Keith already knew that Pitt approved of his conduct and had reportedly described Keith as "remarkably able" and his deployments as "very zealously executed."[42] On the other hand, Keith repeatedly proclaimed that as long as he held the North Sea command, he would remain out of political disputes: "I am unconnected with party or politics, and according to the understanding God granted me, endeavour to discharge my duty to the public." Even so, it disturbed Keith to see problems in the government emerge in the middle of the war, and in May he cynically remarked, "This is a fine moment to be jangling about ministers!"[43] In late April, St. Vincent unsuccessfully asked Keith for his proxy on a vote in the House of Lords. Keith had also received an appeal from one of Pitt's allies, but this one was more discreetly worded: "Mr. Pitt said he thought there might be a delicacy about your acting in Parliament on account of the command you hold, whatever might be your way of thinking."[44] Addington's government fell on 15 May, but Keith played little role in the collapse. He had, as he said, not been directly involved in politics since he returned to active duty in 1803. In this, Keith had matured. He now understood not only the importance of powerful patrons but how to maneuver in political circles. Once he learned that Pitt was to be the new head of government, he quietly gave his moral support. The future was uncertain, but Keith worked to maintain his command, and he could do this only with the support of Pitt.[45]

From its inception, Pitt's ministry appeared weak; Addington's followers had entered the Opposition, and the king refused to allow the supporters of Grenville and Fox into the government. As a result, the cabinet consisted of relative nonentities except Henry Dundas, now Lord Melville, Pitt's appointment as First Lord. Placing his most experienced and trusted lieutenant in the Admiralty conveyed this position's importance. Keith and Melville were lifelong colleagues who had used each other to advance their respective careers, but they were not friends. Melville had proved instrumental in Keith's appointment to command at the Cape and in the Eastern Seas during 1795–96, and he had played a large role in obtaining Keith's Irish peerage in 1797. However, Keith's command in the Mediterranean had highlighted differences between the two, and this was especially apparent following the failure at Cádiz. Still, Melville seemed to have a grudging respect for Keith, which the admiral at least pretended to reciprocate. As far as Keith was concerned, he would serve the new First Lord competently if not happily, but he still refused to mix politics and the naval service, claiming, "I had made it an invariable rule since the year 1792 not to engage in any political career whilst employed on service, thinking it my duty to execute the commands of my superiors faithfully without entering into their motives."[46] This policy was well judged. Keith had never been very effective in politics, whereas success seemed to follow his naval career. A scrupulous nonpartisanship resulted in greater professional security, allowing him to retain his command if the government changed.

Soon after becoming First Lord, Melville questioned Keith about the operations of the North Sea Fleet and asked if he needed additional frigates, gun brigs, and fireships. Commanders rarely refused reinforcements, and Keith responded, "More ships are certainly wanted." Further queries by Melville illustrated one of his greatest faults—the micromanagement of the fleet. He asked Keith if his ships were equipped with hand grenades and fire engines. The admiral responded to such minutiae with restrained sarcasm. Regarding fire engines, he assured Melville, "All the ships in the navy are formally supplied with them"; regarding the grenades, "Seamen throw them as well as any others."[47] Melville's hands-on approach aggravated Keith, but he humored what he considered inane questions, provided that Melville did not infringe upon the fleet's effectiveness. In other areas, however, Keith attempted to dissuade the First Lord, and at times he carefully blocked measures detrimental to the service. The threat of invasion consumed the new First Lord. Keith, relying on decades of experience, viewed the threat with less alarm and attempted to allay Melville's concern: "It always appeared an easier matter to plan an invasion of this country than to carry it into effect and the Nearer the time of Execution the stronger the Difficulties and Dangers will appear."[48]

Even so, French invasion preparations continued. By July 1804, Napoleon had massed more than 1,800 invasion craft between Étaples and Calais, of which 700 were anchored at Boulogne. Napoleon explained that there had not been an engagement between his gunboats and Keith's vessels where the British did not subsequently have to go to the dockyard and refit. Because of this, he confidently believed that he could push aside the small blockading squadrons at the time of the invasion.[49] Although the British did not conceptualize every aspect of the French plan, Melville echoed Napoleon's contention: "I should suppose that *numbers* of vessels must tell." Like St. Vincent with his plan of October 1803, Melville believed that his ships should fight the French "every Inch of their passage in crossing the Sea."[50] To be able to accomplish this, Keith asked Melville for three frigates, six sloops, and two or three cutters, a request that accorded with the Admiralty's sentiment that the North Sea Fleet should obtain the first choice in reinforcements.[51] However, the Admiralty faced many demands, and Melville replied, "In short we are so deficient and will be so for a long time, it is necessary to have recourse to every expedient." The First Lord then offered Keith fifteen armed transports, but three days later his attempt at micromanagement got the better of him. He had to retract the offer after he learned that the transports would need a great deal of work and many additional sailors to make them combat effective. Even without the transports, the number of small vessels in the North Sea Fleet increased during the first four months of Pitt's administration. By September 1804 the North Sea Fleet contained approximately 220 ships of all classes.[52]

With a powerful fleet opposing the massive invasion flotilla, Keith attempted to follow Melville's lead. The First Lord believed that something visible had to be done, since public opinion and the newspapers demanded that the navy destroy or slow the French preparations. Another factor of equal importance was Melville's penchant to use new technology. Although Pitt's government shelved the stone ships expedition, the First Lord looked to other special operations, and Keith remained consistently reserved in his assistance. Boulogne again became the target of attacks, this time involving various types of torpedoes (mines) constructed by Robert Fulton, an inventor who at one time had worked for Bonaparte to construct an underwater vessel. His submarine had alarmed the British government, which sent agents to France to entice Fulton to lend Britain his technological expertise. After secretly arriving in England on 15 May 1804, Fulton assumed the alias Francis and agreed to construct explosive devices for the British.[53] Their first project involved an attack on the ships outside Boulogne. Captain Sir Home Popham worked directly with Fulton in a civilian capacity, and Keith told Popham that "if you are inclined to pursue it at present I have no objection."[54] On the night of 2 October, with Keith, Melville, and Popham present, the British attacked the 150 French vessels outside the harbor at Boulogne. The force included "explosion vessels," similar to fireships but designed to explode, along with boats carrying various types of Fulton's torpedoes. The attack produced several explosions, and the British noted a great degree of confusion, but the French lost only one of their smallest invasion craft with all forty-one hands. Napoleon commented that there was little to fear from such operations, because at worst he would lose one or two boats, but if the British could place these devices within the cramped confines of the harbor, they would cause great damage. Although the British had problems assessing the damage inflicted by the attack, initial reports were favorable, and at Melville's urging, Keith decided to make another attempt.[55]

However, a problem soon surfaced. After the attack, an infuriated Keith addressed Melville about a dinner given by Vice Admiral John Holloway, the admiral at the Downs. At the meal several officers, including Rear Admiral Thomas Louis, commander of the squadron off Boulogne, had disparaged Popham and questioned the success of the recent operation, claiming that one of the mines had actually destroyed a British ship and another had sunk in deep water. Keith declared, "I then put a stop to conversation and desired to know upon what ground such information had been withheld from me." Further investigation revealed that a tow rope on one of the mines had broken. Another sank, and at least one proved defective. As to the failures, Melville responded that the numbers were still well within the acceptable range, given the difficulty of the operation. Rather, it was Louis's behavior that enraged Melville, who ranted, "I have no right to control the private judgement of any officer, but I have a right under certain circumstances to insist that they shall keep their opinions to themselves." He saw Louis as the principal problem and suggested that he could be replaced. Keith's experience and past problems with subordinates colored his response: "I . . . have long much lamented that lax conversation among officers and in the presence of their superiors (not infrequently) which . . . produced . . . the greatest evils which ever befell this country—I mean the mutinies, one of which I had the misfortune to witness." However, Keith believed that "Louis is a good man and will perform his duty correctly." He just needed to curb such conversation.[56] Keith's defense of Louis demonstrates his ability to forgive. Louis was one of the captains who had attacked Keith's conduct off Egypt, yet now Keith protected him when he could have sought revenge. On another level, the incident allowed Keith to learn more about his subordinates and superiors. Melville's enthusiasm for Fulton's mines was startling, but Keith's subordinates disliked the idea. The admiral had to be careful; his own feeling mirrored his officers. He considered the operations expensive and risky, but he could not convey this to Melville.

Melville remained First Lord for only a year. His resignation was a product of rivalries in the navy and his own financial aggrandizement. St. Vincent, while First Lord, had appointed a Commission of Navy Inquiry. Its tenth report became public on 18 March 1805, and it dealt entirely with the Treasurer of the Navy, a post Melville had held during almost all of Pitt's first administration. The contents of the report constituted a damning condemnation of Melville, who had made a fortune out of this office. While members of the Opposition in Parliament used the report to attack the First Lord, Pitt staunchly lent Melville his complete support. It was Keith's view that "the support Pitt gave it must affect him so long as he lives." Parliament voted on a censure motion on 8 April, and a tie resulted in the Commons. The speaker cast the deciding vote against Melville, who then resigned. Keith exclaimed, "I am glad the question went as it did last night." In this case, he broke with his policy of staying out of politics while he held a command. To one of the Prince of Wales's friends, Keith indicated, "The Prince thinks I am disinclined to vote against Lord Melville. I had no such feeling." Keith then recounted, "Myself and my family have met with nothing in that quarter but opposition." Melville had opposed several of Keith's parliamentary elections dating back to the 1770s. More recently, he had contested Keith's nephew's bid for a seat in the Commons, and this election had cost Keith £3,000. Melville's candidates had also opposed Lord Elphinstone twice in his attempts to become a Scottish Representative Peer, and Keith claimed that Melville "has *threatened Lords* who voted for" Lord Elphinstone. As to their relations after he became First Lord of the Admiralty, Keith declared, "I have asked for one favor since he came into office, which has not been granted."[57] Keith's list of complaints reinforced the contention that Keith had no fondness for Melville; he had merely worked with him after Melville joined the Admiralty. It demonstrated Keith's professionalism that he had served for a full year under someone whom he despised. It pleased Keith that Melville had destroyed himself, and the admiral had played no part in the First Lord's dismissal.

Following the resignation of Melville, the position of First Lord remained vacant for three weeks. In part, this was due to the Easter recess, but Pitt's search for an acceptable nominee proved difficult. By mid-April the field had narrowed. One cabinet minister indicated, "As to naval men, Lord Hood was gone by. Lord Gardner has no nerves except on quarter deck. Lord Keith would (from his juniority) strike the flags both of Lord Gardner and Admiral Cornwallis—exclusive of the consideration of his country [Scotland]—so that at last, I fancy, it will be *old* Sir Ch[arles] Middleton." The next day the projections appeared slightly different but still included Keith. At this time another cabinet minister described Keith as "a doubtful sort of politician," and his name subsequently disappeared from consideration.[58] Keith's naval qualifications were never in doubt; however, he had little experience with Admiralty administration and politics. In addition, Keith was junior to several serving admirals, and they would have to stand down before he could sit as First Lord. Cornwallis particularly was a legitimate concern, since he was senior to Keith and had ably commanded the Channel Fleet since the resumption of hostilities in 1803. These reasons led Pitt to select Middleton, but there was one problem—he did not hold a seat in either House of Parliament. Without an election, the only alternative was a peerage, and Middleton was created Baron Barham on 1 May 1805.

The appointment of Barham could have led to personal and professional jealousies, since Keith had also been considered for the position. Worse, Keith's flag flew close to London. Something had to be done to allay possible animosity. Keith wanted to show Barham that he had no hostility, and the First Lord needed a steady presence in the North Sea. Upon his appointment and the confirmation of his title, Keith immediately congratulated Barham, and the new First Lord sent Keith a letter of thanks. Furthermore, the two agreed to maintain a separate private correspondence.[59] This meant that Keith had a trusted ally in Barham. Keith's duties continued with little interruption, with the Texel and Boulogne causing the greatest concern, but there were added wrinkles. Barham explained, "We must get the better of this Don Quixote system of attacking Windmills," and ordered Keith's ships to refrain from engaging the invasion flotilla if it was protected by shore batteries, because their fire severely damaged the British ships.[60] However, this did not mean that Keith should recall his squadrons. More than ever, they needed to be ready to oppose an invasion attempt.

During 1805 the French and Spanish fleets escaped from several of their ports. Napoleon had conceptualized a brilliant plan to disperse the British fleets and bring his ships together in the Western Approaches to the Channel where they could cover the French invasion flotilla as it sailed to Britain. However ingenious, the plan was overly complex for the Age of Sail, since it called for too much coordination and failed to adequately take into account British movements. Napoleon hoped to unite the Spanish fleet at Cádiz with the French ships based at Toulon. This combined fleet would sail to the West Indies, where they would join a French squadron that had sailed from Rochefort. In January the first ships sailed. Although the Toulon and Cádiz fleets combined, they failed to unite with the Rochefort squadron. Furthermore, Napoleon had ordered the French fleet at Brest to sail, but the British blockade prevented this.

The movements of the French and Spanish battle fleets affected Keith's deployments. In July the Admiralty sent ships from the Channel Fleet toward Cádiz, weakening the British presence off Brest. If the combined French and Spanish fleets eluded British squadrons off the coast of Spain and sailed north, the British government feared that they would unite with the French ships at Brest and force the Channel Fleet to withdraw in the face of superior numbers. Accordingly, on 31 July the Admiralty ordered Keith to reinforce the Channel Fleet with five or six ships-of-the-line.[61] Problems occurred, since all but one of these ships were either not manned or in desperate need of repair. Then, within two weeks, Keith's orders changed. The British learned that soldiers had embarked aboard the Dutch ships in the Texel, so instead of sending his ships to the Channel Fleet, Keith reinforced this squadron. This was, in fact, part of Napoleon's plan. He wanted the Texel squadron to sail on a mission of deception and have the British pursue these ships with at least ten ships-of-the-line.[62] This would reduce the strength of the North Sea Fleet at the critical juncture when the combined fleets from Brest, Cádiz, and Toulon arrived off Boulogne to cover the crossing of the invasion flotilla. On 17 August, Keith received intelligence that 16,000 to 18,000 troops were embarked at the Texel and ready to sail. Although this information was accurate, the British had little to fear because the Dutch ships-of-the-line could not sail until the end of the month during the spring tides. These were substantially higher than normal tides and occurred during a new or full moon. In the meantime Keith had three seventy-fours, four sixty-fours, and a fifty-gun ship off the Texel.[63] Both Barham and Napoleon wanted Keith to sail in person off the Texel. The First Lord believed that Rear Admiral Thomas M. Russell, the British squadron commander at the Texel, was of dubious ability and echoed

Keith's critique that "Russell who would do my will for a week is not an officer Your Lordship would choose to continue long in command of the Texel Squadron."[64] Even so, to force Keith to sail, Barham had to issue a threat to take away his flagship: "The demands for line of battle ships are so great that it is impossible to suffer any of them to lay idle." Keith was incensed. He believed that several ships-of-the-line should be kept in the Downs, and he declared there was "no instance where a flag officer of my standing charged with an extensive command, and who is supposed to be in readiness to go to sea at a moment's warning, has been subject to be deprived of his Flagship."[65] Although Keith relented and sailed off the Texel in his flagship during the spring tides, he correctly maintained that his powerful squadron made the chance of action slight. The movement of Keith's flagship also fulfilled part of Napoleon's plan, since he wanted the British to reinforce the Texel squadron to remove one of the very few ships-of-the-line capable of intercepting the French invasion flotilla at Boulogne.[66]

The Dutch did not sail during the spring tides, for the ships from Toulon, Cádiz, and Brest failed to arrive in the Channel. Hostile actions by Austria then caused Napoleon to reconsider the invasion of England. On 2 September he departed Boulogne, and his armies marched east toward the German states and Austria. With Britain having allies on the Continent, Napoleon could no longer threaten England with his army on the Channel coast. These developments did not go unnoticed by Keith. To limit the wear on the British squadron off the Texel, Keith received the Admiralty's permission to send all but a few frigates to Yarmouth until the equinox.[67] While the squadron lay in Yarmouth, Nelson defeated the French and Spanish fleets at Trafalgar, and it became obvious that Napoleon had postponed his planned invasion of England as war with Austria and Russia became a reality.

In late August, as the possibility of a French invasion receded, the Admiralty ordered Sir Sidney Smith to raise the broad pendant and as a commodore take command off Boulogne. This was not the choice of either the Admiralty or Keith; the order came from Pitt and his secretary for war, Robert Stewart, Viscount Castlereagh. Both still relished the advantages of special weapons, particularly William Congreve's new rocket system. In these operations Smith technically served as Keith's subordinate, but he had a fiery independent streak. During early October, Barham and Keith attempted to convince Castlereagh and Pitt of "the folly of the enterprise," or at the very least have Smith sent to the Mediterranean. The First Lord lamented, "There appears to me such a want of judgment in the supporters of this kind of war-fare, that I am wholly at a loss how to account for it."[68] Pitt and Castlereagh realized that opposition was mounting but pressed forward with the opera-tion. "The plans seem determined upon," regretted Keith, "and I was only asked about the means of putting them into execution." He also voiced his decided opinion on the experimental weapons: "Mr. Francis [Fulton] is full of coffers, carcasses and submarine boats, which will not answer here; and Mr. Congreve, who is ingenious, is wholly wrapped up in rockets from which I expect little success, for Mr. Congreve has no idea of the means of applying them professionally."[69] Instead, Keith presented his own plan, claiming, "If the Government really intend to destroy the vessels in Boulogne, it must be done . . . by a dash in the dark night by a few determined *seamen*, well pre-pared to set fire, and return instantly to their boats."[70] Keith's plan received no consideration. It seemed too simple, lacking the spectacular technological edge of Fulton's and Congreve's systems, yet perhaps its greatest flaw was that it could have worked.

Operations continued, but Keith did not trust Smith, who aggravated Keith as he constantly tried to make his command independent of the North Sea Fleet.[71] Smith ranted, "I am to write to Ramsgate [Keith's headquarters] on every proposition." He asserted that if he did this, fleeting targets of op-portunity would slip away.[72] Forcing the commodore to consult Keith cre-ated an administrative roadblock that could not be removed unless Smith's powerful patrons appointed a new officer to command the North Sea Fleet. This seemed unlikely with Keith enjoying the support of the First Lord, who claimed that "it is much safer to employ him [Smith] under command than in command."[73] Even with the obstacles, Smith finally launched an attack on the night of 20 November. The sea was too heavy to use the rockets, so Smith utilized several of Fulton's carcasses. While the rewards were negligible, Brit-ish losses were light.[74] However, Smith's tenure in command off Boulogne was nearing an end. Barham, using Keith to run interference, waited until mid-November to strike at Smith and sow doubt among his patrons. The commodore, Barham accused, had commanded one-third of Keith's fleet for the previous six weeks with no tangible results. In the meantime, Napoleon had released many of the seamen previously assigned to the invasion flotillas, who could now serve on privateers to intercept British trade. Largely because of Smith's operation, Keith lacked the reserves to counter the threat. In ad-dition, two frigates had escaped from Flushing because there was not an adequate blockade force. Barham directed Keith to send cruisers to Norway and the Orkney Islands and explained to Pitt that these orders would have been unnecessary if Keith had had ships to blockade the Scheldt. On 11 December, Smith informed Keith he had received orders to sail to Gibraltar.[75]

While Smith had one-third of the North Sea Fleet under his orders, the British government had decided to land soldiers at the mouths of the Elbe and Weser. The British were forming a continental coalition against France, and they needed to show their commitment. At any rate, the bulk of the French army had withdrawn from the coast. As the British government prepared to land 10,000 troops in northern Germany, Keith supervised the embarkation of the first contingent at Ramsgate in mid-October, with orders to have the transports sail on the first favorable wind. During the embarkation, the plans changed—something that became a constant factor in the operation. The British government seemed to construct the plan as they went along, and the size of the expedition mushroomed. Although this aggravated Keith, he maintained his composure. He had participated in many amphibious operations, and he knew the importance of resolution and steadiness. This was particularly necessary since he received his orders directly from Castlereagh and not the Admiralty.[76] During the ensuing months Keith acted as coordinator, making sure that escorts were available and the convoys were ready and well provisioned. However, Castlereagh left Keith little room for initiative and failed to solicit his professional advice in the planning stages to understand potential problems with the weather. Easterly winds and gale conditions delayed the sailing of the first convoy until early November, and the second convoy did not sail until the end of that month. Keith questioned the logic of conducting such an extensive operation at the approach of the winter season.[77] Indeed, the weather turned deadly in mid-December when the third and fourth convoys, consisting of sixty-seven transports, encountered a severe gale. Many of the transports suffered damage, and eight sank, taking 664 soldiers to watery deaths.[78]

Meanwhile the British government believed their coalition against France was succeeding. Then on 29 December news of Austerlitz and the conclusion of an armistice between France and Austria arrived in London. Keith immediately received instructions to evacuate the soldiers from the Elbe and Weser.[79] Operations proceeded at a rapid pace, and by New Year's Eve, a mere forty-eight hours after receiving the news of Austerlitz, Keith had seven ships-of-the-line and a frigate sailing for the Texel to prevent the Dutch squadron from interfering. For the evacuation itself, he had twenty-two warships either off the North German coast or en route, along with every available transport.[80] The concentration of warships and transports allowed for the rapid reembarkation of the British army. However, the British government slowed the operation because they did not wish to discourage Prussia from joining Britain in an alliance. Throughout January 1806, Britain's soldiers remained in northern Germany awaiting the outcome of their government's discussions with Prussia. Finally on 19 January it was decided to evacuate the troops, and the embarkation continued throughout February until the whole North German venture came to an ignominious end.[81] The navy's role had been both essential and peripheral, and Keith had performed his tasks admirably; this was especially true of the rapid concentration of the forces for the evacuation in late December.

Even though Keith's conduct was commendable, he had been trying throughout Barham's tenure in the Admiralty to obtain a new command, and the First Lord had been attempting to divide the North Sea Fleet. These efforts were not unrelated. The North Sea Fleet had not been Keith's choice; he wanted the Mediterranean Fleet. Just days after Barham became First Lord, Keith wrote that he was coming up to London and would explain "the way which I came to this command (after being refused my former) and my readiness to go to another in the event of an opening."[82] Meanwhile, Barham had begun to study the ramifications of dividing the North Sea Fleet, but he attempted to mollify Keith, assuring him in July that such a division "will not be acted on hastily nor without consideration."[83] The events of late summer and early autumn 1805 that culminated in Trafalgar occupied much of the Admiralty's attention, and the planned division did not resurface until mid-October.[84] By this time Keith no longer wanted the Mediterranean Fleet, for he did not wish to preside over what, in his mind, would merely be the blockade of Cádiz. Instead, Keith indicated that he would happily assume command of the Channel Fleet.[85] Six weeks later he maintained, "A report prevails here . . . of Admiral Cornwallis's resignation. . . . I should like to have the refusal of that command."[86] Meanwhile Keith wrote to Barham to defend the viability of a united North Sea Fleet, pointing out that it lessened correspondence with the Admiralty, promoted effective convoy management, and facilitated the rapid shifting of forces. Barham remained unconvinced. In January the First Lord asserted that the distance from the southern limits of the command to the northern terminus, some 600 to 900 miles, was too great. Furthermore, Keith's headquarters at East Cliff was seventeen miles from his flagship. The fleet contained six junior flag officers located at the Downs, Dungeness, Sheerness, Yarmouth, the Texel, and Leith—again, too high a number. Moreover, dispatches between Keith's command post and his northern flag officers at Yarmouth and Leith were routed though London within a short distance of the Admiralty office. In January 1806, Barham told Keith that the command would be divided into five components. The first would include the area from Beachy Head to Deal and would include the junior admirals at Dungeness and the Downs. The second command would cover the coast from the Thames to Harwich, including the Nore. The third would encompass Yarmouth, and the fourth would include Leith, while the fifth component would comprise the squadron off the Texel. Each of the five would be independent, and Keith's position remained unclear.[87]

This plan never came to fruition, since Pitt died on 23 January and his ministry rapidly disintegrated. As Barham left office, ideas for the division of the North Sea Fleet were temporarily dropped. Likewise, if the outgoing First Lord had another command for Keith, the idea vanished as George III called on Lord Grenville to propose a new cabinet. To Barham, Keith voiced his concern: "Mr. Pitt's death has made many important changes. I respected him very much, although from circumstances we had no political connection. I am sorry you are about to quit the admiralty . . . , for the times require knowledge and constant application. Nothing can persuade me that any man not a seaman is fit for the office in war, I have observed it all my naval life—not a short one now."[88] Keith and Barham had worked together effectively, and they had agreed on most issues with the exception of a unified North Sea Fleet.

The new ministry, often referred to as the Ministry of All the Talents, was led by Lord Grenville and seconded by Charles James Fox. They appointed two successive civilians as First Lords of the Admiralty. Between February and September 1806, Charles Grey served as First Lord, but then the death of Fox in September led to a reshuffling of the cabinet. After much debate Grey, who had lately been created Viscount Howick, became foreign secretary, while Lord Grenville's brother Thomas was invited to lead the Admiralty. Neither of these First Lords pursued Barham's plan to divide the North Sea command, and neither attempted to remove Keith. While the admiral seemed to have very little contact with Grey, the opposite could be said of Thomas Grenville. Upon his appointment, he emphasized his personal connection with Keith and explained that he hoped to make use of Keith's "long experience and acknowledged talents."[89] Grenville carried on a lively private correspondence with Keith, and in return Grenville granted Keith leave to take care of unnamed private concerns and enhanced Keith's patronage powers.[90] Of the six First Lords of the Admiralty during Keith's North Sea command, Grenville caused Keith the least concern and torment.

The overall plan of the Ministry of All the Talents involved the modification of Britain's wartime strategy to sever continental commitments and to focus on colonial ventures. In February 1806 when Grey became First Lord, Keith's ships had nearly completed the withdrawal of the British soldiers from northern Germany. This had been Keith's only connection to coalition warfare on the Continent. The tasks of the North Sea Fleet continued to be based around the defense of the British Isles, the protection of English maritime trade, and the execution of limited raids on the French coast. To accomplish these, the Ministry of All the Talents maintained the North Sea Fleet at eighty-five to ninety vessels excluding gunboats, gun brigs, and hired ships. This was slightly larger than the fleet during the last months of Pitt's administration.[91] Deployments also continued as before with only minor alterations. Although the possibility of a French invasion of England still existed, the threat was minimal except during July 1806, when intelligence reports indicated that Napoleon was moving 72,000 soldiers toward the Channel coast. Keith believed that such a redeployment of soldiers was highly probable, since it would cost no more for the French to quarter them near the coast than anywhere else and the British would certainly take notice of the redeployment and react accordingly. Keith was not alarmed, as he explained: "Plans are always easier made on paper than carried into execution."[92] To counter this threat, Keith's blockade continued basically as before, but the French invasion threat of 1806 resulted from an incorrect intelligence assessment; Napoleon, instead, turned on Prussia.

In addition to blockading the coast, the North Sea Fleet conducted limited attacks on Boulogne with Congreve's rockets, largely mirroring the plans devised during Barham's administration. By mid-1806 Congreve had been developing his rockets for nearly two years, and he believed that his invention warranted several trials. Although there were enthusiastic supporters of the rocketry, Keith was not among them, but he allowed the operation to proceed. The attack finally occurred on the night of 8 October, with his vessels launching four hundred rockets in thirty minutes. There was no effective return fire, and the rockets started a fire among the French naval facilities that burned for three or four hours.[93] Congreve explained to the First Lord that it was "a successful one for a first attempt"; however, he admitted that he could not say with certainty that any French vessels were destroyed.[94] The British could not even determine how many of the rockets reached the harbor. Keith maintained that the weapon would not serve unless the British fired at a large concentration of French ships, since the rockets were extremely inaccurate on land and their accuracy only became worse on the unstable platforms at sea. In late October 1806 he complained, "Neither this plan [Congreve's], nor that of the stone ships, nor of the cattermarrans [Fulton's] ever met my approbation as an officer."[95] On one hand, Keith's intransigence and lack of support had weakened his fleet's ability to use these weapons. Yet a reverse argument could be made that Keith's obstructions saved many lives by preventing sailors from becoming involved in questionable operations.

By 1806 Keith felt unappreciated and disgruntled. He maintained that his command had been frittered away on small projects and bitterly complained, "On no occasion have I ever seen our great naval superiority made use of."[96] However, this was the view of a naval officer. The general public and many in the government relied on the North Sea Fleet as the principal bulwark in the defense of the British Isles from 1803 until 1806. The North Sea Fleet, consisting of more than two hundred vessels, was an impressive morale builder that allowed the people of Britain to believe that Napoleon's invasion flotilla would be defeated at sea and that the British Isles were not endangered. Keith personified the effectiveness of the North Sea Fleet. With decades of experience, success had followed his name, and the Admiralty capitalized on this image. However, this command was unlike his previous appointments; rather than his being an admiral in the traditional sense, the size and complexity of his command forced Keith to act as an administrator. He rarely put to sea, but dealt instead with paperwork and, more important, coordinated the movements of a massive fleet.

These ships maintained their position on the French-controlled coasts throughout the winter of 1806 and the first months of 1807. During this period the Ministry of All the Talents slowly lost power until it was forced from office in March 1807. The new government that emerged contained a large number of former Pitt supporters and immediately attempted to become more active on the Continent, particularly with regard to Russia, which was still battling Napoleon's army in Poland. To assist the Russians, the British deployed a naval squadron in the Baltic.[97] As the British government switched from a defensive posture toward continental commitments, Keith's command fell under the criticism that it had outlived its purpose, and the new ministry revived plans to split the North Sea Fleet into several independent commands. In mid-May 1807, Keith received a flattering letter that cited his excellent service over the previous four years and then ordered him to strike his flag. Keith responded with the hope that his services while commanding in the North Sea had met the government's approval and would lead to consideration for future employment.[98] Within a year the Admiralty had created independent squadrons at Leith, Yarmouth, Sheerness, and the Downs, and maintained a separate squadron off the Texel.[99]

8

"I lead a disagreeable life"

Command of the Channel Fleet (1812–14)

Unemployed after his removal from the North Sea Fleet, Keith collected half pay for nearly five years. Rather than naval service, the highlight of the period was his second marriage, to Hester Maria Thrale of Streatham and Crowmarsh Battle, Oxfordshire. Born on 17 September 1764, she had met George Keith Elphinstone in 1791, two years after the death of his first wife. She was the eldest daughter of the late Henry Thrale, a wealthy local brewer, and Hester Lynch Salusbury Thrale, now Piozzi by a second marriage. Largely owing to her mother's close association with Dr. Samuel Johnson, Hester Maria Thrale received an excellent education, far exceeding her future husband's schooling. Although they had met in 1791, their relationship developed slowly, and they became engaged only in late 1807.[1] Immediately Keith mustered his courage and wrote his future mother-in-law, claiming that "the approbation of a parent is a matter of essential consequence to the General comfort of such a Union." For Keith, never well educated, writing this letter was an unnerving experience. He awkwardly continued, "I hope I know and can appreciate her many Virtues as indeed I ought when I consider she condescends to become the companion of a man who this some Months past his sixtieth year, but whose study it will be to render her time as comfortable as it may during his remaining life."[2] Her mother approved and declared that Keith was "A *good* man, for aught I hear; a *rich* man, for aught I am told; a *brave* man, we have always heard; and a *wise* man, I trow by his choice."[3] As for his new wife, her friend Fanny Burney described her as "another of my faithfullest, &, strange to tell, warmest Friends!—for she bears a character of being not only as fair, but as cold as snow."[4] By the time of their marriage at Ramsgate on 10 January 1808, she was forty-three years old. Although neither of the newlyweds was young, they had one daughter, Georgina Augusta Henrietta Elphinstone, on 12 December 1809. Indicative of Keith's accomplishments, his daughter's sponsors were no less than his personal friends the Prince of Wales and the

Duke of Clarence. Prize money from his naval service as well as sound invest-ments meant that his family had a financial security that few in Britain could boast. In addition to East Cliff near Ramsgate and his Harley Street residence in London, he had several estates including Purbrook Park in Hampshire, Banheath in Dunbartonshire, Stonehaven in north Scotland, and Tullyallan, his favorite estate, at Kincardine on the Forth.[5]

Of the entire Revolutionary Era, the period from 1807 to 1812 was the least notable for Keith. Much of this was attributable to the composition of the government following the demise of the Ministry of All the Talents in 1807. While Keith had generally maintained cordial relations with those in power, particularly on the Admiralty Board, this did not continue after his removal from command of the North Sea Fleet. Since he had been headquartered for four years in close proximity to London, Keith had made enemies there, and his close relationship with Thomas Grenville while Grenville was First Lord likely alienated the subsequent ministry. Keith explained, "No sooner was I removed from the command than that the House [of Commons] failed to Reply to any Letters when My Secretary had occasioned to address to it thus it appears Politicians are not confined to Higher Circles."[6]

Career prospects improved following the Prince of Wales's appointment as regent with limited powers in 1811, and he reportedly called Keith and several others his "old friends." Princess Charlotte, writing about her father the Prince of Wales, claimed, "I never saw any one talk of Ld. Keith so well as he does."[7] To be sure, the prince had little patronage power as long as the ministry appointed by his father remained in office, but Keith contended, "It is impossible things can long remain as they are and I am one who thinks the King will never recover *Health* nor *Mind*." This proved an accurate forecast. George III did not regain his health, and the Prince of Wales received full royal powers in February 1812. He immediately decided to reward Keith.[8] With Keith's seniority in the service and his previous record, there were few available options, but one possibility was the Channel Fleet. This was tradi-tionally seen as the most prestigious command in the Royal Navy, and for someone in his mid-sixties it was an excellent way to conclude a career now spanning more than fifty years. Although official correspondence is lacking, there is some evidence that the Admiralty, probably at the prince regent's instigation, had decided to dismiss the commander of the Channel Fleet so that Keith could receive the command. Keith's mother-in-law claimed, "The Regent has just Superseded Sir Charles Cotton, and given the Command of *his* Channel Fleet to my Lord Keith; when the Baronet [Cotton] dropt down dead in an Apoplexy; and never heard the Event." In another letter she claimed, "I congratulate Sir Charles Cotton on his happy Removal and Escape from being superseded." Although these statements can be viewed as the meandering gossip of an old lady, Cotton died at 1:30 a.m. on 23 February, and on the next day the Admiralty appointed Keith to replace the deceased admiral.[9] The speed of the appointment lends credence to the argument that Cotton had indeed been superseded and definitely indicates that Keith was under consideration for a command.

Keith did not immediately travel to Plymouth and join his new command; instead, he remained in London for six weeks commanding the Channel Fleet by having his dispatches routed to the Admiralty Building and thence to his Harley Street residence. The Admiralty deemed this acceptable since Keith was ill and the dispersed nature of French forces in the region posed little threat to Britain. The once powerful French fleet at Brest numbered only one operational line-of-battle ship, five frigates, and one corvette. On the other hand, they had four ships-of-the-line and two corvettes at Lorient along with a pair of frigates on the Loire, and two dismantled frigates at Les Sables d'Olonne. On the Charente at Rochefort the French had finished building a three-decked line-of-battle ship, while nearby at the Île d'Aix the French had two ships-of-the-line and three corvettes. Furthermore, they had three frigates in the Gironde estuary, and at Pasajes near San Sebastián they had a frigate and two smaller vessels. Although the French naval forces in the region were scattered and weak, their future appeared promising, as they were building ten ships-of-the-line and three frigates. To oppose these, the Channel Fleet comprised fifteen ships-of-the-line, fourteen frigates, and ten smaller vessels.[10] These were arrayed from Cape Finisterre to Brest.

The first crisis occurred with Keith still in London. On 9 March 1812, Vice Admiral Zacharie J. Allemand sailed with four ships-of-the-line from Lorient to attack a British East India convoy and return to Brest. Allemand reached the open sea, eluding effective pursuit. On 18 March, with the whereabouts of the French squadron still a mystery, Keith deployed five ships-of-the-line off Brest and four ships-of-the-line at Basque Roads, the vast island-protected anchorage off Rochefort and La Rochelle. Although Allemand did not capture any of the ships in the East India convoy, the British failed to engage his squadron, and he slipped into Brest during a southwest gale.[11] The failure to bring the French squadron to battle could be attributed to several circum-

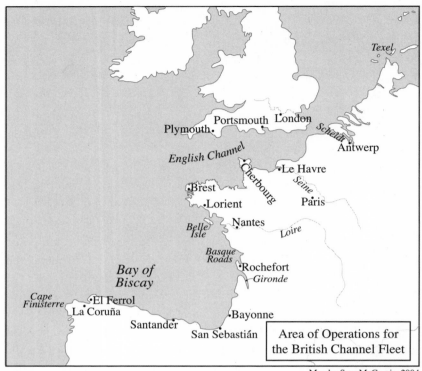

Map by Sara McCranie, 2004

Map 11. Area of Operations for the British Channel Fleet.

stances. The changeover in command from Cotton to Keith had brought disruption. The British did not have enough ships to effectively blockade all of the French ports. Finally, Keith's presence in London proved inefficient, so during the crisis the Admiralty ordered him to Plymouth to exercise greater control over his fleet. However, his health remained poor, and he remained in London.[12] Although Keith's presence at sea could have helped in the management of the crisis, it probably would not have altered the results, since the French arrived at Brest undetected in the midst of a storm while the British were battling the elements and not looking for Allemand.

In early April Keith had recovered sufficiently to travel, but upon arrival at Plymouth he had a relapse that kept him ashore until the end of the month. By now his behavior had upset the Admiralty Board, who sent a letter strongly urging him to join the squadron off Brest. Keith responded that his health had prevented it earlier, but he now felt better and would sail when his flag-ship was ready for sea. Even when Keith was younger, he had never been very healthy; now that he was in his sixties, the hard years of naval service had exacerbated his chronic health problems. This would be a constant theme during his command of the Channel Fleet, and he would spend more of his time at Plymouth with his wife than aboard the cold and damp ships off Brest or at Basque Roads.[13]

Although Keith was ill, he still attended to his new command. On 23 April he appealed to the Admiralty for a new set of instructions because his orders were dated 11 August 1809. Keith claimed that changes to French deployments in the region had made his current orders obsolete. The Admiralty immediately issued new instructions directing Keith to personally command the squadron off Brest and have another squadron under a subordinate admiral stationed off Basque Roads. Keith's primary duty was to blockade the French ports and pursue their squadrons if they escaped. In addition, he was to annoy French trade and protect British commerce. Finally, he was to assist in operations on the north coast of Spain.[14] Almost as soon as Keith received these instructions, he began to modify them, since there were never enough frigates in his command. Furthermore, he decided to remain ashore instead of off Brest and placed Rear Admiral Sir Harry Neale, his second in command, off this port. He then ordered Rear Admiral P. C. Durham, the junior flag officer, to Basque Roads. Keith told Neale that he must pursue any French squadron that sailed, and if its destination was unknown, he should assume that it was headed for Ireland. Durham was cautioned to avoid being surprised by the French. Keith especially worried that his squadron at Basque Roads would be crushed between the French ships at the Île d'Aix and the ships from Brest.[15]

Keith had commanded the Channel Fleet for little more than two months when Britain faced a grave crisis. Spencer Perceval, the head of government, was assassinated in May. The ensuing chaos culminated in the cabinet's resignation. After two and a half weeks a new ministry was formed under Robert Banks Jenkinson, 2nd Earl of Liverpool. Most believed that this government would not survive, but the ministers remained in office until 1827, twelve years after Keith resigned from his last fleet command. The composition of the cabinet was very similar in views and in personnel to the Perceval ministry. At the Admiralty, Robert Saunders Dundas, 2nd Viscount Melville, became First Lord. Although the new First Lord was the son of Henry Dundas, who had acted as both Keith's patron and an opponent, an excellent working relationship developed between Keith and the younger Melville. Several naval officers who served on the Board also became important allies. Although the Admiralty could not always give the material assistance Keith requested, he received their steadfast support.

Operations for the Channel Fleet changed little following the appointment of Melville, and for the first time since Keith had assumed command, there were no French warships at sea. Instead, attention shifted toward the north coast of Spain in late May when the Admiralty secretly ordered Keith to dispatch Commodore Sir Home Popham to the area with a small squadron and a battalion of marines. Popham, an eccentric and brilliant but often erratic officer, was to cooperate with the Spanish guerrillas and tie down French troops by making frequent attacks on their coastal garrisons.[16] Popham began his operation in mid-June, and it came as a sudden blow to General of Division Marie-François Caffarelli, commander of the Armée du Nord. This operation was part of Wellington's complicated plan to divert French attention from his main attack against Marshal Auguste Marmont's Armée de Portugal.[17] Describing his operations, Popham claimed, "I profited from the panick which appeared to have seized all the Enemy's posts. . . . The march of the French in such force in different directions, is the strongest and most unequivocal proof of the great advantage which this squadron has proved to be of to the common cause; our object is to distract the Enemy by rapid movements, followed by strong demonstrations."[18] Popham's operation prevented Caffarelli from sending substantial reinforcements to Marmont and contributed to Wellington's victory at Salamanca on 22 July. Wellington wrote to Popham, "I beg leave to congratulate you upon the success of your operations. They have been great use to me." He ended with an appeal, "I trust, therefore, you will not discontinue" the raids.[19]

Keith approached this operation with little of Wellington's enthusiasm, instead worrying about the safety of his men and ships. In early July he commended Popham for his discretion and recommended "that you do not engage in any operations of too tedious and extensive a nature." By the end of the same month Keith's message had changed: "Thirty days have elapsed since the date of your last communication. . . . I cannot avoid expressing my surprise at this inattention." It turned out that Popham had corresponded directly with the Admiralty. Keith recounted to the First Lord, "I was no more surprised in my life."[20] Then he complained that Popham had violated his instructions by retaining ships not under his orders and diverting others. Keith even threatened to replace his subordinate. When Popham explained the reasons for his behavior, Keith demonstrated a degree of tolerance and approved of his decisions, but this did not placate him; only news of Popham's success tempered his feelings.[21]

In the meantime, the British navy continued to operate on the littoral, attacking the remaining French strongholds on the Spanish coast, but it took until the middle of August for Keith, the Admiralty, and the British government to fully appreciate the navy's important role in preventing Caffarelli's troops from joining Marmont at Salamanca. At the urging of Wellington and the War Office, Keith received orders to reinforce Popham's squadron with a second battalion of marines. Understanding the overall importance of the mission, Keith declared, "There is indeed not a moment to be lost as the term for carrying on operations . . . upon that coast must soon end unless we are able to maintain a good harbor on that coast which is dangerous with west and northwest winds."[22]

In general, Keith's independence was limited by decisions of both the Admiralty and the War Office, as well as Wellington's requests. When the Channel Fleet commander received instructions, it was his duty either to forward them to Popham or to dispatch additional forces to the region. In essence, he served as the intermediary, while the government slowly crafted its policy. This irked Keith, who in several previous commands had the authority to authorize similar operations. Even minor requests for Congreve's rockets and mortars now required Admiralty approval.[23] The overall effect was that Popham and Keith had to anticipate their needs or delay operations for weeks while the British government pondered its policy and even cleared their decisions with Wellington. This only slowed the already slow response and added to the paper trail.

Popham's squadron remained active between late August and October, carrying out numerous and diverse operations until Wellington withdrew his army into winter quarters in Portugal. This left Popham isolated on the north coast of Spain. In any case, the prevailing winds and winter storms made it almost impossible to sustain active operations. Popham wanted to return to Britain, but at Wellington's instigation Keith ordered him to "remain on the North Coast of Spain so long as it can be of the least use to the operations of Lord Wellington."[24] Popham complied, but on 7 December he informed Keith that Wellington's last communication was dated 1 November. He felt used and claimed, "I rather think when he pressed so strongly to remain on this coast it was in the contemplation that he should not go beyond Vallado-lid or certainly Salamanca." At this time Keith drafted orders to withdraw the bulk of the squadron, which Popham accomplished in late December.[25] Thus ended the first major period of cooperation between Wellington's army and Keith's Channel Fleet. While evidence indicates that the operation prevented Caffarelli's Armée du Nord from reinforcing Marmont at Salamanca, the suc-cesses of 1812 set standards that the British navy failed to match during 1813 and 1814.

In addition to assisting Wellington's army in the Peninsula, the Channel Fleet became a tangential player in the War of 1812. The Royal Navy had been searching for British subjects aboard American ships, provoking fervent protests by the United States government and its people. Equally vexatious to the United States, and more damaging economically, were trade restric-tions resulting from the French Continental System and the British Orders in Council. The power of the Royal Navy coupled with the development of a United States merchant fleet willing to trade with both Britain and France exacerbated problems. Keith understood this, but his ships had orders to pre-vent the Americans from trading with the French. However, his complete views on the subject remain obscure with the exception of a written tirade to one of his captains following the plundering of an American brig. In Keith's mind, this was unlawful and offensive and not to be repeated.[26] On the other hand, Melville warned Keith, "The American Government are proceeding at great lengths in a way of provocation, with a view probably to . . . produce irritation against this country, and undoubtedly such dangerous conduct may involve us in a quarrel."[27] Melville's assessment was prophetic. The Americans had unresolved grievances against England, and a declaration of war came on 18 June.

The British government reacted quickly, ordering the navy to bring all American ships into port. Keith's responsibilities multiplied as his ships detained numerous American merchant vessels sailing for Europe. How-ever, Keith likely welcomed the situation, since prize money from captured American ships would enrich him as well as his officers and men. On the other hand, American privateers conducted an effective war on British com-merce, and the area patrolled by the Channel Fleet was not immune to these attacks.[28] In addition to privateers, the warships of the United States Navy outfought their British opponents in several engagements early in the war.

The confidence of the Royal Navy was damaged by some of its worst setbacks since 1793, and the Admiralty eventually required its frigates to sail in pairs and avoid single engagements with the larger, better armed American warships. This requirement, coupled with the loss of several frigates, produced a severe British frigate shortage between 1812 and 1814 and severely complicated Keith's deployments.[29]

Along with fighting the Americans, Keith still had to maintain an effective blockade of several French ports including Brest. In August 1812 there were thirteen frigates in the Channel Fleet, but Keith needed more. He had five on the north coast of Spain, two off Basque Roads, and two off the Gironde estuary. This left him only two to cover Brest and two to refit in port. Several months later the Admiralty "temporarily" removed frigates from Keith's command to protect convoys to America. When the Admiralty detached frigates, they were not always replaced, and in July 1813 Keith commanded only eight frigates. Disgusted, Keith declared, "Of frigates, the whole number do not account to so many as the Enemy have in Brest alone."[30] The problems mounted when the Admiralty ordered Keith to dispatch small squadrons in 1812 and 1813 to search for American frigate squadrons reportedly sailing in the Atlantic.[31] As the war with America grew in intensity, French naval activities increased in late 1812. Shorter days and foul weather allowed their ships to more easily elude Keith's blockade squadrons. When two French frigates sailed from the Loire on 25 November, Keith had to gamble, since he had too few frigates of his own "to execute the different services." In effect, Keith had no reserves. His ships nearly ran out of water while they unsuccessfully awaited the return of the French squadron.[32]

If Keith had trouble destroying even small French squadrons, the situation only became more difficult during 1813. In June, British naval intelligence indicated that the French outnumbered the Channel Fleet. Several factors exacerbated the situation. Unlike the French, the British had to keep ships off the north coast of Spain. Of Keith's thirty-three total warships, eleven were in port for repairs, water, and victuals or were en route. Quantitatively, the number of warships in the Channel Fleet declined by 12 percent between April 1812 and mid-1813 while the number of French ships ready for active service in the region increased by 35 percent.[33]

While the war with the United States and concerns over the French fleet occupied much of Keith's attention, operations in support of Wellington's army expanded in 1813 when the weather became more acceptable for conducting land operations in Iberia. Instead of Popham, Keith had a new subordinate in the region of whom he wrote, "I have explained to Sir George Collier as fully as I can the nature of the service he is going upon and I think he understands it perfectly."[34] In May Wellington's armies advanced from Portugal and outmaneuvered the French as they attempted to withdraw, forcing a battle at Vitoria on 21 June. It was a disaster for the French, who lost 8,000 men and 149 guns. With the defeat, the French position on the Biscay coast became untenable.

After this success on the battlefield, Wellington's advances brought his army to the Biscay coast of Spain and into direct contact with Keith's command, but it quickly became evident that neither Collier nor Keith nor the Admiralty could provide the resources Wellington demanded. The advance from Portugal meant that the army needed the navy to establish forward supply bases on the coast and protect convoys from Lisbon and Britain, but organizing these efforts took time, and an agitated Wellington complained, "For the first time I believe it has happened to any British army, that its communication by sea is insecure."[35] It was true that the navy faced a serious predicament in 1813. Active operations since 1793 had decreased the experienced manpower pool through attrition, and added deployments resulting from the War of 1812 stretched the navy's resources to the limit.[36] In addition, Wellington's 1813 campaign opened when an unusually large number of the Channel Fleet's ships were in port undergoing repairs.[37] Blame remains hard to ascribe. Keith did not know the specifics of Wellington's plan. On 3 July, two weeks after Vittoria, he received Wellington's letter to Collier dated 6 May outlining the expectations for his squadron. Realizing that his current strength was too weak to provide the level of assistance that Wellington demanded, Keith immediately dispatched all the available small vessels, but it took time for them to reach the Spanish coast. Conditions improved over the next three weeks, and by 21 July Collier's total force had grown from six to fourteen vessels, but Wellington still considered this force inadequate and claimed that the navy "will be responsible for any failure that may occur."[38]

This failure did occur at San Sebastián.[39] In July a detachment of Wellington's army began siege operations against the French garrison in this coastal fortress located on a small peninsula jutting into the Bay of Biscay. The navy's role in the siege was both necessary and peripheral. Collier remained in the region with a small squadron blockading the fortress. This proved a thankless task, since other French bases were nearby and storms disrupted the blockade, allowing the French to receive supplies during the entire siege. Yet the Admiralty wanted to pretend that the blockade was a success, and as late as 3 September, Melville claimed that "the naval blockade has not to any considerable degree been broken."[40] This statement was made either from ignorance or in an attempt to cover up the navy's failure. During this period Keith remained curiously silent. He could not contradict his superiors, but he realized that the nature of the coast and the weather limited the blockade's effectiveness.

Unlike Keith, Wellington railed that the blockade was "notorious to the whole world." The interservice animosity became even more pronounced after 25 July when the French decisively defeated the first major British assault on San Sebastián. Now the navy became the convenient scapegoat. An enraged Wellington lambasted the failure: "In the attack of a maritime place, some assistance has generally been received by the army from the navy; but the naval force on this coast is too weak to give us any of the description we require."[41] Rather than attacking Keith, Wellington sent a very harsh letter to the First Lord which declared, "And I believe that nobody will deny, that either we have not sufficient naval means, or that they are misapplied."[42]

Keith became a pawn in this struggle between the Admiralty and Wellington. He could see both sides, given his past experience in joint operations. The army needed naval support, and every day that it was delayed, Wellington's casualty lists lengthened. On the other hand, fitting, manning, and victualling new ships took time. Keith claimed, "I have constantly given that service the preference, and left in other stations fewer vessels than either their lordships' [the Admiralty's] orders or even prudence demanded."[43] This statement held credence since he did not have an adequate number of ships blockading the Gironde, Lorient, and the Loire during the summer of 1813. At the Gironde and Lorient the French had a ship-of-the-line and a frigate, and at the Loire they had three frigates. Keith worried that the French would send at least one of these squadrons to surprise Collier's command off San Sebastián and inflict losses that the navy could not easily replace. To counter this threat, Keith wanted to deploy a ship-of-the-line off San Sebastián. This corresponded with Wellington's views, but the Admiralty considered such warships too large to operate in the bight of the Bay of Biscay. In mid-August Keith finally decided to have the *Ajax* (74) make a short demonstration off San Sebastián to intimidate the French. Wellington approved of the operation but wished that Keith would permanently station this ship off the coast.[44] Collier disagreed: "I must still maintain my opinion that this is not an anchorage for a ship of the line." He may have had personal motives: most captains commanding ships-of-the-line were senior to him and would supersede his authority. Melville sided rather sarcastically with Collier: "Our Military officers . . . seem to consider a large ship within a few hundred yards of the shore off San Sebastian as safe in its position and as immovable by the winds and waves as one of the Pyrenean Mountains."[45] Ultimately the *Ajax*'s mission proved a success. The French lookouts at San Sebastián sighted her as she sailed with three frigates, six brigs, and nine transports, causing the fortress commander to worry about an amphibious assault.[46] Keith, though, had no intention of allowing for such an assault on San Sebastián. The surf and the strength of the fortress made this too risky an operation.[47] Keith merely wished to have a larger ship make a demonstration in the area. In late August, Keith proposed a second mission, this time by two ships-of-the-line. He explained, "The service is so important that something must be risked."[48]

Keith declared, "I hope the San Sebastián service may terminate soon and well[;] it will be a great relief to our Branch."[49] On the very day he penned these words, the allies made a second major assault on San Sebastián, and after sustaining extremely heavy casualties, they gained control of the city. The last French bastion surrendered on 8 September. Victory brought little consolation to Keith because of continued animosity between the army and the navy. In an effort to improve matters, Melville decided to dispatch a flag officer to meet with Wellington, but Keith was too ill to travel. Indeed, the lack of personal contact between the two commanding officers was a continuing problem in relations between the army in Iberia and the Channel Fleet, and it stemmed in part from Keith's poor health. Instead of the fleet commander, Rear Admiral T. Byam Martin, the commander at Plymouth, met with Wellington five days after the surrender of San Sebastián. Martin recognized that the British naval squadron on the north coast of Spain needed reinforcements.[50] However, he soon returned to Britain, leaving Collier in command of the squadron.

Wellington saw Martin's mission for what it was—an attempt by the Admiralty to defuse criticism—and ten days after the meeting, Wellington complained that Martin brought only promises, not reinforcements. Disgruntled, Wellington had to accept inadequate deployments—he had no authority to interfere with naval operations.[51] From the navy's perspective, the lack of ships in the Channel Fleet made it difficult to provide Wellington with greater support, and in October a member of the Admiralty declared to Keith, "You have all we can spare for the Coast of Spain. . . . can you not relieve a Brig or two on stations where smaller vessels will do?" Robbing one part of his command to meet the demands of another was not the best way to conduct operations, but this was Keith's only choice. Even with shifting forces, Keith still lacked the necessary ships and told Collier, "You must endeavour to supply the wants of the army as well as you can with the means which the Lord Commissioners of the Admiralty have enabled me to place at your disposal."[52]

In an attempt to compensate for his weak squadron, Keith asked Collier to "call Lord Wellington's attention to the necessity of a greater degree of system being observed" in the sailing of convoys. Particularly, he was to avoid situations where the navy had to escort single ships.[53] Keith described his reasoning: "I have had much experience in conjunct service of this nature, and always found it impossible to satisfy calls of the different Departments, because the heads of them never acted in concert. . . . I have had occasion to observe this is too much the case in the service entrusted to Sir George R. Collier's direction."[54] Keith wanted a senior officer placed at Wellington's headquarters to coordinate convoys. Melville considered this an excellent idea but wanted an army officer to fill the position. When Wellington learned of the idea, it threw him into a rage, since a request for better management of convoys implied that his subordinates were to blame. He refused to appoint an officer, since Collier was rarely more than fifteen miles from his headquarters and had never mentioned irregularities with the convoys.[55] Keith's suggestion to Wellington had been necessitated by the navy's weakness or perhaps the Admiralty's inability to concentrate its forces, and the situation became more desperate as the autumn and winter weather approached.

During the summer months of 1813, Keith had largely stripped his command of small vessels to meet Wellington's requirements on the north coast of Spain. This was possible because there was a lack of activity in the French ports and because the long days coupled with the absence of stormy weather allowed for a more effective blockade. Intelligence, however, indicated that French naval strength continued to increase. Keith worried that the French frigates would attempt to harass British trade as they had done over the previous two winters, and he asked the Admiralty for five frigates and four sloops to meet the threat. These reinforcements were not forthcoming, and Keith's concerns were soon realized beyond his expectations. The size and the intensity of the French campaign that began in late September 1813 and continued until April 1814 dwarfed the naval campaigns of the previous two years. In the first phase, three pairs of French frigates sailed. One pair departed from the Texel on 30 September, while a second pair of frigates slipped out of Cherbourg undetected on 20 October for a six-month cruise off the coast of Africa. The last pair of frigates left the Scheldt also on 20 October, avoiding the British blockade squadron and disappearing into the North Sea. Ships of the Channel Fleet captured the frigates from the Texel, but only after they had been crippled in a gale. The other four frigates remained at large to prey on British trade.[56]

In addition, the large French squadron at Antwerp became more active during the last months of 1813, in response to a June 1813 order from Napoleon requiring that nine ships-of-the-line sail from the Scheldt before it froze over for the winter. This operation became more important as the allied armies advanced across the German states, and in early November the Admiralty became aware of the plan. Even though Antwerp was not within the limits of Keith's command, it still affected his operations, since the Admiralty decided to take ships from the Channel Fleet to help form a squadron off St. Helens. However, by the end of November the Admiralty claimed, "Our last accounts however all agree in stating that they are dismantling and unmanning all their large ships at Antwerp." These reports proved correct, and by mid-December the Admiralty had begun to break up the squadron at St. Helens.[57]

Among the concerns over the French fleet at Antwerp, the French frigates at sea, the war with America, and the deployments off the northern coast of Spain, the shortage of ships crippled the ability of Keith's fleet to conduct blockade operations. Between November 1813 and the end of the war with France in April of 1814, Keith grappled with the lack of resources and the intensification of French naval activities. While he decided to keep his ships concentrated at Basque Roads and Brest, this left a total of only two frigates and two sloops to watch the three French anchorages at the Loire, Lorient, and the Gironde.[58] The inadequate size of Keith's blockade squadrons allowed two frigates to sail from the Loire on 24 November 1813; a week later another pair sailed from the Gironde, and in January 1814 three frigates sailed from Lorient. However, blame should not rest entirely with Keith. The Admiralty had ordered him to detach frigates and ships-of-the-line to escort convoys. And Wellington had, of course, pressed the Admiralty to increase the size of the squadron supporting his military operations. These factors reduced the size of Keith's blockade squadrons. Keith even had difficulties at Brest; these and the winter weather allowed four French frigates to slip past the blockade in November and December. By February 1814, eleven French frigates remained at sea. In March the French still had eight frigates at large attacking British trade, and Keith's fleet had proved almost powerless to stop them.[59]

Meanwhile, the squadron supporting Wellington's army continued to be a major drain on Keith's resources. Unlike in the winter of 1812, the army continued operations into December by advancing across the Pyrenees and into the south of France where, after a short respite, active campaigning resumed in early 1814. To support these operations, the navy maintained its patrols and escorted convoys. It still had an inadequate number of warships, but its operations were becoming more effective. The length of coastline under patrol was shrinking as Wellington advanced into France, while the size of the squadron remained steady. Another important factor was the replacement of Collier. Although neither Keith nor Wellington attempted to blame him for the navy's many failures during 1813, he had acted questionably on several occasions and was not very assertive with either Wellington or Keith. While his health was the ostensible reason for his replacement, this merely allowed him to resign gracefully, since he had powerful patrons including members of the royal family.[60] In this instance, a capable junior officer had received an important command that was beyond his level of expertise. Blame should be ascribed to both Keith and the Admiralty for maintaining him in command. Since both Keith and Melville wanted someone more senior on the coast, Rear Admiral Charles V. Penrose received orders in early 1814 to assume command of the squadron.[61]

Operations by Wellington's army were nearing an end, but the navy still had important work to do. The final operation for the Channel Fleet in conjunction with the army occurred at the end of March on the Gironde. Near the mouth of the estuary, the French had anchored a seventy-four-gun line-of-battle ship, two corvettes, several privateers, and a few gunboats. As early as 17 January, Keith explained to Melville that his ships might need to attack this French squadron in support of Wellington's planned advance. In February Penrose reiterated this point: "The navigation of the river will be directly wanted." He asked Wellington for as much notice as possible so "that the requisite force might again be prepared."[62] These two comments demonstrate that the navy had learned to be prepared, and neither Keith nor Penrose wished to be accused of failing to zealously support the army.

Two months after Keith had first mentioned the possibility of sending ships into the Gironde, Wellington asked Penrose if this could be done. Of particular importance, supply lines for the British army would be simplified if they could secure the Gironde estuary and the Garonne River that linked the estuary and Bordeaux. This led Melville on 27 March to suggest to Keith: "I think that so many things, may occur very speedily on the French coast, which would be more satisfactorily arranged and provided for on the spot than by reference to your Lordship at Plymouth or to us in London, that I cannot help wishing you were there."[63] Keith immediately prepared to sail for the Gironde, and Melville ordered him to secure its navigation. To accomplish this task, Penrose and Keith assembled a substantial squadron consisting of nine warships including a ship-of-the-line and two frigates. The plan involved a simultaneous attack against the ships in the estuary and the shore batteries that protected their anchorage. Everything was ready by 6 April, but on that date the French burned the ships to prevent their capture.[64]

In the meantime, the First Empire rapidly disintegrated. While Wellington's army had driven across southern France, the armies of Prussia, Austria, and Russia had invaded eastern France. Napoleon had attempted to check their advances, but the allies captured Paris, and on 31 March all sides agreed to an armistice. Napoleon, realizing the hopelessness of the situation, abdicated on 6 April.

With the conclusion of hostilities, Keith's duties were still far from over. His fleet remained on a war footing until Napoleon sailed for exile on Elba in late April. Following Napoleon's departure, Keith received orders to begin paying off ships' companies, but the Admiralty declared itself unable to revert to a peacetime establishment because of "the unjust and unprovoked aggression of the American Government."[65] For the next four months, Keith's primary responsibilities included getting the Portuguese troops home; shipping supplies to Britain; and repatriating or redeploying British troops to Ireland, England, Canada, and the United States. This was a massive operation, and ordnance stores alone required nearly fifty transports. On 10 June, Keith met with Wellington to discuss the embarkation of the remainder of his army, but it was a slow process. After dispatching three convoys to America, he had only two transports remaining in the Gironde. Two weeks later Keith claimed,

"We are quite idle for want of ships, all I have are in Ireland or England with men there are 20,000 more to send home."[66]

The work of these months wore on Keith's health and nerves. By now he was nearing seventy and had suffered through many punishing years of service at sea. He wanted to leave France and return to Scotland, or at the very worst to London. To his sister he described his stay in Bordeaux as "tired with music, constant cooking, little room and prodigious expense in the Hotel." Conditions did improve during his last month in France when he, his servants, and his staff were invited to live in a nobleman's house which Keith described as "very superb in all respects."[67] Still, he concluded, "I am very desirous for getting home. I lead a disagreeable life here and see nothing but extreme folly and vanity, and for anything I am doing here I might as well go to Paris and make a fool of myself like many others."[68]

While the representatives of the allied nations determined the future borders and the government of France, Keith continued to oversee the removal of Wellington's army. One positive note occurred in June. Keith was advanced in the peerage to viscount. This title demonstrated the government's esteem for a lifetime of service that was rapidly nearing an end. In mid-July Keith received permission from the Admiralty to allow Penrose to assume command of the remnants of the Channel Fleet. He then sailed aboard the *Queen Charlotte* (110) and anchored at Plymouth on 20 July. On the evening of 29 July 1814, Keith struck his flag.[69]

He had held command of the Channel Fleet for slightly more than two years. This was the senior post, which traditionally protected England from France and her major naval base at Brest. However, the importance of the Channel Fleet had changed, and between 1812 and 1814 the two largest French fleets rode at anchor at Antwerp and Toulon. While the Channel Fleet had lost part of its raison d'être, a new mission had emerged involving operations on the north coast of Spain. This was a major undertaking and became the most demanding assignment in Keith's command. Severe storms battered the region and created one of the most dangerous lee shores in Europe. The mission had been incredibly complex, and Wellington found the navy wanting. Several of the naval officers serving on the coast were mediocre, and the Admiralty proved arrogant and unyielding, while Keith's leadership was questionable. A simple visit with Wellington might have resulted in a mutual understanding, but Keith entrusted this to his subordinates.

As commander in chief of the Channel Fleet, Keith remained at Plymouth for the great majority of the period; this was similar to the system he had utilized in the North Sea. Rather than a traditional fleet commander, Keith worked as a good administrator, juggling his limited forces in an attempt to cover as many threats as possible. Moreover, staying in port was easier on his old and frail body than service at sea. The Admiralty probably should have replaced Keith, since he was exhausted and often unable to coordinate the entire strategic position from Plymouth. A combination of patrons inside the Admiralty, his friendship with the regent, and his seniority likely prevented his removal. Although claiming that Keith failed would be too harsh, blockade operations by the Channel Fleet had generally proved unsuccessful. While the bulk of the French warships remained in port, it is noteworthy that much of this was part of Napoleon's strategy. These ships caused the British to incur great expense in maintaining the blockade and prevented the employment of these ships elsewhere. When French squadrons occasionally sailed, they moved in and out of Keith's area of operations virtually at will, especially during the winter. This was, in part, due to the lack of flexibility in the Channel Fleet. The initiative of Keith's subordinates was limited by definite instructions, few frigates, and geographic constraints. Even Keith did not have complete authority to alter all of his deployments, because considerations involving Wellington's army prevented the redeployment of the squadron on the northern coast of Spain. The Admiralty should also accept some of the blame, since they failed to provide the Channel Fleet with an adequate number of frigates and smaller vessels, leaving Keith with a command that was continually under strength.

"I am doing my best to nab Nap!"

The Fates of Keith and Napoleon (1815–23)

With peace, Keith largely withdrew from public life. But in 1815 Europe again drifted toward war, forcing the admiral to return to active service in his sixty-ninth year. The crisis that led to renewed hostilities began on 26 February 1815 when Napoleon Bonaparte and a number of followers slipped away from Elba, landed on the French Mediterranean coast, and then advanced toward Paris. News of Napoleon's return reached London on 11 March. Keith wrote to his mother-in-law, "Report runs that the News from France is unfavourable, No Activity among the People, too much among the Troops." Events in France continued to deteriorate; the Bourbon king, Louis XVIII, lost control and fled Paris on 19 March. The next day, Napoleon arrived and took over the government. The leaders of the other European states looked on these developments with horror, and on 25 March they formed the Seventh Coalition and prepared for war.[1]

As Napoleon mobilized his armies, the allies massed their resources, and this led the Admiralty on 28 April 1815 to reappoint Keith to command of the Channel Fleet. Keith, however, lingered in London, since the French navy remained unprepared for hostilities, and it was late May when Melville caustically remarked, "We are sending off some orders today which we should have preferred addressing to your Lordship rather than any of the junior flags." Keith soon proceeded to Plymouth.[2] One of his major tasks was maintaining a squadron off Quiberon Bay so as to be able to support a Royalist revolt against Napoleon. However, Keith expressed misgivings: "I do not believe all the Royalists tell me, for it always ends 'give me money and arms.'" The Admiralty had similar doubts, and it was not until 23 June that Keith received official sanction to support the Royalists. By this time Napoleon's forces had shattered Royalist resistance, and Waterloo had already taken place.[3]

In addition, the Channel Fleet had to be very careful about stopping ships at sea, since the British government did not sanction the capture of French merchant ships; only warships and vessels carrying soldiers, arms, and ammunition were subject to seizure. On 17 June, Melville assured Keith that the British government would soon issue a proclamation allowing his warships to make any French ship a prize of war. The First Lord suggested to Keith, "If any of your cruisers are about to sail, whose departure might be deferred for a few days, they might as well be detained till after you receive official communication." On 21 June the government issued this document, but Napoleon had been defeated at Waterloo on 18 June and hostilities would soon end, rendering this order to capture French ships unnecessary.[4]

Waterloo changed the mission of the Channel Fleet. The decisiveness of the victory forced Napoleon to renounce his imperial authority on 22 June. Two days later, news of Waterloo reached Keith at Plymouth. Realizing that the loss might cause Napoleon to flee France, Keith immediately ordered every available vessel to blockade the French coast from Brest to Bayonne. Several days later the Admiralty repeated this order. Keith had gained a head start by anticipating governmental policy, and within ten days he had thirty ships "seeking for Bonny on the sea." In this instance Keith had taken the initiative, and the Admiralty approved: "You have done, as you always do, quick right and the Board approves your proceedings."[5] By 30 June additional information arrived in England about the possible escape of Napoleon, and the Admiralty reported to Keith that "the likelihood of such an event is much increased."[6] While the hunt continued, rumors about Napoleon's whereabouts abounded, and in a letter to his wife on 6 July, Keith jested, "I have not got Bonny yet, my dear, but a rumour ran that I had, and that he was at Windsor's Hotel, to which place all Plymouth and Dock repaired."[7] On 14 July the Admiralty commented to Keith that "it will be exceedingly difficult, if not impossible, to stop him if he embarks like Hamlet 'naked and alone.'"[8] However, these, like all instructions issued by the Admiralty and Keith during the first half of July, were superseded in the rush of events.

Meanwhile in France, the provisional government had placed several frigates at Napoleon's disposal. The new French leaders unsuccessfully appealed to the British government to grant their former emperor safe passage aboard one of these warships. Before Napoleon received an unfavorable response from the British government, he traveled to Rochefort, where the frigates rode at anchor. He arrived on 3 July but found a small squadron under Captain Frederick L. Maitland of the *Bellerophon* (74) in the offing. These ships had been dispatched to blockade the port by Rear Admiral Sir Henry Hotham, the commander at Quiberon Bay. The presence of the British navy disconcerted Napoleon, and he pondered his situation for the next week. The British and Prussians had shattered his army at Waterloo, and he had renounced his title as emperor of France. In Rochefort it had become apparent that the provisional French government wanted him to leave the country quickly, but the British navy blocked his exit. If the former emperor wished to travel incognito, there was little risk of capture, but Napoleon wished to travel in a style becoming the former ruler of France. On 10 July he sent a delegation to see if Maitland would allow his ships safe passage, but the British captain refused on the grounds that their two countries were at war.[9]

Napoleon learned on 11 July that Louis XVIII had returned to Paris. This meant that he needed to sail from Rochefort. Many alternatives were studied, and several French officers spoke with Maitland about the possibility of the Royal Navy transporting Napoleon to Britain. Louis Marchand, Napoleon's valet, recorded that "the captain of the *Bellerophon* had assured them he would be welcomed there." Emmanuel de Las Cases, also with Napoleon, maintained that "several [British] captains who were present expressed themselves to the same effect, that there was not the least doubt of Napoleon's meeting with all possible respect and good treatment." The choices for Napoleon were limited. Henri-Gatien Bertrand, Napoleon's grand marshal, understood that the former ruler planned to "go voluntarily to England as an ordinary citizen to enjoy the protection of the laws" of Britain. Napoleon boarded the *Bellerophon* on 15 July and sailed for England.[10] Maitland dispatched the *Slaney* (20) to sail ahead to warn Keith, the Admiralty, and the British government. During the voyage to England, Maitland drafted a letter to Keith. Choosing his words carefully, he did not date the document until the eighteenth, three days after Napoleon had boarded his ship. He maintained that the former emperor could have escaped unnoticed aboard any small vessel; instead, he was now in British custody. Napoleon, to the contrary, believed he had come aboard the *Bellerophon* with the understanding that he would receive asylum in England. For his part, Maitland apparently lied, claiming that he had made no promises since "I had no authority to make any sort of stipulation as to the reception he was to meet with."[11]

On 22 July the *Slaney* anchored at Plymouth with news of Napoleon's imminent arrival aboard the *Bellerophon*. In addition, Napoleon had sent a representative aboard the *Slaney* to deliver a personal letter to the prince regent asking to receive protection under English law. Keith sent the letter to

London but detained the French representative.[12] Two days after the arrival of the *Slaney*, the *Bellerophon* anchored at Torbay, and Keith sent a public and a private letter to Napoleon. The public letter explained that he was to remain aboard the warship, while the other privately thanked Napoleon for the kind treatment of Keith's nephew James Drummond Elphinstone, a captain in the 7th Hussars, who had been captured on 17 June during Wellington's retreat from Quatre Bras.[13]

The same day that the *Bellerophon* arrived at Torbay, the British cabinet met to decide Napoleon's fate, and on the following day Melville explained that Napoleon would be sent to St. Helena escorted by a naval squadron under Rear Admiral Sir George Cockburn. Keith received orders to read all Napoleon's mail and then send it to the Admiralty; their "Prisoner," as Melville termed it, was to be treated like a captured general officer, not an emperor. In Plymouth, Keith refused to meet with Napoleon until he received these instructions from Melville. This led Emmanuel de Las Cases to complain, "It was evident that our company was shunned, our conversation avoided."[14] Rather, Keith claimed, "I felt awkward as he [Napoleon] had sent repeatedly desiring me to see him," and the admiral had been unsure how to treat the prisoner. Maitland had conveyed a message that Napoleon "considered himself as an individual and expected no honour or public attention beyond that of a prisoner of war."[15] Once Napoleon's status had been determined, Keith met with him on 28 July. An important topic of the conversation was Napoleon's future, but Keith, lacking instructions from his government, declined to comment, leading Marchand to describe it as a half-hour "courtesy visit," while General of Division Albine de Montholon claimed that Keith "came only for a few minutes, and said nothing."[16] Keith's description of the meeting corresponds with the other descriptions in recording that nothing substantive was said about Napoleon's future; however, Keith claimed, "We talked on many subjects—of Toulon, Egypt, East Indies, etc." After the meeting the Admiral concluded, "He looks like a man in perfect health, thick calves, thin ankles, clear eyes and thin mouth—like as possible the picture."[17]

On 30 July, Keith was notified by Melville that Major General Sir Henry Bunbury, an undersecretary of war, was traveling to Plymouth for an official interview with Napoleon. Keith and Bunbury were to signify His Majesty's determination that the prisoner be transported to St. Helena.[18] Just before noon on the thirty-first, the two officers boarded the *Bellerophon* for an audience with Napoleon. After exchanging pleasantries, they delivered a copy of the government's instruction. The document was in English, and Napoleon asked the officers to translate it into French. Never competent with foreign languages, Keith slowly and uncomfortably translated the first few lines until Napoleon took the letter from him and suggested that Bunbury read the remainder. The prisoner did not pay close attention, nor did he ask for a copy of it in French. Instead Napoleon made a solemn protest against the handling of his case. He claimed that he had entered the *Bellerophon* in good faith that the British would treat him according to the laws of their country. He maintained, too, that he was not an official prisoner of war and declared, "If he [Maitland] had told me I was to be a prisoner, I should not have come. . . . I demand to be received as an English citizen." Napoleon then explained, "In St. Helena I should not live three months. With my habits and constitution it would be immediate death. . . . No, I will not go to St. Helena. Botany Bay is better than St. Helena. If your Government wishes to put me to death, they may kill me here." Bunbury and Keith remained silent. They were not authorized to enter into discussion, and Napoleon decided to make a formal protest to the British government, which Keith relayed to London. Napoleon asked to remain aboard the *Bellerophon* until he received a response. Although Bunbury was noncommittal, Keith seemed to think that the government would grant the delay until they had studied the protest. In any case, the admiral was aware that it would be at least a week before the squadron was ready to sail to St. Helena, and this would allow the government time to review the complaint. Keith and Bunbury took their leave after approximately forty-five minutes, but as they made their way to their barge, Napoleon asked Keith to meet with him in private.[19] Excusing himself from Bunbury, the admiral returned, and Napoleon sought his advice. Keith later claimed, "I replied, 'I am an officer and have discharged my duty. I have left the heads of my Instructions with you, in order that you may observe upon them if you consider it necessary.'" He refused to say any more without Bunbury's presence. Napoleon again insisted that he should not be sent to St. Helena. Keith "observed, 'Sir, it is surely preferable to being confined in a smaller space in England, or being sent to France, or perhaps to Russia.' 'Russia! God forbid!' was his [Napoleon's] reply." The interview then came to an end.[20] Afterwards Keith characterized Napoleon's mood as "hot, agitated, verbose, and repeatative in the extreme." Although Napoleon was repetitive, verbose, and even agitated, descriptions by Bunbury, Marchand, Las Cases, Montholon, and Gourgaud indicate that "hot" was too strong a term.[21]

Meanwhile, in Plymouth Sound, Napoleon had become a spectacle. Between five and six o'clock every evening, he walked the quarterdeck of the *Bellerophon* to take some fresh air, and every day boats with sightseers attempted to get close enough to see the man who had been their sworn enemy for so many years. His mere presence excited the onlookers and led Keith to comment that "there is no nation so foolish as we are!"[22] With so many curious sightseers, the prisoner's security became a critical issue, leading Keith to station guard boats to keep the public at least three hundred yards away. Even so, the measure often proved impossible to enforce.[23] To his daughter he wrote, "I wish he was sent away, for I am plagued to death; the women go near the ship and the guard boats have been desired to fire."[24]

Napoleon's presence in Plymouth posed a number of daunting problems. He could escape or die, but the worst threat became the British court system. Late on the night of 2 August, Keith received a telegraphic message from the Admiralty: "*Tonnant—Bellerophon*—frigate—sail—Start." Keith immediately prepared to raise his flag aboard the *Tonnant* (80) and ordered the *Bellerophon* and a frigate to the Start. This location was close to Plymouth, just twenty miles to the east, but more isolated from the public.[25] While the ships prepared to sail, one Alexander Mackenrot arrived in Plymouth. According to Melville, he was a shady character: "His menace is silly and impudent and empty. . . . Sir A[lexander] Cochrane is prosecuting him for a scurrilous libel, and the most charitable opinion which can be formed respecting him is that his intellects are not altogether sound."[26] First Mackenrot attempted to locate Keith at home. "What a mercy," Keith wrote, "I left the house before the constable came to it."[27] Only James Meek, his secretary, was present. Mackenrot identified himself and explained that he had a subpoena for Napoleon to testify as a witness in the Court of the King's Bench. Meek realized the potential repercussions of the summons and explained that Keith had gone for the day. Mackenrot immediately went in search of the admiral, while Meek hastened to join Keith aboard the *Tonnant*. This situation was a sticky one. Keith believed that if he received the court summons, he was legally bound to deliver it to Napoleon, and the prisoner would be detained until November while the case was brought to trial. According to Admiralty instructions, Keith could not for any reason send Napoleon ashore; however, this ran counter to constitutionality and legal procedure. The admiral now prepared to thwart the will of the court. If Mackenrot failed to deliver the summons, Napoleon could not be considered subpoenaed. Since the summons would have to be received by Keith before being presented to the prisoner, the admiral, in effect, went on the lam. From the *Tonnant*, he boarded his barge and had his boat crew row him to a nearby frigate, where he remained only a short time before the barge put him ashore at Cawsand Bay. There he spied the *Prometheus* (18) entering Plymouth. Keith had his barge carry him out to the passing vessel, which he ordered to come about and steer for the Start. At 8:00 p.m. he finally boarded the *Tonnant*, which had slipped out of the harbor while Mackenrot pursued Keith. In the end, as Meek put it, "in all probability great inconvenience, both to the public and himself, [was] thereby avoided." However, Keith had ignored the laws of the kingdom. In this instance the admiral's views corresponded with those of Melville, who ventured, "We may possibly have to apply to Parliament for their sanction to what we are doing respecting Bonaparte and the safe custody of his person, but we must do our duty in the meantime."[28]

After Mackenrot failed to locate Keith on 3 August, he sat down on the following day in King's Arms Tavern near Plymouth Dock and wrote a letter to the commander of the Channel Fleet. In the last paragraph he reminded Keith that evasion of the subpoena "would amount to a high contempt against that honourable Court." He ended by stating that he would be in town until the evening of fifth, and he enclosed a copy of the writ for Keith's perusal. The letter reached Keith aboard the *Tonnant*, and he requested Melville's advice on how to evade the letter of the law.[29] Keith asked "whether it is better to take no notice of the letter at all, as it cannot be proved that it was delivered and is only a copy; or to state that I got it at sea at a given time and place so long after the date that no reply could be made to the letter as I was out of the kingdom at the time."[30] To avoid Mackenrot, Keith remained aboard the *Tonnant* at the Start. However, he took the subpoena more seriously than the Admiralty did. Since Napoleon was technically a prisoner of war, a legal advisor indicated that a writ that dealt with a private case had no authority and could not release Napoleon from military detention. Still, the Admiralty worried that they might not be able to continue to manipulate the English legal process, and Napoleon did not consider himself a prisoner of war. The government decided that the best course would be for Cockburn to quickly sail for St. Helena. Meanwhile the ships waited at the Start, and Keith complained to his daughter that "very ill behaviour obliged me to put to sea . . . to wait the arrival of Sir G. Cockburne." To his wife he accurately summed up the Mackenrot episode: "I should have been had up before the Justice; and Bony under my wing till November next!" Afterwards Lord Liverpool, the head of government, pushed an act through Parliament in early 1816 to legitimize the government's conduct. This technically cleared Keith and the others of any wrongdoing, but moral questions remained. Besides, this law was promulgated nearly a year after Mackenrot first raised the legal questions.[31]

On 6 August Cockburn's flagship, the *Northumberland* (74), joined the squadron. The seas were too heavy for movement between the ships, so the squadron anchored at Berry Head south of Torbay. Napoleon realized he would soon sail for St. Helena, so he dispatched one of his aides to the *Tonnant* to provide Keith with a list of those who would accompany him into exile. Instead of a surgeon, Napoleon wished to take Las Cases as his secretary. Keith agreed, but his orders had specified that the former emperor be accompanied by a doctor. It was decided that the *Bellerophon*'s surgeon would serve in that capacity. On the evening of the sixth, Keith, with Cockburn and Meek as witnesses, met with Napoleon in his cabin aboard the *Bellerophon* to inform him that he would be transferred the next morning to the *Northumberland*. Napoleon again protested, but Keith maintained that "we could only listen to the remarks he had made, but were not authorized to answer them."[32]

Early the next morning, Napoleon sent Keith another letter of protest hand-delivered by Las Cases, who later recounted, "Admiral Keith, a fine-looking old man, of highly polished manners, received me with great politeness, but he carefully avoided touching on the subject of the protest." However, Las Cases was not to be detoured and claimed that Napoleon was in no condition to travel, since his legs were swollen. Keith responded that the Start was an unsafe anchorage and the squadron needed to sail. Las Cases, who had served in the French navy, agreed with Keith, but again protested the British conduct. He next asked if Napoleon would be deprived of his sword. Keith said no, but the remainder of his followers would be disarmed. Las Cases claimed, "A secretary who was writing near us, observed to Lord Keith . . . that the order [for the transfer to the *Northumberland*] stated that

Napoleon himself was to be disarmed; upon which the Admiral drily replied . . . 'mind your business, Sir, and leave us to ourselves.'" By leaving open the possibility that Napoleon could retain his sword, Keith demonstrated a degree of honor and understanding not granted by the British government. However, the interview was not over, and Las Cases continued to protest while "Lord Keith listened . . . with marked impatience." Las Cases pressed the point that they had boarded the *Bellerophon* voluntarily because "Maitland said he had been authorised to bring us to England . . . voluntarily and in confidence." After this comment, Las Cases related that "the Admiral's ill humour and even anger broke forth, and he replied sharply, that if such were the case Captain Maitland must have been a fool, for his instructions contained nothing of the kind." Las Cases then withdrew, offering his own conclusion that "his Lordship's conscience rendered [it] somewhat painful to him" to send Napoleon to St. Helena.[33]

The failure of Las Cases's personal appeal was predetermined, since Keith had no choice but to follow his government's orders. During the morning of the seventh, the British began to transfer Napoleon's baggage to the *Northumberland*, and Keith boarded the *Bellerophon* to disarm the French. He confiscated all firearms, but as indicated in his conversation with Las Cases, he had considerable misgivings about demanding Napoleon's sword. Keith decided to ask for the former emperor's sword to determine his resolution. If he resisted, he would keep it, but if he was willing to hand it over, which Keith believed unlikely, then the admiral would take possession of the weapon. Montholon described the scene: "Lord Keith, at length resigning himself to the execution of an order which was at variance with the whole of his long and brilliant military career, approached the Emperor, and said in a voice subdued by lively emotion—'England demands your sword.'" As for Napoleon's response, "the terrible expression of his eye was the only reply. . . . The old admiral was astounded; his tall figure shrunk; his head, white with years, fell upon his breast like that of a criminal shrinking before the sentence of his judge. The Emperor retained his sword."[34] Then, according to Keith, the prisoner declared that he would not leave voluntarily. Keith asked him if he would have to use force, but Napoleon responded, "Oh no! but you shall order me." Later that day as Napoleon prepared to transfer ships, he exclaimed to Keith, "What! do you take the trouble to come too?" Later Keith described the trip across to the *Northumberland*: "He talked of St. Helena,

... asked if that was the *Tonnant* of Aboukir? If the *Bellerophon* was old? Why I changed my name from Elphinstone, which he knew me by ever since Toulon?"[35] Once Napoleon boarded the *Northumberland*, the vessels destined for St. Helena parted company with the rest of the squadron. Several hours later, Keith ordered the remaining ships to steer for Plymouth.[36]

At Plymouth the excitement of Napoleon's visit lingered, and Keith claimed, "All you see in the papers is nonsense about Bony."[37] However, he had almost completed his duties. Melville complimented the Admiral: "I should not do justice . . . if I did not express to your lordship our entire approbation of your proceedings on this occasion."[38] Keith had served his country and had gained Napoleon's respect—a contention both Las Cases and Marchand seemed to support. The admiral said of the emperor, "He was anxious no doubt about his fate, but always temperate and civil; even funny, and jocose at times."[39] The prisoner had disagreed with his treatment, but he understood that it was not Keith's decision. When he made a special request for Las Cases to accompany him, the admiral granted his wish. Keith also let Napoleon retain his sword. On the other hand, Keith functioned as the Admiralty wished, even breaking English law by refusing to deliver the subpoena to Napoleon. Melville knew he had someone absolutely reliable who would carry out his orders. The prisoner had to be disposed of quickly and quietly, although (or perhaps because) some Englishmen, along with Napoleon himself, wished to draw attention to the "illegal" actions of the British government. With Napoleon sailing to St. Helena, Keith's duties came to an end. At sunset on 19 August, Keith struck his flag for the final time and went ashore.[40] The sun was finally setting on a career that had begun in 1761, eight years before the birth of Napoleon Bonaparte. Fifty-four years later, the last act of Keith's career was to send the French emperor to his final exile. The wars of the French Revolution and Napoleon had finally come to an end. Keith had played a prominent role, but he was almost seventy and ready to retire from public life.

The last eight years of Keith's life were dull in comparison to his previous existence but hardly less unsettling. No longer would he command fleets operating over thousands of square miles of ocean; instead he adjusted to the bucolic life of the gentry. In 1815 he began to liquidate his properties in England. Part of this money went to finance a major construction project at his favorite estate of Tullyallan, at Kincardine on the Forth River, which contained several thousand acres of fields and forests with three lochs. Keith had a residence constructed to match the size and beauty of this estate. To realize the project he chose William Atkinson, who designed a Gothic castle of approximately one hundred rooms. In addition to being an architect, Atkinson was a noted horticulturist, and he planted his ideas in Keith, who became obsessed with the extensive and beautiful gardens surrounding the residence. During the first phases of construction, Keith lived at Purbrook Park, Hampshire. Then in 1819 he returned to Scotland to oversee the last stages of work, which was finally completed in 1820. The following year Keith sold his Harley Street residence in London. This was his last property in England, and for the remaining two years of his life, he stayed close to his beloved Tullyallan.[41]

The withdrawal of Keith from public life was influenced by his family and particularly by the embarrassing actions of Margaret Mercer Elphinstone, his daughter by his first marriage, whom a friend described as having "a warm heart, but a cool head—nevertheless."[42] She had grown up without the attention of either parent. Her mother died when she was too young to remember, and naval service took Keith away. Not until she was in her early teens did she see her father on a regular basis. Keith's relationship with the Duke of Clarence and the Prince of Wales introduced Margaret to the royal family. She quickly became close friends with Princess Charlotte, the Prince of Wales's daughter. With education and friends of high birth, Margaret Mercer grew up in a very different environment than her father, who had spent his teenage years in the dark, damp, and cramped confines of a midshipman's berth. In 1815 she met General of Division Charles-Auguste Flahaut de la Billarderie, a charismatic French officer and once the lover of Napoleon's stepdaughter, Hortense de Beauharnais.[43] Flahaut had fled to England following the Hundred Days. One evening at a party, Margaret began to flirt with him to vex another, but she soon became enamoured of Flahaut. By January 1816 a friend recounted, "Miss Mercer has very distinctly set her cap at him, and if he is well advised he will marry her."[44] There remained one problem with this romance. Her father loathed him, since he was French, Catholic, and reputedly the illegitimate son of Talleyrand. A female cousin supposedly described it as "the *national* evil," while a second cousin reputedly could not "name the subject at all, I am told, from the Horrour at its thought!" Keith concurred and described his daughter as "this infamous made woman." Soon a friend claimed that "all sorts of people are at war with it, for the Father's sake."[45] To reconcile with her father who was then in Edinburgh, Margaret departed London and traveled north. Although Keith considered meeting his daughter, he learned from a friend that her fiancé had decided on a foreign education for any children born of the union. Keith concluded that "she is infatuated and the Baron is very angry."[46] Keith refused to meet Margaret and immediately left Edinburgh, crossed the Forth, and returned to Tullyallan. The more the family's opinion turned against the marriage, the more Margaret's determination grew. On 20 June 1817 the two were married in a small private service in Edinburgh. Margaret had become Madame la comtesse de Flahaut.[47]

The members of the family were livid, and Keith ultimately changed his will, disinheriting his daughter. She would not receive any wealth from her father's estate. This led a friend to claim, "Miss Mercer has just married Flahaut, and for that has given up an inheritance of £30,000 a year."[48] Even so, she was not destitute, as she received an income of £6,000 annually from her mother's estate. In addition to monetary emoluments, Keith had obtained from Parliament in 1803 a modification to the patent of his title, since it did not appear that he would have any male heirs. By this action the patent, upon Keith's death, would be extended to Margaret and then to her male heirs. However, this involved only the barony, and in 1815 Keith claimed, "I was anxious to have the Title of Viscount convey'd to my Daughters in place of the Barony." Keith dropped these plans following Margaret's marriage to prevent his daughter from inheriting the title. Despite his rage and resentment, upon his death she became Baroness Keith. However, she never had a male heir, so the title became extinct upon her death in 1860.[49]

Bitterness dominated the last years of Keith's life. As late as 1819 a friend wrote, "Lord Keith has not yet forgiven! nor admitted to his presence, M[me] de Flahaut, L[ad]ʸ K[eith] however, who acts with the highest honour in this business, thinks he will finally relent, though ever remain cruelly wounded by the alliance."[50] This prediction proved accurate. Flahaut was extremely charming, Margaret was his favorite daughter, and slowly the couple gained Keith's acceptance. Still, he refused to rewrite his will and "completely disinherited *her*" and "left the whole of his property to her children—That is to her son when he comes of Age—if she has none to Georgina's son—Then to the daughters in succession."[51]

While thoughts of betrayal and dissatisfaction played on Keith's mental health, pain tormented his last months. Lady Keith, being many years younger than her husband, could take care of her frail admiral, but this depressed her. Especially she worried that he had become a recluse. In early 1823 she recounted to a friend, "I often wonder how Ld. K[eith] who has a strong and a cultivated mind too—can like to live so entirely secluded from all the society he has been accustomed." This seclusion vexed her, as it distanced her too from society. She questioned how Lord Keith could deal with "People so entirely his Inferior in all respects with whom he never can confide except only [in] affairs of business." Yet she sympathized with her husband's age or perhaps his final illness by describing the "weakness and Languor [that] pain and sickness will produce" when she lamented, "Poor man he has . . . been entirely absorbed and occupied by his Health and thinking from Hour to Hour what [to] . . . take or do to relieve . . . pain." In mid-February 1823 Lady Keith described Keith as "infinitely better" to the point that "I begin to hope life may . . . be even prolonged for a few years." However, Lord Keith's body had faced too many rigors, and of his impending death, she later claimed that "it was impossible long to be averted."[52]

With summer of 1823 approaching, the improved climate eased concerns over Keith's health. Moreover, Keith enjoyed the companionship on his estate of a learned relative, George Skene Keith, who was the grandson of George Keith, 10th Earl Marischal—the man whom Lord Keith honored with his title in the peerage. George Skene was both a preacher and a noted writer, primarily on agricultural subjects. Although he was several years Lord Keith's junior, he died suddenly on 7 March, and Lady Keith declared that this "shocked and distressed us severely." The funeral was held on the morning of 10 March, and Keith, his wife, and his younger daughter, Georgina, attended. After the service, Keith reportedly said to his wife, "I believe the best thing I could do now would be to bury myself down beside the poor doctor." Several hours later, his wish came true. Later Lady Keith described her husband's final moments, claiming that he had been well all day. "The last dreadful scene came upon me so suddenly that at first I could hardly believe the sad Conclusion." His melancholy wife related that he "was sealing his Letters, when he fainted—and never revived—You may well imagine what must have been the Horrour of such a scene to poor Georgina and me." Distraught at his passing, Lady Keith was assisted by Lord Keith's nephew, Rear Admiral Charles Elphinstone Fleming, who arrived to visit at about the time of his uncle's death. Torn by the suddenness and finality of her loss, the widow allowed Fleming to handle the arrangements, claiming "it was so *very* fortunate for me to have him here at the Time—as he broke the Account to the Old Lady," meaning his favorite sister Mary Elphinstone. Fleming then sent for Madame de Flahaut "who arrived the next morning with the Count." Keith was buried on the grounds of Tullyallan at his family mausoleum.[53]

His obituary in *Gentleman's Magazine* claimed that Keith was "taught at an early age to contend with the three boisterous elements, fire, air, and water."[54] Taking these lessons, he served his country for more than fifty-four years. Few could match the diversity and longevity of his service.

Conclusion

"He has generally stood high in estimation, as an officer."

Keith lived a long, complex, and full life, but was it successful? He never commanded a fleet in a major engagement. He often seemed more hated than loved, and some even questioned his competence. And at the end, his health deteriorated, and he believed that his daughter had betrayed him. He did have many faults, but few British admirals could match Keith's contribution to the wars of the French Revolution and Napoleon. Yet historians have neglected his influential role. Although he never had a truly spectacular or defining moment, he held almost every major fleet command in the Royal Navy, including its two most prestigious appointments—the Channel and Mediterranean Fleets. In all, Keith held fleet commands for approximately ten years. The diversity and longevity of his naval service meant that Keith played a major, if underappreciated, role in the implementation and the crafting of British naval strategy.

The longevity of Keith's career resulted from the construction of a powerful patronage network. Although the system extended down to Keith's subordinates, the more influential elements expanded upward into the ranks of the senior admirals, the Admiralty, the cabinet, and the royal family. One of Keith's colleagues, Sir William Hotham, claimed that Keith "had been long and frequently employed, but seems to have been more indebted to his rank and family connexions for his commands."[1] This is true, but Keith manipulated the system better than most. Hotham failed to understand that Keith was born with few connections; instead, he developed these over his entire career. In the period of peace following the War of American Independence, Keith developed lasting relationships with several members of the royal family, including the Duke of Clarence and the Prince of Wales. The latter, as prince regent in 1812, rewarded Keith with command of the Channel Fleet, but Keith did not rely solely on the royal family. Captain John Jervis, later the Earl of St. Vincent, was his first commander in 1761 and served as an influential patron until 1804. It was his support that secured Keith's position as a subordinate flag officer in the Mediterranean Fleet during late 1798. Then in 1803, when St. Vincent was First Lord of the Admiralty, he chose Keith to command the North Sea Fleet. Keith was astute and savvy enough to understand the political side of patronage. Once St. Vincent was forced to resign as First Lord in 1804, Keith did not try to protect his former patron but instead found a new one. Keith created a tangled and constantly changing web of powerful supporters. In many cases this did not rest on friendship or even admiration. For example, in 1804 and 1805 while Keith commanded the North Sea Fleet, the First Lord of the Admiralty was Henry Dundas, 1st Viscount Melville, whom Keith personally loathed. However, Melville was not unusual in being seen merely as a means to enhance Keith's career. All officers utilized a system of patronage for advancement; an officer who did not might never become even a lieutenant. What strikes one about Keith is his understanding of the system. This resulted in an inherently flexible approach to finding patrons, coupled with a willingness to use almost any means to further his career. What Keith realized was that other qualified officers existed, and if he did not work the system correctly, he would find himself unemployed and someone else would receive command.

Naval success beginning in the War of American Independence demonstrated Keith's competence and his ability to succeed. Upon his return from the Cape of Good Hope in 1796, Keith was created a baron in the Irish peerage. After his accomplishments in the Mediterranean, and particularly off Egypt in 1801, he was created a peer of the United Kingdom. Although still a barony, his new title was much more prestigious than an Irish one. Then, at the conclusion of hostilities in 1814, Keith was advanced in the peerage to a viscountcy of the United Kingdom.

These were remarkable accomplishments for a man who began with a limited education and no financial resources. In 1764 Keith appealed to his father, claiming, "I have not had a farthing to have my shirts washed."[2] He would not remain poor. Keith seemed to attract money during his career, beginning with a generous gift of £2,000 from his great-uncle in the late 1760s. The bulk of his fortune, however, came from prize money. This was the distribution of proceeds of the sale of captured ships and property taken from Britain's enemies. As a captain during the War of American Independence and as an admiral during the Revolutionary Era, Keith's success in collecting prize money became legendary. Other officers were not so fortunate. Nelson sniped, "Lord Keith Loves a little money, and a great deal much better."[3] Keith's ships took more than a hundred prizes during the American Revolution. Between one-quarter and three-eighths of the prize money was his, and it came to at least £20,000. For his command at the Cape of Good Hope and the Indian Ocean, Keith wrote his sister, "My prizes are numerous and in 10 years they may turn out £40 or £60,000."[4] In fact, they exceeded £60,000, and Keith's Mediterranean command yielded even more.[5] Yet the exact total of the Mediterranean prizes is difficult to ascertain, since the disbursements occurred very slowly. In 1812, more than £58,000 of the total prize money from the Egyptian Campaign of 1801 remained unpaid.[6] Keith's share of the North Sea prizes was much less—as of the end of 1806, it totaled only about £12,000—but it was still almost double Keith's standard pay while he held this command.[7] Then there were the prizes taken while Keith commanded the Channel Fleet.[8] When freight money was added, a conservative estimate places Keith's lifetime earnings at more than £250,000.[9]

Prize money translated into wealth that Keith invested in estates and his family. This again evoked a mixture of admiration and disdain. Admiral Collingwood observed, "But it is a true Scotch principle, to claim every thing and get what they can, or Lord Keith would not have been so rich by many a good estate."[10] At one point Keith had an estate in England and three in Scotland, including his favorite, Tullyallan at Kincardine, for which he paid £57,500.[11] In addition to his estates, Keith had houses in London and at East Cliff. However, he invested nearly as much in his family. Margaret Mercer Elphinstone, his favorite daughter, was reportedly bequeathed in his original will an annual stipend of £30,000.[12] Keith was "much attached" to Mary Elphinstone, his sister, and she took care of "his then only Daughter during his absence at sea."[13] Keith, not his parents or other siblings, paid Mary's expenses, and he included her in his will.[14]

On the other hand, Keith later disinherited Margaret when, in his mind, she ignored his wishes. This impinged on his honor and could not go unpunished. Keith did maintain a code of honor, though this honor occasionally seemed to be at variance with his actions. He disinherited his daughter, but he rewarded his sister's dedication to that daughter by including her in his will. He let Napoleon keep his sword against the government's wishes but abided by the government's orders and unhesitatingly sent Napoleon to St. Helena. He ransomed the ships in the harbor at Genoa but arrested his purser during the War of American Independence for abusing a prisoner. All of this made perfect sense to him. His first duty was to his superiors, and orders, even if questionable, were meant to be followed. Prize law, however dubious, allowed him to ransom the ships at Genoa, and prize law, if followed, was a mode to reward those who served the Crown faithfully. There was also an honor between individuals, and for Keith, here resided the real boundaries of honor. Although France was his country's longtime enemy, Napoleon was also a respected opponent. Keith respected his prisoners as well as his sailors. He refused to honor his daughter because she had refused to honor him.

Although Keith had a sense of honor, he was also arrogant, abrasive, and often uncompromising. Especially when he commanded in the Mediterranean and the Eastern Seas, Keith's power was almost supreme, and there was little government oversight. He was dictatorial in his relations with the Dutch in the Cape Colony, and perhaps he was even worse at Genoa in 1800 when he dealt with the Austrians and the Genoese, ignoring their interests and objectives. This was the result of an overinflated ego. Keith represented the power of the navy and wished to enhance it, but he had a difficult time sharing it. Working with the army at Cádiz in 1800, he had to assist Abercromby. It seemed that the army had taken a predominant role, and Keith resented this, especially following failures by British land forces and successes by British naval forces during the first years of the war. He was unreasonable and perhaps haughty when assisting Wellington's army. Keith had a difficult time understanding that by 1812 the army had become dominant in government strategic thinking, and the navy's mission was to support the army. The role reversal was disquieting to one who had served the navy for nearly his entire life. Prize money also warped Keith's attitude. Pay in the navy was low and was meant to be augmented by the distribution of prize money, which became a self-perpetuating preoccupation for Keith. The British government did not disparage Keith's obsession with prize money as long as it did not noticeably interfere with naval operations. A clash of interests was something that Keith carefully avoided. In the Eastern Seas, his prizes were the product of direct orders from the British government, but in the Channel Fleet, he was accused of "filling his pockets."[15]

Keith mixed self-interest and dedication to provide a composite image of a competent, well-connected, rich, arrogant and sometimes uncompromising officer; however, he developed this image after long years of service aboard cold, damp, and disease-ridden ships. This deadly environment afflicted everyone who served during the Age of Sail. By the time Keith was twenty-five, he had chronic health problems which only grew worse as he aged, and this affected his ability. Long voyages seemed to make his health worse. There is no record that he was a hypochondriac, and his illnesses impeded his ability to command. Indeed, when he led the North Sea and Channel Fleets, he remained primarily ashore. In the past it was not uncommon, especially in the Channel Fleet, for the commander to remain in port for short periods, but Keith, with the government's approval, permanently set up headquarters ashore. This unusual arrangement had its hazards. Keith was isolated from the operations conducted by his ships. No instance better exemplifies this than his glaring lack of personal involvement with the operations on the north coast of Spain. His decision to remain at Plymouth may have prevented the development of an effective relationship with Wellington. However, commanding from a fixed position ashore had its advantages as well. It kept Keith healthy. His subordinates always knew where to locate their commander. Finally, the administrative aspects of his command functioned almost flawlessly. The paperwork, records, and bookkeeping that fleet administration entailed were startling, especially when Keith commanded more than two hundred vessels of the North Sea Fleet. Still, Keith's poor health and his need to command from an isolated position ashore were liabilities that detracted from flexible fleet operations. It is not too extreme to state that his poor health should have prevented him from commanding the Channel Fleet.

Serving ashore did not endear Keith to his subordinates, and this was a nagging problem throughout his career. Although most respected him, Hotham claimed that it was unpleasant to serve under Keith.[16] Several officers deservedly charged Keith with incompetence following the failure to land Abercromby's army at Cádiz in 1800. But in fairness, some of the problems were not of the admiral's making. In the North Sea command, the Admiralty sent him some of the navy's most difficult officers, and he handled them well. After working to quell the Great Mutinies in 1797, Keith's ideas became more pronounced. In his mind, the outbreak of the mutinies could largely be blamed on the officers. His first commander had been St. Vincent, a man noted as a harsh but fair disciplinarian. Keith tried in his own way to maintain the same standards of fairness. In the North Sea, he claimed, "The punishments in the Lynx [16] were frequent, and far too severe without trial."[17] In the Channel Fleet, Keith maintained, "Flogging appears to lose its effect by too frequent repetition." Instead he recommended that his officers punish minor offenses creatively. Keith offered an example for habitual drunkenness: "Throw their grog into the sea before them."[18] He was particularly concerned that his captains would become petty tyrants and mete out punishments that were too strict for the offense. Common seamen seem to have respected Keith, and this was best exemplified by their positive response to him during the Great Mutinies of 1797.

Success with prize money did not necessarily translate into other naval accomplishments. Especially during the cruise of Admiral Bruix, Keith never could bring the Combined Fleet of French and Spanish warships to battle, but he came close on two occasions. At Saldanha Bay on the South African coast, he forced a Dutch fleet to surrender. Although taking an entire fleet intact was a coup, a naval battle would have garnered more distinction, but the Dutch seamen were mutinous and refused to fight. Keith wanted to command a fleet in battle, but this proved elusive. In 1805 following Trafalgar, Keith dropped pleas to return to the Mediterranean because there was little chance of fighting a fleet engagement.

Naval dominance did not rest solely on great naval battles. In twenty-two years of war during the Revolutionary Era, there were only six major fleet engagements. Instead, Keith was evidence that control of the sea was an important measure of British naval superiority. It was this that allowed the British government to deploy armies anywhere it chose and allowed the British merchants to trade. Keith also demonstrated that maintaining this naval dominance was made tedious by continuing British naval weaknesses. Privateers, single warships, and small squadrons from France, Spain, and America could never be entirely destroyed. Even with hundreds of warships, the British navy remained too small to meet its global commitments. All Keith's commands contained fewer ships than was believed prudent, so he was forced to prioritize his objectives and hope his enemies did not capitalize on his weakness. The Mediterranean command illustrated what the British could do with minimal resources. Keith maintained a powerful fleet off the Egyptian coast and deployed highly mobile squadrons to protect the remainder of the Mediterranean, hoping that French and Spanish naval squadrons would be incompletely or poorly utilized. In the Channel command Keith again operated without an effective reserve, with more damaging results. In all his commands, Keith was rarely aggressive; instead, he tried to husband his ships carefully and maximize their usefulness. Even though this approach did not always succeed, he had no choice. Britain's command of the sea was tenous, and there were too many threats and too few of his ships to protect Britain's interests adequately.

Often, what gained control of the sea was not British naval dominance but the failure of her enemies. Keith's career offers a number of such instances. During his pursuit of Admiral Bruix, the French admiral avoided the British and did not attempt to achieve his objectives. More glaring, the flotilla Napoleon built for an invasion of England was never tested. Keith believed that the French were incapable of mounting such an operation, not that the British were capable of stopping an invasion. A similar situation existed while Keith commanded the Channel Fleet. Napoleon rarely ordered his ships to sea, but as long as these ships remained fitted out in port, they forced the British to maintain a vigilant blockade. Here too, British operations seemed deficient, and the porous blockade allowed small squadrons to sail almost at will. An attempt to control the world's sea lanes meant that the British in fact controlled none in their entirety, yet France failed to challenge British naval dominance effectively during the Revolutionary Era. This gave the British superiority by default.

Britain's control of the sea, no matter how tenuous, allowed the navy to conduct operations with both the British and the allied armies. No admiral during the Revolutionary Era equaled Keith's diverse experience in supporting joint operations.[19] In the American Revolution, he commanded British naval forces operating ashore in conjunction with the British army at Charleston. General Sir Henry Clinton, the British commander, complimented Captain Elphinstone in his dispatches to London. Later at Toulon, Elphinstone served ashore with notable success. At the Cape of Good Hope in 1795, a near perfect level of cooperation existed between the army and the navy, much of it was the result of Elphinstone's judicious conduct. In 1800 at Genoa, cooperation with the Austrians was effective; only after the Austrian defeat at Marengo did relations suffer. Later the same year, at Cádiz, Keith sustained one of his greatest failures. Peculiar for Keith, a lack of initiative and inflexibility contrasted sharply with his previous conduct in joint operations. He partially redeemed his reputation in 1801, commanding on the coast of Egypt. In 1805 his fleet landed a British army in northern Germany and almost immediately had to withdraw it following the defeat of Britain's continental allies. Keith again proved flexible in this difficult and hastily conceived operation. It was also Keith's duty, between 1803 and 1805, to combat the most concerted French joint operation of the Revolutionary Era. Although the invasion of England never occurred, Keith's powerful but surprisingly outnumbered North Sea Fleet constantly plied the water in defense of England. Finally, Keith's role in supporting land operations on the north coast of Spain was a prolonged version of the Cádiz debacle. Between 1812 and 1814 he provided Wellington with reticent support and dealt with an inflexible Board of the Admiralty. The diversity and scope of these joint operations afforded Keith a tremendous wealth of knowledge, yet his worst failure was this last assignment. Age, intransigence, and a dearth of resources constituted major impediments that prevented Keith from breaking the deadlock between Wellington and the Admiralty.

Keith was an officer willing to blame others when he could, and at times he preferred to avoid responsibility. Not a likable man and unsavory to some, he demonstrated absolute and almost rigid loyalty to his patrons. This accounted for the longevity of a career marred by more than one blemish. An associate in 1795 most accurately described Keith's character, "He is cautious but active and decided. . . . He risks nothing. If it succeeds he adds much to his reputation, and if it fails it takes neither from his force nor his fame."[20] His superiors knew they had someone steady and loyal in command, not one to take unnecessary risks. He could not be accused of being charismatic or of having Nelson's instinct to bring Britain's enemies to battle and then destroy their fleets. At the same time, the Admiralty could trust him in a sustained and arduous command. He was not a loser, but neither was he spectacular; rather, he was an important functionary who had the good judgment and luck to have influential patrons, to receive important and lucrative appointments, and to fulfill his orders with a minimum of problems. Even though he had some reprehensible personal traits, these were shared by many of his contemporaries. His country benefited by his loyal service over a period of fifty-four years, and England would remain the world's greatest naval power for the next hundred years, thanks to men like George Keith Elphinstone, Viscount Keith.

Abbreviations

ADM	Admiralty Office Papers, The National Archives, London.
Barham	Barham, *Letters and Papers of Charles, Lord Barham, Admiral of the Red Squadron, 1758–1813.*
BL	British Library, London.
CN	Bonaparte, *Correspondance de Napoleon 1er.*
DLN	Nelson, *The Dispatches and Letters of Vice Admiral Lord Viscount Nelson.*
FN	Kerry, ed., *The First Napoleon: Some Unpublished Documents From the Bowood Papers.*
HMC	Historical Manuscripts Commission.
IO	India Office, London.
KP	Perrin and Lloyd, eds., *The Keith Papers: Selected from the Papers of Admiral Viscount Keith.*
LCG3	Aspinall, ed., *The Later Correspondence of George III.*
LSV	St. Vincent, *Letters of Admiral of the Fleet the Earl of St. Vincent whilst the First Lord of the Admiralty, 1801–1804.*
Markham	Markham, ed., *Selections from the Correspondence of Admiral John Markham during the Years 1801–4 and 1806–7.*
MCVC	Londonderry, ed., *Memoirs and Correspondence of Viscount Castlereagh.*
Meek MSS	MSS Meek's Draft on the Life of Keith, NMM KEI/47.
NAS	National Archives of Scotland, Edinburgh.
NDAR	Clark et al., eds., *Naval Documents of the American Revolution.*
NLS	National Library of Scotland, Edinburgh.
NMM	National Maritime Museum, Greenwich.
Paget	Paget, *The Paget Papers: Diplomatic and Other Correspondence of the Right Hon. Sir Arthur Paget, G.C.B: 1794–1807.*
POW	Aspinall, ed., *Correspondence of George, Prince of Wales, 1770–1812.*
RCC	Theal, ed., *Records of the Cape Colony.*
Spencer	Spencer, *Private Papers of George, Second Earl Spencer, First Lord of the Admiralty, 1794–1801.*

Notes

Introduction. "A man of rank in society"

1. Log of the *Barfleur* [Keith's flagship], 3, 4 May 1799, ADM 51/1268, pt. 8; Hotham, *Pages and Portraits*, 2:32; Proceedings of the Squadron of H.M. Ships under the Orders of Keith, 3 May 1799, *KP*, 2:41.

2. Private signals were designed for identification; these combinations of flags and gunshots, supposedly known only to other British warships, were used extensively when two ships or squadrons sighted each other (Hill, *Prizes of War*, 253).

3. Log of the *Barfleur*, 4 May 1799, ADM 51/1268, pt. 8; Proceedings of the Squadron of H.M. Ships under the Orders of Keith, 4 May 1799, *KP*, 2:42.

4. David G. Chandler in *Dictionary of the Napoleonic Wars* (216) asserts that Nelson and St. Vincent were the most important admirals of the period.

5. Brian Lavery writes, "The Mediterranean fleet was one of the most important commands in the navy, overshadowed only by the Channel fleet" (*Nelson's Navy*, 249).

6. MSS Meek's Draft on the Life of Keith, NMM [hereafter cited as Meek MSS], KEI/47/1–3.

7. Allardyce, *Memoir*.

8. *Dictionary of National Biography*, s.v. "George Keith Elphinstone," 6:739.

9. Lavery, "George Keith Elphinstone."

10. *Markham*, 102–76.

11. *FN*, 138–78.

12. *KP*, vols. 1–3. Vol. 1 was edited by W. G. Perrin, vols. 2–3 by Christopher Lloyd.

13. Knight, *Manuscripts in the National Maritime Museum*, 1:55–56.

Chapter 1. "My liking the sea very well": Education and Advancement—His Early Naval Career (1746–82)

1. Gascoigne to Clementina Fleming, 13 Aug 1761, NAS, GD 156/6/8/3; Fraser, *Elphinstone Family Book*, 1:262–68; Allardyce, *Memoir*, 1–7; Lavery, "George Keith Elphinstone," 377–78.

A number in parenthesis following a ship's name—e.g., the *Prince George* (90)—indicates how many guns the ship carried. For British warships, the number is generally taken from David Lyon's *Sailing Navy List*.

2. Gascoigne to Clementina Fleming, 29 Aug, G. K. Elphinstone to Charles Elphinstone, 5 Nov 1761, NAS, GD 156/6/8/4, 8; N.A.M. Rodger, *Wooden World*, 260; N.A.M. Rodger, "Patronage and Competence," 239; Ross, "Naval Officer," 71.

3. Muster book of the *Gosport*, January Report, ADM 36/5655; Keith Elphinstone to Clementina Fleming, 7 Mar [1762], NAS, GD 156/6/8/15; Lavery, *Nelson's Navy*, 88; N.A.M. Rodger, *Naval Records for Genealogists*, 18–20.

4. Journal of the Proceedings of the *Gosport*, NMM, KEI/L/126A; Keith Elphinstone to Clementina Fleming, 7 Mar 1762, NAS, GD 156/6/8/15.

5. Keith Elphinstone to Clementina Fleming, 14 May [1762], NAS, GD 156/6/8/28; Jenkins, *French Navy*, 141.

6. Keith Elphinstone to Charles Elphinstone, 9 May 1764, NAS, GD 156/6/8/2; Journal of the Proceedings of the *Juno* & *Lively*, NMM, KEI/L/126A.

7. Marischal to William Elphinstone, 2 Jul 1765, IO, MSS EUR F89/131.

8. Marischal to William Elphinstone, 6 Feb 1766, IO, MSS EUR F89/131.

9. Allardyce, *Memoir*, 8–10.

10. Marischal to William Elphinstone, 27 Dec 1768, IO, MSS EUR F89/131.

11. Keith Elphinstone to Clementina Fleming, 15 Aug [1769], NAS, GD 156/6/8/25; Meek MSS, KEI/47/1/13–14.

12. Keith to Peter Spiers, 22 Jan 1816, NAS, GD 22/1/327.

13. Lieutenant's Examination, George Keith Elphinstone, Dec 1769, ADM 1/163.

14. Keith Elphinstone to Clementina Fleming, 24 Dec 1769, NAS, GD 156/6/8/12.

15. Ibid.; N.A.M. Rodger, *Wooden World*, 282.

16. Keith's Journals on the *Gosport*, *June*, and *Lively*, NMM, KEI/L/126A; Lavery, *Nelson's Navy*, 93.

17. Elphinstone to Adam, 9 Aug 1782, Meek MSS, KEI/47/1/43–45.

18. Meek MSS, KEI/47/1/16–17; Perrin, *KP*, 1:3; Denis to Elphinstone, 24 Apr 1774, *KP*, 1:16–17; Allardyce, *Memoir*, 12–14; Ross, "Naval Officer," 79.

19. Denis to Elphinstone, 30 Apr 1774, *KP*, 1:18–19.

20. Although any naval officer in command of a ship received the courtesy title of captain, the term post captain meant a real captain and indicated that the officer had the authority to command any post (or rated) ship with at least twenty guns (King, *A Sea of Words*, 339).

21. This subject will be explored in chapter 2.

22. Admiralty List, 1 Jun 1776, ADM 8/52; *London Chronicle*, 9–12 Mar 1776; Allardyce, *Memoir*, 23–24; N.A.M. Rodger, *Wooden World*, 19; Syrett, "Admiral Rodney," 416.

23. Log of the *Perseus*, 16 Aug 1776, ADM 51/688, pt. 1; Elphinstone to Howe, 10 Nov 1776, *KP*, 1:46–48; Admiralty to Elphinstone, 23 Jul, Elphinstone to Smith, 11 Aug 1776, *NDAR*, 6:149–50, 493–96.

24. Journal of the *Perseus*, 26 Sep 1776, *NDAR*, 6:1018; Howe to Stephens, 22 Feb 1777, *NDAR*, 7:1258–60; Elphinstone to Howe, 10 Nov 1776, *KP*, 1:46–48; Serle, *American Journal*, 14 Oct 1776, 123–24.

25. The American Prohibitory Act, 22 Dec 1775, in Jensen, *Documents*, 9:853; Lavery, *Nelson's Navy*, 116.

26. Marischal to William Elphinstone, 6 Nov 1774, IO, MSS EUR F89/131.

27. Narrative of Andrew Hamond, 27 Jan–18 Mar 1777, *NDAR*, 8:149–50.

28. Autobiography of Joshua Barney, 4 Jan 1777, *NDAR*, 7:860.

29. Meek MSS, KEI/47/1/23; Young to Stephens, 10 Mar 1777, *NDAR*, 8:77–78; Prize List for the American Squadron, 1 Jan–22 May 1777, *NDAR*, 8:1056–57.

30. Meek MSS, KEI/47/1/23; Journal of the *Perseus*, 8 Jul 1777, *NDAR*, 9:252; *Gazette of the State of South Carolina*, 30 Jun 1777. The thirty-four men equaled approximately 20 percent of the ship's company.

31. Journal of the *Perseus*, 27 Jul 1777, *NDAR*, 9:343–44.

32. Journal of the *Perseus*, 7 Sep 1777, *NDAR*, 9:893.

33. Journal of the *Perseus*, 7 Dec 1777, *NDAR*, 10:683; Fanshawe to Elphinstone, 24 Oct, 26 Nov 1777, *KP*, 1:75–76; *Gazette of the State of South Carolina*, 2 Dec 1777.

34. Fanshawe to Howe, 13 Feb 1778, in Davies, *Documents*, 15:42–47.

35. Howe to Elphinstone, 3 Jun, Elphinstone to Howe, 20 Aug 1778, *KP*, 1:101–2, 125–28.

36. Prevost to Clinton, 11 Jul 1778, HMC, *American Manuscripts*, 1:271–73.

37. Toyn to Elphinstone, 17 Jul, Elphinstone to Prevost, 20 Aug 1778, *KP*, 1:108–9, 12–28. During the war for America, the British constructed an array of galleys. These were not galleys in the traditional sense, as they were not oceangoing vessels. Instead, they were gunboats mounting several heavy guns and were propelled by oars. See Lyon, *Sailing Navy List*, 214.

38. Elphinstone to Wright, 19 Aug 1778, Wright to Elphinstone, 26 Aug 1778, *KP*, 1:124–25, 130–31.

39. Prevost to Clinton, 16 Sep 1778, HMC, *American Manuscripts*, 1:293–94.

40. North to Sandwich, 30 Apr 1778, in Sandwich, *Private Papers*, 2:39–40; Meek MSS, KEI/47/1/25.

41. Allardyce, *Memoir*, 32–33.

42. Log of the *Perseus*, 23 Nov 1779, ADM 51/688; Lavery, *Nelson's Navy*, 207.

43. Account of vessels seized as prizes by the *Perseus*, 22 May 1777–22 Nov 1779, NMM, KEI/2/4.

44. Log of the *Perseus*, 26 Dec 1779, 17 Jan 1780, ADM 51/688; Ewald to Baron [?], 29 Feb 1780, in Uhlendorf, *Siege of Charleston*, 21; Tilley, *British Navy and the American Revolution*, 172–74.

45. Arbuthnot to Elphinstone, 4 Feb 1780, *KP*, 1:145; Clinton, *American Rebellion*, 160; Syrett, *Shipping*, 54.

46. Ewald, *Diary of the American War*, 11 Feb 1780, 195.

47. Diary of Captain Johann Hinrichs, 18 Feb 1780, in Uhlendorf, *Siege of Charleston*, 183, 189; Bain, "Siege of Charleston," 13–14 Feb 1780, 484.

48. Meek MSS, KEI/47/1/28; Hamond to Elphinstone, 26 Mar 1780, *KP*, 1:153–54.

49. Meek MSS, KEI/47/1/29; Clinton, *American Rebellion*, 162–63; Syrett, *American Waters*, 137–38.

50. Duncan to Elphinstone, 14 Apr 1780, *KP*, 1:1643–65.

51. Arbuthnot to Elphinstone, 15 Apr 1780, *KP*, 1:167–68.

52. Elphinstone to Arbuthnot, 12 May 1780, *KP*, 1:173–74.

53. Syrett, *American Waters*, 140.

54. Willcox, "Arbuthnot, Gambier, and Graves," 268.

55. Clinton to Elphinstone, 22 Mar 1780, *KP*, 1:151.

56. Clinton, *American Rebellion*, 172.

57. Meek MSS, KEI/47/1/32; Namier and Brooke, *House of Commons, 1754–1790*, 2:400. This topic will be explored in chapter 2.

58. Log of the *Warwick*, 25 Dec 1780–6 Jan 1781, ADM 51/1049, pt. 8; Elphinstone to Stephens, 7 Jan 1781, in Allardyce, *Memoir*, 53–54; Syrett, *European Waters*, 128.

59. William Feilding to Basil Feilding, 30 Jun 1781, in Balderston and Syrett, *Lost War*, 209; Graves to Stephens, 20 Aug, Graves to Admiralty, 27 Sep 1781, in Chadwick, *Graves Papers*, 32–35, 112.

60. Tilley, *British Navy and the American Revolution*, 248–63; Tunstall, *Naval Warfare in the Age of Sail*, 172–75.

61. Elphinstone to Adam, 15 Oct 1781, Meek MSS, KEI/47/1/34.

62. Syrett, *American Waters*, 216–17.

63. Graves to Stephens, 29 Oct, Observations of Elphinstone, 27 and 28 Oct 1781, in Chadwick, *Graves Papers*, 137–39, 143–44.

64. William Feilding to Basil Feilding, 13 Jun 1782, in Balderston and Syrett, *Lost War*, 215–17.

65. Syrett, *American Waters*, 219–20, 222–23.

66. Carleton to Leslie, 27 May 1782, HMC, *American Manuscripts*, 2:500; Syrett, *American Waters*, 225.

67. Log of the *Warwick*, 14–16 Jul 1782, ADM 51/1049, pt. 8.

68. William Feilding to Basil Feilding, 2 Aug 1782, in Balderston and Syrett, *Lost War*, 218; Jenkins, *French Navy*, 180.

69. Digby to Elphinstone, 5 Aug 1782, *KP*, 1:88.

70. Elphinstone to Adam, 9 Aug 1782, Meek MSS, KEI/47/1/43–45.

71. Log of the *Warwick*, 13–15 Aug 1782, ADM 51/1049, pt. 8; Digby to Stephens, 8 Oct 1782, *Barham*, 1:400–401; William Feilding to Basil Feilding, 8 Oct 1782, in Balderston and Syrett, *Lost War*, 220–21.

72. Digby to Carleton, 7 Oct 1782, HMC, *American Manuscripts*, 3:154.

73. William Feilding to Basil Feilding, 9 Nov 1782, in Balderston and Syrett, *Lost War*, 222.

Chapter 2. "If I were well it would be a wonder": Personal and Career Prospects (1774–94)

1. Brown, "'Strugalls and Corruption,'" 112.

2. Elphinstone to Lord Elphinstone, 11 Dec 1773, NAS, GD 156/6/8/14.

3. Minutes as to Scotland in the 1774 Election, 13 Dec 1773, State of Contested County Elections in Scotland, 30 Jun 1774, in Robinson, *Parliamentary Papers*, 7, 19.

4. Elphinstone to Lord Elphinstone, 11 Dec 1773, NAS, GD 156/6/8/14.

5. *Journals of the House of Commons*, 12 Dec 1774, 35:38; ibid., 10 Nov 1775, 35:436–37.

6. Ibid., 7 Nov 1780, 38:14; ibid., 13–14 Feb 1781, 38:203, 205; Edith, Lady Haden-Guest, "Dunbartonshire," in Namier and Brooke, *House of Commons, 1754–1790*, 1:477; Allardyce, *Memoir*, 50–52. After 1770, disputed elections were handled by a select committee modeled on the idea of a jury. In the Commons a quorum of one hundred had to be achieved. Then the jury was selected by lot. One hundred members' names were placed in six urns, and names were drawn until twenty-five were chosen. Each side then struck six names from the list and appointed one representative of its choosing. The committee would hear the petition, and its decision would be final. It was very difficult to pack such a committee. See Lawson, "Grenville's Election Act," 221.

7. Elphinstone to Adam, 18 Oct 1781, Meek MSS, KEI/47/1/35; Elphinstone to Mary Elphinstone [hereafter called Mary], 8 May 1782, NMM, KEI/46/4.

8. Christie, "Opposition," 60, 66; Fraser, *Elphinstone Family Book*, 1:264.

9. Shelburne to the King, the King to Shelburne, 13 Mar 1783, in Fortescue, *Correspondence of King George*, 4:274.

10. Parliamentary Election of 1784: Scotland, in Robinson, *Parliamentary Papers*, 100; "Dunbartonshire" (see note 6), 1:477–78.

11. William Feilding to Basil Feilding, 13 Jun 1782, in Balderston and Syrett, *Lost War*, 215–17.

12. Prince of Wales to Prince Frederick, 17 Jan 1783, *POW*, 1:101–2.

13. Deutsch, "Moral Trespass in Georgian London," 640–41; Edith, Lady Haden-Guest, "George K. Elphinstone," in Namier and Brooke, *House of Commons, 1754–1790*, 2:400. Christie, "Opposition," 66–67, indicates gambling drew Elphinstone into the prince's personal circle of friends. Although plausible, the report is undocumented.

14. Elphinstone to Mary, 8 May 1782, NMM, KEI/46/4.

15. Reminiscences and Notes of Martin, William to Martin, 31 Jan 1786, William Henry to Martin, 31 Jan 1786, Elphinstone to Martin, 3 Feb [1786], in Martin, *Letters and Papers*, 1:20–22, 208–10.

16. William to Prince of Wales, 8 Feb, Elphinstone to Prince of Wales, 31 Mar 1787, *POW*, 1:276–79.

17. Nelson to William, 27 Jul 1787, *DLN*, 1:250–51.

18. William to Elphinstone, 3 Jan 1787, *LCG3*, 1:268n.

19. Elphinstone to Prince of Wales, 31 Mar 1787, *POW*, 1:278–79.

20. Ibid.

21. Voting records, George K. Elphinstone, in Ginter, *Voting Records*, 2:478.

22. Clarence to the King, 1 Jun, Pitt to the King, 20 Jun 1789, *LCG3*, 1:419–21, 426.

23. William to Prince of Wales, 4 Jul 1787, *POW*, 1:316–18.

24. Allardyce, *Memoir*, 58; Cokayne, *Complete Peerage*, 9:446, 49; Habakkuk, "Marriage Settlements," 24; Clay, "Marriage, Inheritance," 505.

25. Notes from Lord Keith's Marriage Contract with Miss Jane Mercer, NAS, GD 132/338; Clay, "Marriage, Inheritance," 505, 511; Habakkuk, "Marriage Settlements," 23.

26. Elphinstone to Adam, 9 Aug 1782, Meek MSS, KEI/47/1/43–45; William to Prince of Wales, *POW*, 1:408–9; Allardyce, *Memoir*, 58.

27. Adam to Elphinstone, [Mar/Apr 1789], in Ginter, *Whig Organization*, 49; Ginter, "Financing of the Whig Party," 421.

28. Morthland to Adam, 7 and 9 Feb 1789, Millar to Adam, 9 Feb 1789, in Ginter, *Whig Organization*, 33–34, 37–41; D. G. Henry, "Glasgow Burghs," in Thorne, *House of Commons, 1790–1820*, 2:602.

29. Morthland to Adam, 7 Feb 1789, in Ginter, *Whig Organization*, 33–35.

30. Elphinstone to Mary, 11 Dec 1789, NMM, KEI 46/7.

31. Cunynghame to Adam, 20 Dec 1789, in Ginter, *Whig Organization*, 139–40.

32. Elphinstone to Mary, 12 Jan 1791, NMM, KEI/46/8.

33. Elphinstone to Prince of Wales, 18 Jan 1791, *POW*, 2:136–37.

34. Elphinstone to [Eleonora] Adam, 7 Mar, Elphinstone to Mary, 1 Apr 1791, NMM, KEI/46/10–12.

35. Elphinstone to [Eleonora] Adam, 7 Mar 1791, NMM, KEI/46/10.

36. Elphinstone to [Eleonora] Adam, 28 Apr, 12 May 1791, NMM, KEI/46/14–15.

37. Ehrman, *Younger Pitt*, 2:208, 238, 241, 257.

38. Admiralty to Elphinstone, 29 Jan, 17 Apr, Hood to Elphinstone, 7 May 1793, NMM, KEI/3; Elphinstone to Mary, 29 May 1793, NMM, KEI/46/19; Elphinstone to Payne, [Mar/Apr 1793], *POW*, 2:347.

39. Elphinstone to Mary, 6 and 12 Jul, 28 Aug 1793, NMM, KEI/46/22, 26; Log of

the *Victory*, 23 May 1793, in J. Rose, *Lord Hood*, 104; N.A.M. Rodger, *Wooden World*, 107.

40. Order of Battle of Sailing, 17 May 1793, NMM, KEI/3; Elphinstone to Mary, 29 May 1793, NMM, KEI/46/19.

41. Elphinstone to Mary, 14 Jun, entry 18 Jun 1793, NMM, KEI/46/21; Hood to Elphinstone, 10 and 11 Jun, 9 Aug 1793, NMM, KEI/3; Nelson to Mrs. Nelson, 23 Jun 1793, in Naish, *Letters to His Wife*, 83–84.

42. Crook, *Toulon*, 126, 141; Brun, *Guerres maritimes*, 2:224–25.

43. Log of the *Princess Royal*, 28 Aug, Log of the *Britannia*, 28 Aug, Hood to Stephens, 29 Aug 1793, in J. Rose, *Lord Hood*, 105–7, 126–27.

44. Elphinstone to Mary, 28 Aug 1793, NMM, KEI/46/26.

45. Hood to Elphinstone, 28 Aug, Elphinstone to Hood, 30 Aug 1793, *KP*, 1:181–84; Graham to Cathcart, 19 Aug [misdated], 7 Sep 1793, in Delavoye, *Graham*, 46, 49.

46. Graham to Cathcart, 7 Sep 1793, in Delavoye, *Graham*, 49–50; J. Rose, *Lord Hood*, 30.

47. Elphinstone to [Mary], 21 Sep 1793, NMM, KEI/46/27.

48. Elphinstone to William Elphinstone, 2 Oct 1793, NMM, KEI/46/28; Phipps, *Armies*, 3:113.

49. Graham to Cathcart, 27 Sep 1793, in Delavoye, *Graham*, 65–66; Weinzierl, "Claude-Victor Perrin," 17–18.

50. Graham to Cathcart, 2 Oct 1793, in Delavoye, *Graham*, 71–72.

51. Ibid.; Elphinstone to William Elphinstone, 2 Oct 1793, NMM, KEI/46/28.

52. Elphinstone to Mary, 20 Oct 1793, NMM, KEI/46/30; Elphinstone to Graham, 13 Nov 1793, NLS, MSS 3,598, 51–52.

53. Elphinstone to Graham (see note 52); Elphinstone to William Elphinstone, 22 Nov 1793, NMM, KEI/46/35.

54. Elphinstone to William Elphinstone, 13 Dec 1793, NMM, KEI/46/37; Bonaparte to Minister of War, 14 Nov 1793, *CN*, 1:15; "Siége de Toulon: Août-Decémbre 1793," *CN*, 29:22.

55. Elphinstone to Mary, 29 Dec 1793, NMM, KEI/46/39.

56. Elphinstone to Mary, 20, 29 Dec 1793, NMM, KEI/46/38–39; "Siège de Toulon: Août–Decémbre 1793," *CN*, 29:22–23; Hood to Dundas, 20 Dec 1793, in J. Rose, *Lord Hood*, 158–59.

57. Elphinstone to Mary, 20 Oct 1793, NMM, KEI/46/30.

58. Nelson to Fanny, 12 Oct 1793, *DLN*, 1:333.

59. Hood to Elphinstone, 1 Jan 1794, NMM, KEI/3; Elphinstone to William Elphinstone, 20 Jan 1791 [1794], Elphinstone to Mary, 19 Mar 1794, NMM, KEI/46/9, 41; Meek MSS, KEI/47/1/98.

60. Clowes, *Royal Navy*, 4:192–93; Lavery, *Nelson's Navy*, 99.

61. Elphinstone to Mary, 31 Mar, Apr 1794, NMM, KEI/46/42, 44; Meek MSS, KEI/47/1/98.

62. Elphinstone to Mary, postmarked 2 Jul 1794, NMM, KEI/46/48.

63. Derry, *Politics*, 95; O'Gorman, *Whig Party*, 206–8.

Chapter 3. "Things go remarkably well": From the Cape of Good Hope to Mutiny (1794–97)

1. Meek MSS, KEI/47/1/98; Collingwood to Carlyle, 9 Jul 1794, in Collingwood, *Correspondence*, 51–53. John descended from the Elphinstones of Sowerby, and Sir George descended from the Lord Elphinstones (Graham, "Footnote").

2. Collingwood to Carlyle, 3 Aug 1794, in Collingwood, *Correspondence*, 53–54; N.A.M. Rodger, "Patronage and Competence," 239–41. According to Rodger, "followers" benefited the service and were condoned by the Admiralty since the benefits largely outweighed any detriment to the service. However, Rodger acknowledges that this system was open to abuse.

3. Line of Battle, 7 Aug 1794, NMM, KEI/3; Saxby, "Blockade of Brest," 26–27.

4. Elphinstone to Mary, 11 Oct 1794, NMM, KEI/46/61.

5. Elphinstone to Mary, 22 Jan 1795, NMM, KEI/46/67.

6. Saxby, "Blockade of Brest," 27.

7. Elphinstone to Mary, 4 and 22 Jan 1795, NMM, KEI/46/66–67.

8. Elphinstone to Mary, postmarked 28 Jan 1795, NMM, KEI/46/68.

9. Dundas to Grenville, 16 Nov 1794, HMC, *Fortescue*, 2:645–46; Cabinet Minute, 8 Feb 1795, *LCG3*, 2:300–301; Harlow, "British Occupations," 8:170–71; Philips, *East India Company*, 89; Ehrman, *Younger Pitt*, 2:561.

10. Sunter, *Patronage and Politics*, 8–9; Philips, *East India Company*, 60, 336; Allardyce, *Memoir*, 84–85.

11. Elphinstone to Mary, 7 Mar 1795, NMM, KEI/46/70.

12. N.A.M. Rodger, *Wooden World*, 303.

13. Perrin, *KP*, 1:215–16.

14. Elphinstone to Admiralty, 23 Mar, Admiralty to Elphinstone, 25 Mar, Cornwallis to Elphinstone, 26 Mar 1795, *KP*, 1:248–50.

15. Instructions from the Horse Guards to Clarke, 4 May 1795, Elphinstone to Admiralty, 4 Jul 1795, *RCC*, 1:38–39, 106–8; Perrin, *KP*, 1:216.

16. Elphinstone to [Mary], 2 Apr 1795, NMM, KEI/46/73; Elphinstone's Journal, 10 Jun 1795, *KP*, 1:256; Craig to Dundas, 16 Jun 1795, Elphinstone to Admiralty, 4 Jul 1795, *RCC*, 1:51–52, 106–8.

17. Prince of Orange to Governor of the Cape, 7 Feb, Craig to Dundas, 16 Jun 1795, *RCC*, 1:28, 52–56; Theal, *History of South Africa*, 4:315–18.

18. Elphinstone to Sluysken, 13 Jun 1795, *KP*, 1:264.

19. Elphinstone's Journal, 14 Jun, Elphinstone to Dundas, 17 Jun 1795, *KP*, 1:266, 270–74.

20. Elphinstone's Journal, 20 and 28 Jun 1795, *KP*, 1:277, 302; Elphinstone and Craig to Sluysken and Council, 29 Jun 1795, *RCC*, 1:91–92; Theal, *History of South Africa*, 4:323–24.

21. Elphinstone's Journal, 1 Jul 1795, *KP*, 1:313.

22. Elphinstone's Journal, 11, 14, 22, 26, and 27 Jul 1795, *KP*, 1:332, 335–36; Craig to Dundas, 21 Sep 1795, *RCC*, 1:148–50.

23. Elphinstone to Craig, 26 Jul 1795, *KP*, 1:336–38; Theal, *History of South Africa*, 4:329.

24. Elphinstone to Craig, 27 Jul 1796, *KP*, 1:339; Theal, *History of South Africa*, 4:229–30.

25. Elphinstone's Journal, 3, 4, 5, and 7 Aug 1795, *KP*, 1:343–34; Elphinstone to Dundas, 18 Aug 1795, *RCC*, 1:113–16; Allardyce, *Memoir*, 96.

26. Elphinstone's Journal, 9 Aug 1795, *KP*, 1:345; "Account of the Cape of Good Hope," *Naval Chronicle*, 5:420.

27. Elphinstone to Dundas, 12 Sep 1795, *RCC*, 1:119–21.

28. Elphinstone to Dundas, 23 Sep 1795, *RCC*, 1:157–58.

29. Elphinstone to Mary, 22 Sep 1795, NMM, KEI/46/75.

30. Craig to Dundas, 21 Sep 1795, *RCC*, 1:148–50.

31. Clarke to Dundas, 23 Sep 1795, *RCC*, 1:160–63.

32. Elphinstone to Mary, 10 Nov 1795, NMM, KEI/46/77.

33. Elphinstone to Mary, 22 Sep 1795, NMM, KEI/46/75.

34. Elphinstone to Mary, 10 Nov 1795, NMM, KEI/46/77; Anne Barnard to Dundas, 24 Aug 1797, in Barnard, *Letters*, 59; Craig to Dundas, 9 Oct 1795, 14 Feb 1796, *RCC*, 1:182–84, 329–31; Theal, *History of South Africa*, 5:1–2.

35. Elphinstone to Mary, 10 Nov 1795, NMM, KEI/46/77; Elphinstone to Blankett, 12 Nov, Elphinstone to Admiralty, 13 Nov 1795, *KP*, 1:391–95.

36. Parkinson, *Eastern Seas*, 80–82. Parkinson included in his text a letter from Elphinstone to Rainier that stated, "On my arrival here upon the 10th I took upon me the command of His Majesty's Ships & Veſſels employed on a particular service including all the Indian Seas." Parkinson gives the date of this letter as 10 August, but Elphinstone did not arrive anywhere on that date. On the contrary, he had been at the Cape since 10 June.

37. Shore to Dundas, 5 Nov 1795, in Furber, *Private Record*, 79–83.

38. Parkinson, *Eastern Seas*, 84–85, 94–95. Parkinson chastised Elphinstone for failing to combat this menace, since it disrupted trade routes from Calcutta and Madras. However, his argument is weak, for he acknowledges that Rainier had not adequately addressed the threat before sailing to the Moluccas.

39. Shore to Dundas, 7 Feb 1796, in Furber, *Private Record*, 93–95.

40. Admiralty to Elphinstone, 13 Feb, Elphinstone to Admiralty, 24 and 25 Jun, 3 Aug 1796, *KP*, 1:396, 417–25, 436–38.

41. Elphinstone to Rainier, 23 Jul 1796, NMM, KEI/L/136/73–83. The French frigates with Sercey were the *Forte* (44), *Seine* (36), *Vertu* (40), and *Régénérée* (36).

42. Admiralty to Elphinstone, 25 Feb, Elphinstone to Admiralty, 25 Jun, Elphinstone to Spencer, 10 Jul 1796, *KP*, 1:421–25, 423n, 431–33; Elphinstone to Dundas, 24 Jun 1796, *RCC*, 1:391–93.

43. Elphinstone to Admiralty, 19 Aug 1796, *KP*, 1:453–56.

44. Elphinstone to Lucas, 16 Aug, Lucas to Elphinstone, 16 Aug, Articles of Capitulation, 17 Aug 1796, NMM, KEI/136/L/91–94, 98–105; Craig to Dundas, 19 Aug 1796, *RCC*, 1:433–37; Elphinstone to Lucas, 16 and 17 Aug, Elphinstone to Shore, 19 Aug 1796, *KP*, 1:440–43, 453–57.

45. Elphinstone to [Mary], 19 Aug 1796, NMM, KEI/46/82.

46. Lucas to Elphinstone, 17 Aug 1796, NMM, KEI/136/L/108–9.

47. Craig to Dundas, 29 Aug 1796, *RCC*, 1:445–50. Manning problems were not unusual for the Dutch fleet, which had suffered such deficiencies since the 1780s; see Bruijn, *Dutch Navy*, 214.

48. Elphinstone to Mary, 19 Aug 1796, NMM, KEI/46/83.

49. John Elphinstone to Elphinstone, 21 Jun, Elphinstone to Pringle, 26 Jul 1796, *KP*, 1:412–13, 433.

50. Elphinstone to Pringle, 5 Oct 1796, NMM, KEI/L/136/163–77; Ships commanded by Elphinstone, [Sep 1796], *KP*, 1:458; Elphinstone to Nepean, 1 Nov, Pringle to Admiralty, 13 Nov 1796, *RCC*, 1:477–78, 482–83; Spencer to Dundas, 26 Mar 1796, *Spencer*, 1:241–43.

51. Narrative of Proceedings on Board H.M.S. *Monarch*, n.d., *KP*, 2:3–5; Elphinstone to Secretary of Admiralty, 23 Dec 1796, *KP*, 2:5.

52. Elphinstone to Secretary (see note 51); Tone, *Life*, 22–23 Dec 1796, 662–63; Desbrière, *Projets et tentatives*, 1:195; Guillon, *France et l'Irlande*, 249–53.

53. Narrative (see note 51); Elphinstone to Secretary of Admiralty, 24 Dec 1797, *KP*, 2:6.

54. Elphinstone to Mary, 25 Dec 1796, NMM, KEI/46/85.

55. Journal of Bouvet, 24–25 Dec 1796, in Guillon, *France et l'Irlande*, 274; Tone, *Life*, 26–27 Dec 1796, 668, 671. This was the remainder of Admiral Kingsmill's squadron consisting of one sixty-four-gun ship-of-the-line and several frigates that had been deployed to protect homeward-bound convoys. They had all suffered in the storms and had anchored at Cork. See Notes by Lord Spencer on the failure of the fleet to intercept Hoche's expedition, *Spencer*, 1:392.

56. Elphinstone to Mary, 27 Dec 1796, NMM, KEI/46/86; Elphinstone to Secretary of Admiralty, 27 Dec 1797, *KP*, 2:8.

57. Secretary of Admiralty to Elphinstone, 3 Jan 1797, *KP*, 2:11; Arthur, *Remaking of the English Navy*, 68–69.

58. Log of the *Monarch*, 31 Dec 1796–3 Jan 1797, *KP*, 2:2–3; Intelligence sent to Lord Lieut. Governor of Ireland, 30 Dec 1796, *KP*, 2:9–10.

59. Jackson to Keith, 6 May 1800, *KP*, 2:394.

60. McCahill, "Scottish Representative Peers," 284.

61. *Journals of the House of Commons*, 20 Oct 1796, 52:46; ibid., 23 Dec 1796, 52:231; R. G. Thorne, "Stirlingshire," in *House of Commons, 1790–1820*, 2:581–88.

62. Richards, "Creations of Peers," 53.

63. Portland to the King, 3 Feb 1797, *LCG3*, 3:539–40; Dundas to Elphinstone, 20 Nov 1796, in Allardyce, *Memoir*, 133–34. There is some confusion over the date of his creation. Allardyce (135) claims that it was 7 March, Aspinall (*POW*, 3:318n) that it was 8 February. The latter's information appears the more accurate, as there exist documents that predate 7 March where Elphinstone is referred to as Lord Keith (Dundas to Keith, 17 Feb, Keith to Prince of Wales, 18 Feb 1797, *POW*, 3:318, 322).

64. Prince of Wales to Pitt, 8 Feb 1797, *POW*, 3:313–16; Ehrman, *Younger Pitt*, 3:162–64.

65. Parnell to Scully, 19 Mar 1821, in Scully, *Catholic Question*, 643–44.

66. Dundas to Keith, 17 Feb, Pitt to Keith, 18 Feb, Keith to Prince of Wales, 19 Feb 1797, *POW*, 3:318, 320, 322.

67. Prince of Wales to Pitt, 23 Feb, Pitt to Keith, 26 Feb 1797, *POW*, 3:325–26.

68. Keith to Mary, 24 Feb 1797, NMM, KEI/46/93.

69. Dundas to [Keith], 18 Mar 1797, *POW*, 3:328.

70. Hibbert, *George IV*, 1:177.

71. Lavery, *Nelson's Navy*, 142.

72. Declaration of Richard Parker, *Spencer*, 2:160–73; Examination of Mr. John Snipe, 3 Jun 1797, *KP*, 2:17; "Memoirs of Peter Cullen, esq.," 12 May 1797, in Thursfield, *Five Naval Journals*, 83; Wells, *Insurrection*, 87–88; Ehrman, *Younger Pitt*, 3:27.

73. *London Chronicle*, 25–27 and 27–30 May 1797.

74. King's Reply, 27 May 1797, *LCG3*, 3:579–80; *London Chronicle*, 30 May–1 Jun 1797.

75. Keith to Dundas, 24 Jun 1797, BL, Add. MSS 41,081, 1–3; Keith to Spencer, 2 Jun 1797, *KP*, 2:15–16; *London Chronicle*, 1–3 Jun 1797. Several authors have indicated that the Admiralty sent Keith to the Nore as second in command with the expectation that he would take on many of Buckner's duties. Yet these authors provide no documentation for this deduction. See Manwaring and Dobrée, *Floating Republic*, 193; Dugan, *Great Mutiny*, 261.

76. Keith to the Men at the Nore, 6 Jun 1797, in Allardyce, *Memoir*, 143–45.

77. Keith to Dundas, 24 Jun 1797, BL, Add. MSS 41,081, 1–3.

78. Keith to Mary, 2 Jul 1797, NMM, KEI/46/107; [Admiral] King to Spencer,

27 Jun 1797, *Spencer*, 2:159–60; Examination of Mutineers from the *Repulse*, 10 Jun, Examination on the *Ardent*, 10 Jun, [Keith] Memo to Captains and Commanders at the Nore and Sheerness, [22 Jun 1797], *KP*, 2:20–22, 22–23, 25; Wells, *Insurrection*, 89.

79. [Keith] Memo to All Officers, 22 Jun 1797, *KP*, 2:24–25.

80. Admiralty to Keith, 26 Jun 1797, *KP*, 2:25.

81. [Admiral] King to Keith, 5 Jul, Keith to King, 5 Jul 1797, *KP*, 2:26–28; Wells, *Insurrection*, 106.

82. Keith to King, 5 Jul 1797, NMM, KEI/L/158/16–17.

83. Keith to Mary, 5 Jul 1797, NMM, KEI/46/108.

84. Keith to Bridport, 7 Jul 1797, NMM, KEI/L/158/21.

Chapter 4. "Reflecting on human events and their uncertainty": Escaping the Stigma of an Affront (1797–99)

1. Keith to Spencer, 20 Jul, Spencer to Keith, 30 Jul 1797, in Morriss and Saxby, *Channel Fleet*, 256–57, 260.

2. Ryan, "Blockade of Brest," 186.

3. Keith to Mary, 10 [Aug], 12 Sep, 18 Oct, 3 Nov, with addendum for 5 Nov 1797, NMM, KEI/46/115, 120, 126, 128. The woman's name is abbreviated exactly as in the letter.

4. Keith to Mary, 3 Nov 1797, NMM, KEI/46/128.

5. Admiralty to Bridport, 11 Nov 1797, in Morriss and Saxby, *Channel Fleet*, 271–72.

6. Memo on Lord Keith, 1 Dec 1797, NLS, MSS 9,733, 12; Keith to Bridport, 25 Nov 1797, in Morriss and Saxby, *Channel Fleet*, 273.

7. Keith continued to dismiss the disagreement as "conjecture" for the remainder of his life (Meek MSS, KEI/47/1/196–98).

8. Memo on Lord Keith, 1 Dec, Keith to Dundas, 2 Dec 1797, NLS, MSS 9,733, 12–14 (underlined by Keith).

9. Keith to [Mary], 19 Nov 1797, NMM, KEI/46/130.

10. Keith to Dundas, 12 Feb 1798, BL, Add. MSS 41,081, 5–6. Keith was misinformed. Admiral Frederick did not die until the following year.

11. Spencer to Keith, 15 and 19 Feb 1798, in Morriss and Saxby, *Channel Fleet*, 283.

12. Keith to Dundas, 13 Jun 1798, BL, Add. MSS 41,081, 9–10.

13. Keith to Stuart, 14 Feb 1799, NLS, MSS 7,199, 45–46.

14. St. Vincent to Clinton, 27 Feb 1781, in Hatch, "Letters," 102.

15. St. Vincent to Nepean, 22 Sep 1800, NMM, NEP/5/168–69.

16. Keith to Mary, 18 Dec, entry 22 Dec 1798, NMM, KEI/46/137; Meek MSS, KEI/47/1/201–2; Log of the *Foudroyant*, ADM 51/1270, 4.

17. Keith to Mary, 18 Dec, entry 22 Dec 1798, NMM, KEI/46/137; Keith to Stuart, 14 Feb 1799, NLS, MSS 7,199, 45–46.

18. Keith to Mary, 23 Jan, entry 24 Jan 1799, NMM, KEI/46/142; A. Rodger, *Second Coalition*, 97.

19. Keith to Mary, 23 Jan 1799, NMM, KEI/46/142.

20. Keith to Mary, 23 Jan, entry 30 Jan 1799, NMM, KEI/46/142.

21. Keith to [Mary], 3 Jan 1799, NMM, KEI/46/139; St. Vincent to Spencer, 13 Feb 1799, *Spencer*, 4:43–45; Cochrane, *Autobiography*, 28, 31.

22. St. Vincent to Nepean, 13 Feb 1799, NMM, NEP/5/19–20.

23. Directory to Bruix, 15 Mar 1799, Jonquière, *Égypte*, 5:136–38.

24. Saxby, "Escape of Admiral Bruix."

25. Extract from the Log of the *Barfleur*, 3–4 May 1799, ADM 1/399; Lord Grenville to Thomas Grenville, 25 May 1799, HMC, *Fortescue*, 5:65–66.

26. Extract from the Log of the *Barfleur*, 4 May 1799, ADM 1/399.

27. Smyth, *Captain Philip Beaver*, 125.

28. Cochrane, *Autobiography*, 32.

29. Meek MSS, KEI/47/1/219.

30. Extract from the Log of the *Barfleur*, 4–5 May 1799, ADM 1/399.

31. Keith to St. Vincent, 7 May 1799, ADM 1/399.

32. General Memo, 6 May 1799, NMM, STE/2/8.

33. Keith to Spencer, 6 May 1799, Meek MSS, KEI/47/1/215–17; Extract from the Log of the *Barfleur*, 5 May 1799, ADM 1/399.

34. Keith to Mary, 6 May 1799, NMM, KEI/46/156.

35. Proceedings of the Fleet, 6 May 1799, ADM 1/399.

36. Keith to Mary, 21 May 1799, NMM, KEI/46/158.

37. Thomas Grenville to Lord Grenville, 28 May, Lord Grenville to Thomas Grenville, 3 Jun 1799, HMC, *Fortescue*, 5:71–72, 78–80; Spencer to St. Vincent, 10 May, 27 Jun 1799, *Spencer*, 3:80–82, 4:51–55.

38. Keith to Spencer, 6 May 1799, Meek MSS, KEI/47/1/215–17.

39. St. Vincent to Nepean, 10 May 1799, ADM 1/399.

40. Keith to Mary, 11 May 1799, NMM, KEI/46/157; Keith to St. Vincent, 7 May 1799, Meek MSS, KEI/47/1/215–17.

41. Keith to Mary, 27 May entry, NMM, KEI/46/159; Log of the *Barfleur*, 10–11 May 1799, ADM 51/1268, pt. 8; St. Vincent to Spencer, 10 May 1799, *Spencer*, 3:80–82.

42. Log of the *Barfleur*, 18–20 May 1799, ADM 51/1268, pt. 8; Duckworth to St. Vincent, 11 May 1799, Meek MSS, KEI/47/1/228–30.

43. Meek MSS, KEI/47/1/230–31; Information by Capt. Bowen of the *Caroline*, 27 May 1799, *KP*, 2:43–44; Clowes, *Royal Navy*, 4:383–84; Carlan, *Navios en secuestro*, 36.

44. St. Vincent to Nepean, 31 May 1799, NMM, NEP/5/37–38.

45. St. Vincent to Nepean, 31 May 1799, ADM 1/399.

46. Orders to Keith, 3 May 1799, *KP*, 2:44; Cochrane, *Autobiography*, 33; A. Rodger, *Second Coalition*, 114–15.

47. Log of the *Barfleur*, 7 Jun 1799, ADM 51/1268, pt. 8; St. Vincent to Keith, 5 Jun 1799, *KP*, 2:45.

48. Keith to Mary, 8 Jun 1799, NMM, KEI/46/160.

49. Log of the *Barfleur*, 8 Jun 1799, ADM 51/1268, pt. 8.

50. Keith to Mary, 8 Jun 1799, NMM, KEI/46/160.

51. Log of the *Barfleur*, 9 Jun 1799, ADM 51/1268, pt. 8.

52. St. Vincent to Keith, 3 Jun 1799, *KP*, 2:44.

53. Cochrane, *Autobiography*, 34.

54. Keith to Mary, 8 Jun 1799, NMM, KEI/46/160.

55. Collingwood to Blackett, 17 Aug 1799, in Collingwood, *Correspondence*, 100–101.

56. St. Vincent to Nelson, 11 Jun, St. Vincent to Spencer, 16 Jun 1799, in St. Vincent, *Memoirs*, 1:482–84.

57. Log of the *Barfleur*, 18 Jun 1799, ADM 51/1291, pt. 2; Markham to Keith, 19 Jun 1799, *Naval Chronicle*, 2:346.

58. Log of the *Barfleur*, 20–27 Jun 1799, ADM 51/1291, pt. 2; Keith to Mary, 29 Jun 1799, NMM, KEI/46/163; Keith to Nelson, 27 Jun 1799, in Allardyce, *Memoir*, 170–71.

59. Log of the *Barfleur*, 7–8 Jul 1799, ADM 51/1291, pt. 2; Krajeski, *Shadow of Nelson*, 31–33; Keith to Mary, 13 Jul 1799, NMM, KEI/46/164.

60. Keith to Mary, 13 Jul 1799, NMM, KEI/46/164.

61. Keith to Spencer, 11 Aug [Jul] 1799, *Spencer*, 3:94–95.

62. Keith to Mary, 13 Jul 1799, NMM, KEI/46/164; Keith to Nepean, 11 Jul 1799, ADM 1/400; Keith to Nelson, 9 Jul 1799, *DLN*, 3:414–15.

63. Nelson to Keith, 14 and 19 Jul, Nelson to Spencer, 13 Jul 1799, *DLN*, 3:408–9, 411, 414–15; Nelson to Spencer, 15 Jul 1799, *Spencer*, 3:90–91.

64. Duckworth to Keith, 2 Aug 1799, Meek MSS, KEI/47/1/269.

65. Nelson to Fanny, 24 Aug 1799, in Naish, *Letters to His Wife*, 488–89; St. Vincent to Keith, 7 Jul 1799, *KP*, 2:48–49; Pettigrew, *Nelson*, 1:285.

66. Keith to Nepean, 16 Jul 1799, ADM 1/400.

67. Keith to Nepean, 18 Jul 1799, ADM 1/400.

68. Journal of Keith, 18–31 Jul 1799, ADM 1/400; Log of the *Barfleur*, 18–31 Jul 1799, ADM 51/1291, pt. 2; Keith to Nelson, 15 Jul 1799, *KP*, 2:50.

69. Keith to Spencer, 11 Aug [Jul] 1799, *Spencer*, 3:94–95; Cochrane, *Autobiography*, 35.

70. St. Vincent to Keith, 16 Jul 1799, Meek MSS, KEI/47/1/257; Nepean to Nelson, 20 Aug 1799, *Spencer*, 3:53–54.

71. Nepean to Nelson, 20 Aug 1799, in Pettigrew, *Nelson*, 1:293–94.

72. Spencer to Pitt, 5 Aug 1799, *Spencer*, 3:11–13.

73. State of the Enemy's Fleet in Brest, 13 Aug 1799, ADM 1/400; Keith to Kingsmill, 14 Aug 1799, *KP*, 2:58.

74. Keith to Nepean, 30 Jul, List of Ships under the Command of Lord Keith to Nepean, 7 Aug 1799, ADM 1/400; Admiralty to Keith, 16 Aug 1799, ADM 3/123; Log of the *Barfleur*, 16 Aug 1799, ADM 51/1291, pt. 2; Admiralty to Bridport, 19 Aug 1799, NMM, KEI/24/1; Spencer to the King, 17 Aug 1799, *LCG3*, 3:241.

75. Directory to Bruix, 15 Mar, Bruix to Talleyrand, 13 May, Talleyrand to Bruix, 17 May 1799, Jonquière, *Égypte*, 5:136–38, 156, 160–61; Barras, *Memoirs*, 3:506.

76. Keith to Mary, 11 May 1799, NMM, KEI/46/157.

77. Collingwood to Blackett, 17 Aug 1799, in Collingwood, *Correspondence*, 100-101; Cochrane, *Autobiography*, 34.

78. Nepean to Nelson, 20 Aug 1799, in Pettigrew, *Nelson*, 1: 293-94.

Chapter 5. "I am a great loser": Keith in the Western Mediterranean (1800)

1. Keith to Mary, 10 Aug 1799, NMM, KEI/46/167.

2. Bridport to Nepean, 31 Aug 1799, ADM 1/113.

3. Keith to Mary, 27 Aug 1799, NMM, KEI/46/174.

4. Keith to Mary, 28 Aug, 10 Sep 1799, NMM, KEI/46/175, 180; Keith to Dundas, 18 Nov 1799, NLS, MSS 9,733, 17–18; Admiralty to Keith, 15 Nov 1799, ADM 2/922; Meek MSS, KEI/47/1/312.

5. Keith to Mary, 22 Nov 1799, NMM, KEI/46/189; Meek MSS, KEI/47/1/313, 319; Nelson to Keith, 7 Jan 1800, *DLN*, 4:170–72.

6. Keith to Mary, 18 Jan 1800, NMM, KEI/46/196.

7. Keith to Mary, 3 and 9 Feb 1800, NMM, KEI/46/197–98; Keith to Paget, 6 May 1800, *Paget*, 1:200.

8. Keith to Louis, 12 Feb 1800, NMM, ELL/139; Nepean to Keith, 30 Mar 1800, NMM, KEI/L/32/79; Meek MSS, KEI/47/1/335; Keith to Nepean, 20 Feb 1800, ADM 1/401.

9. Keith to Nepean, 20 Feb 1800, *Naval Chronicle*, 3:401–2; Clowes, *Royal Navy*, 4:418–19. This was the same Perrée who was captured off Toulon in June 1799.

10. Nelson to Keith, 18 Feb 1800, *Naval Chronicle*, 3:402–3.

11. Keith to Graham, 20 Feb 1800, NLS, MSS 3,600, 160–61.

12. Nelson to Keith, 24 Feb 1800, *DLN*, 4:191.

13. Nelson to Keith, 28 Feb, Nelson to Troubridge, 10 Mar 1800, *DLN*, 4:196–97, 203–4; Keith to Nelson, 20 Mar 1800, *KP*, 2:163.

14. Dixon to Troubridge, 31 Mar 1800, *KP*, 2:164–66.

15. Young to Keith, 11 May 1800, NMM, KEI/18/5.

16. Keith to Paget, 20 Apr, 6 May 1800, BL, Add. MSS 48,397, 16, 23; Nepean to Keith, 9 May, Nelson to Keith, 11 Jul 1800, *KP*, 2:94, 123.

17. Keith to Nepean, 6 Jan 1800, ADM 1/401; Keith to Louis, 5 Jan 1800, NMM, ELL/139; Keith to Mary, 1 Feb 1800, NMM, KEI/46/197.

18. Keith to Melas, 11 Mar 1800, *KP*, 2:72.

19. Keith to Nepean, 17 Mar 1800, ADM 1/401; Keith's Journal of the Fleet, 17 Mar 1800, ADM 50/36; Keith to Mary, 17 Mar 1800, NMM, KEI/46/202; Keith to Paget, 17 Mar 1800, BL, Add. MSS 48,397, 7; Parsons, *Nelsonian Reminiscences*, 40–41; Account of John Baird (Carpenter) transmitted by Lord Keith to Admiralty, "Loss of the Queen Charlotte," *Naval Chronicle*, 3:299–300.

20. Keith to Minto, 17 Mar 1800, NMM, ELL/139.

21. The head count varied with the source. Keith to Paget, 17 Mar, addendum 18 Mar 1800, *Paget*, 1:189, put the number saved at 157. Extract from Keith's Journal, 18 Mar 1800, *KP*, 2:76, said those rescued totaled 11 officers and 143 men out of 790 aboard. "List of officers from the ships company saved from the wreck," 19 Mar 1800, *Naval Chronicle*, 3:301–2, said 11 officers and 148 men were saved.

22. Keith to Mary, 25 Mar 1800, NMM, KEI/46/205.

23. Keith to Minto, 17 Mar 1800, NMM, ELL/139. The first time this occurred was at Toulon in 1793.

24. Keith to Mary, 17 Mar 1800, NMM, KEI/46/202. Keith's first wife had died, as had his parents, so he had to rely on his sister Mary to provide him with items from home.

25. Spencer to Keith, 12 Apr 1800, NMM, KEI/18/5; Lavery, *Nelson's Navy*, 43.

26. Keith's Journal of the Fleet, 4 Apr 1800, ADM 50/36; Keith to Paget, 20 Apr 1800, *Paget*, 1:194–96; Thiébault, *Journal*, 11, 13 Apr 1800, 1:157–58, 169; Marshall-Cornwall, *Marshal Massena*, 105–6.

27. Keith to Minto, 10 May 1800, NMM, ELL/139.

28. Keith to Paget, 16 Apr 1800, BL, Add. MSS 48,397, 15; Report on Intercepted French Correspondence provided by Melas, 14 Apr, Keith to Admiralty, 9 May 1800, in Gachot, *Histoire*, 379, 382–84.

29. Keith to St. Julien, 16 May 1800, ADM 1/402; Keith to Melas, 17 May, Melas to Keith, 23 May 1800, Meek MSS, KEI/47/1/472–74.

30. Keith to Paget, 19 May 1800, BL, Add. MSS 48,397, 29; Keith to Masséna, 14 May 1800, *KP*, 2:95–96; Thiébault, *Journal*, 30 Apr 1800, 1:222. Moral questions linger about Keith's decision to prevent the Genoese from leaving the city during the siege, since thousands died of malnutrition. However, Keith's decision was legally grounded. A notice of blockade for Genoa had been issued on 5 January. By definition, the residents should not have been able to flee by ship: "the nature of cargo on

board such ships is irrelevant; it is solely the fact that the ship is endeavouring to enter or leave a blockaded port or coast that is material" (Colombos, *Law of the Sea*, 714).

31. Keith to Paget, 19 May 1800, BL, Add. MSS 48,397, 29; Keith to Nepean, 21 May, Keith to Masséna, 21 May, Masséna to Keith, 21 May 1800, *KP*, 2:97–99.

32. Keith to Paget, 19 May 1800, *Paget*, 1:223–24.

33. Keith's Journal of the Fleet, 2 Jun 1800, ADM 50/36; Keith to Nepean, 4 Jun 1800, *KP*, 2:105–7.

34. Keith to Paget, 5 Jun 1800, *Paget*, 1:228–29.

35. Keith to Mary, 2 Jun 1800, continued 4 Jun, NMM, KEI/46/219.

36. Masséna, *Mémoires*, 4:236.

37. Keith to Graham, 6 Jun 1800, NLS, MSS 3,602, 17.

38. Keith to Mary, 8 Jun 1800, NMM, KEI/46/220; Keith to Nepean, 10 Jun 1800, *KP*, 2:112–13; Thiébault, *Journal*, 4 Jun 1800, 1:323.

39. Spencer to Keith, 29 Mar, Keith to Spencer, 1 May, 5 Jun 1800, *Spencer*, 4:112–14, 117–18, 122–23.

40. Keith to Paget, 19 May 1800, *Paget*, 1:223–24.

41. Keith to Mary, 8 Jun 1800, NMM, KEI/46/220.

42. Ibid.

43. Keith to Mary, 22 Jun 1800, NMM, KEI/46/221; Convention between Austria and France, signed at Alessandria, 16 Jun 1800, in Parry, *Consolidated Treaty Series*, 55:229–34; Keith to Nepean, 22 Jun 1800, *KP*, 2:117–19.

44. Keith to Nepean, 17 Jun 1800, ADM 1/402; Abercromby to Keith, 9 May, Keith to Abercromby, 1 Jun, Keith to Bentinck, 17 Jun 1800, *KP*, 2:92, 101–3, 115–16.

45. Spencer to Keith, 17 Aug 1800, NMM, KEI/18/5.

46. Keith to Paget, 20 Jun 1800, *Paget*, 1:232–33.

47. Wyndham to Paget, 24 Jun 1800, *Paget*, 1:233–34; Bonaparte to Masséna, 24 Jun 1800, *CN*, 6:488; Convention (see note 43), 55:229–34.

48. Keith to Nepean, 22 Jun 1800, Meek MSS, KEI/47/1/517–20.

49. Bentinck to Keith, 16 Jun 1800, Meek MSS, KEI/47/1/512.

50. Keith to Minto, 8 Jun 1800, NMM, ELL/139; Minto to Hamond, 1 Mar 1803, NMM, KEI/18/5.

51. Keith's Journal of the Fleet, 22 Jun 1800, ADM 50/36.

52. Minto to Hamond, 1 Mar 1803, NMM, KEI/18/5.

53. Bulletin de l'Armée de Reserve, 21 Jun 1800, *CN*, 6:480–82; Buckingham to Lord Grenville, 3 Jul 1800, HMC, *Fortescue*, 6:260; Petrie, *Prize Game*, 19–20. The £25,000 was viewed differently by all involved. The French considered it a bribe. The British considered it a ransom that eventually would be distributed as prize money to the officers and men involved in the operation. The Austrians later challenged this

claim in British prize courts, demanding part of the prize money. This still remained under litigation in 1803 (Minto to Hamond, 1 Mar 1803, NMM, KEI/18/5).

54. Keith to Mary, 22 Jun 1800, NMM, KEI/46/221.

55. Minto to Keith, 16 Jul 1800, NMM, KEI/18/5; For the negative interpretations of Keith's conduct at Genoa, see Hohenzollern to Suchet, 21 Jun 1800, *Le Moniteur Universal*, 29 Jun 1800, 1130; Bulletin de L'Armée de Réserve, 21 Jun 1800, *CN*, 6:488; Masséna, *Mémoires*, 4:256.

56. Keith to Minto, 23 Jun 1800, NMM, ELL/139.

57. Keith to Mary, 22 Jun 1800, NMM, KEI/46/221.

58. British casualties at Genoa excluding those lost on the *Queen Charlotte* were two officers and five seamen wounded; the Neapolitan forces cooperating with the British lost five seamen killed and twenty wounded (Keith to Nepean, 4 Jun 1800, ADM 1/402).

59. Wyndham to Paget, 24 Jun 1800, *Paget*, 1:233–34.

60. Troubridge to Keith, 23 Jun 1800, *KP*, 2:174–75; John Moore, *Diary*, 4 Jul 1800, 1:365.

61. Dundas to Abercromby, 5 May 1800, *KP*, 2:87–91; Ingram, *Commitment to Empire*, 373–75.

62. Keith to Nepean, 3 Jul 1800, ADM 1/402.

63. Young to Ann Young [wife], 22 Sep 1800, BL, Add. MSS 46,712, 12.

64. Keith to Paget, 20 and 23 Jul 1800, BL, Add. MSS. 48,397, 45–46, 50–52; Acton to Keith, 4 Jul 1800, ADM 1/402; H. Bunbury, *Narratives*, 43–46.

65. Keith to Paget, 20 Jul 1800, *Paget*, 1:253–54; H. Bunbury, *Narratives*, 43–46.

66. Keith's Journal of the Fleet, 7 Aug 1800, ADM 50/36; Armistice between Austria and France signed at Parsdorf, 15 Jul 1800, in Parry, *Consolidated Treaty Series*, 55:251–56; Dundas to Abercromby, 31 Jul 1800, *KP*, 2:134–35.

67. Keith's Journal of the Fleet, 13–14 Sep 1800, ADM 50/36; Keith to Nepean, 22 Sep 1800, ADM 1/403; Meek MSS, KEI/47/2/637; Admiralty to Keith, and encl. 1: Dundas to Abercromby, 31 Jul 1800, *KP*, 2:133–38.

68. Lavery, "George Keith Elphinstone," 390–91; A. Rodger, *Second Coalition*, 214; Mackesy, "'Most Sadly Bitched,'" 42.

69. Admiralty to Keith and encl. (see note 67), my emphasis; Harding, "Sailors and Gentlemen," 40–41.

70. Local intelligence from a harbor pilot, 26 Sep 1800, ADM 1/403; Minutes dictated by Abercromby of what passed between him and Keith, in Dunfermline, *Abercromby*, 233–37; Bickerton to Keith, 19 Sep 1800, *KP*, 2:138–39.

71. Keith to Abercromby, 8 Oct 1800, Meek MSS, KEI/47/2/658–62; Report of the British Consul in Tangiers, 27 Sep 1800, NMM, KEI/18/5.

72. Graham Hamond to Andrew Snape Hamond, 13 Oct 1800, Andrew Snape Hamond Papers, Duke University; Bickerton to Keith, 19 Sep 1800, *KP*, 2:138–39.

73. Young to Keith, 25 Oct 1800, NMM, KEI/18/5; Keith to Spencer, 22 Sep 1800, *Spencer*, 3:372–3.

74. Keith to Abercromby, 8 Oct 1800, Meek MSS, KEI/47/2/658–62; Keith to Paget, 16 Oct 1800, *Paget*, 1:272–73; Minutes (see note 70).

75. Dundas to Abercromby, 31 Jul, Abercromby to Keith, 8 Oct 1800, *KP*, 2:134–35, 144–45.

76. Keith's Journal of the Fleet, 2–5 Oct 1800, ADM 50/36.

77. Conference, Keith, Abercromby, Bickerton, Captains Morris and Elphinstone, and Colonels Abercromby and Anstruther, 5 Oct 1800, in Dunfermline, *Abercromby*, 228–29; Minutes (see note 70).

78. Minutes (see note 70).

79. Keith to Abercromby, 8 Oct 1800, Meek MSS, KEI/47/2/658–62; A. Rodger, *Second Coalition*, 214.

80. Dundas to Abercromby, 31 Jul, encl. 1 in Admiralty to Keith, 31 Jul 1800, *KP*, 2:134–35. The section left out of the quote reads: "or the Naval Officer who may be appointed by the Lords Commissioners of the Admiralty."

81. Keith to Spencer, 29 Oct 1800, *Spencer*, 4:134.

82. Keith to Abercromby, 8 Oct 1800, Meek MSS, KEI/47/2/658–62.

83. Dunfermline, *Abercromby*, 229–30.

84. John Moore, *Diary*, 7 Oct 1800, 1:377–78.

85. Ibid., 78.

86. Memo, Cochrane, 4 Oct 1800, NLS, MS 2569, 34–35; A. Rodger, *Second Coalition*, 215.

87. Keith's Orders, 6 Oct 1800, in A. Anderson, *Journal*, 80–81.

88. Abercromby to Keith, 6 Oct, Keith to Abercromby, 6 Oct 1800, *KP*, 2:142–43.

89. A. Anderson, *Journal*, 7 Oct 1800, 81–83; John Moore, *Diary*, 7 Oct 1800, 1:379.

90. Keith to Abercromby, 8 Oct 1800, Meek MSS, KEI/47/2/658–62; Abercromby to Keith, 8 Oct 1800, *KP*, 2:144–45.

91. Keith to Nepean, 7 Oct 1800, ADM 1/403; Mackesy, "'Most Sadly Bitched,'" 53.

92. Young to Keith, 25 Oct 1800, NMM, KEI/18/5; Spencer to Keith, 23 Oct 1800, *Spencer*, 4:133–34.

93. Keith to Mary, 7 Oct 1800, NMM, KEI/46/231; Mackesy, "'Most Sadly Bitched,'" 46–47.

94. Samuel Hood to Lord Hood, Nov 1800, in Laughton, "Hood," 255–58; Collingwood to Carlyle, 7 Dec 1800, in Collingwood, *Correspondence*, 117–19.

95. Smyth, *Captain Philip Beaver*, 189.

96. Spencer to Keith, 27 Dec, Young to Keith, 27 Dec 1800, NMM, KEI/18/5; Admiralty to Keith, 27 Dec 1800, *KP*, 2:256–57.

97. Dundas to Spencer, [27 Dec 1800], *Spencer*, 4:143.

98. Mackesy, *Victory*, 7.

99. Dundas to Keith, 27 Dec 1800, *KP*, 2:149–50.

100. Keith to Spencer, 12 Feb 1801, *Spencer*, 4:144–47.

101. Keith to Markham, 30 Dec 1803, *Markham*, 128.

102. Keith to Paget, 23 Jul 1800, *Paget*, 1:256–57.

103. Young to Spencer, 11 Sep 1800, *Spencer*, 4:291–92.

Chapter 6. "An arduous task to perform": Keith and the Egyptian Campaign (1801)

1. Admiralty to Keith, Dundas to Abercromby, 6 Oct 1800, *KP*, 2:240–43; Ingram, *Commitment to Empire*, 380–81; Ingram, "Geopolitics," 444–46; Ehrman, *Younger Pitt*, 3:407–9; Fedorak, "Catholic Emancipation," 59–60.

2. Keith to Nepean, 27 Oct 1800, ADM 1/403; Moore to his father, 1 Apr 1801, James Moore, *Life*, 2:372–76.

3. Keith to Admiralty, 11 Nov 1800, *KP*, 2:252; Collingwood to Carlyle, 7 Dec 1800, in Collingwood, *Correspondence*, 117–19; Mackesy, *Victory*, 41.

4. Young to Ann Young, 12 Jan [1801], BL, Add. MSS 46,712, 17.

5. Journal of the Fleet, 9 and 16 Nov, 2 and 8 Dec 1800, ADM 50/36; Keith to Paget, 27 Nov 1800, BL, Add. MSS 48,397, 82; Keith to Admiralty, 21 Dec 1800, Meek MSS, KEI/47/2/37.

6. Meek MSS, KEI/47/2/38; Inglis to Young, 18 Jan 1801, in Laughton, "Operations," 338–39; Keith to Admiralty, 11 Jan 1801, *KP*, 2:258–59; Parsons, *Nelsonian Reminiscences*, 42–44.

7. Young to Keith, 20 Nov 1800, NMM, KEI/18/5.

8. Keith to Paget, 18 Dec 1800, BL, Add. MSS 48,397, 87–88; Keith to Nepean, 12 Dec 1800, ADM 1/403.

9. Keith to Admiralty, 29 Nov 1800, Meek MSS, KEI/47/2/684–87.

10. Louis to Keith, 7 Feb 1801, ADM 1/404; Bonaparte to Lucien Bonaparte, 15 Jan 1801, in Bonaparte, *Lettres inédites*, 1:19; Bonaparte to Talleyrand, 4 and 13 Feb 1801, *CN*, 7:4, 24–27; Admiralty to Keith, 27 Dec 1800, *KP*, 2:256–57.

11. Barlow to Keith, 20 Feb 1801, *KP*, 2:366–67.

12. General Memorandum, signed Captain Young, 13 Dec 1800, NMM, STE/2; Bonaparte to Ganteaume, 2 Mar 1801, *CN*, 7:72–73.

13. Keith to [Mary], 13 and 21 Jan 1801, NMM, KEI/46/239–40.

14. Grand Vizir to Keith, [prior to landing in Egypt], Chiaush Bashi [supreme commissary to the Porte] to Keith, 30 Jan 1801, Kapudan Bey to Keith, 15 Jan 1801

[misdated 1800], NMM, KEI/15/1, 2, 3; A. Anderson, *Journal*, 14 Jan 1801, 194. Shaw, *Between Old and New*, passim; Lewis, "Impact," 108–10.

15. Keith to Paget, 15 Feb 1801, *Paget*, 1:310–11.

16. Young to the Captains of the Fleet, 4, 6, and 7 Feb 1801, BL, Add. MSS 46,714, 10, 14; Meek MSS, KEI/47/2/127. The landing craft came in three varieties: the flat-boat carried between fifty and sixty soldiers; the ship's launch carried approximately twenty men; the rowboats carried eight to ten; see A. Anderson, *Journal*, 8 Mar 1801, 218–19.

17. Journal of the Fleet, 27 Oct, 2 and 3 Nov 1800, ADM 50/36; Keith to Smith, 24 Oct 1800, in Barrow, *Smith*, 1:336–38; Hallowell to Keith, 31 Oct 1800, Keith to Admiralty, 21 Jan 1801, *KP*, 2:245–48, 259–60; John Moore, *Diary*, 24 Jan 1801, 1:397–98.

18. Distribution of Boats, 4 Oct 1800 [misdated], Composition of the Marine Battalion, signed by Young, 21 Feb 1801, NLS, MSS 2,569, 48–49, 106; Meek MSS, KEI/47/2/121; Keith to Abercromby, 4 Feb 1801, *KP*, 2:262–63.

19. Keith to Nepean, 22 Feb 1801, ADM 1/404.

20. Keith to [Mary], 16 Feb 1801, NMM, KEI/46/242.

21. Journal of the Fleet, 22 Feb 1801, ADM 50/36; Meek MSS, KEI/47/2/115, 24; Extract of Instructions from Dundas to Abercromby, 6 Oct 1800, *KP*, 2:242–43.

22. Journal of the Fleet, 7 Mar 1801, ADM 50/36; Keith to Paget, 5 Mar 1801, *Paget*, 1:324–25; John Moore, *Diary*, 6 Mar 1801, 2:2; A. Anderson, *Journal*, 1, 2 Mar 1801, 214.

23. Journal of the Fleet, 3 Mar 1801, ADM 50/36; Warren to Nepean, 14 Dec 1800, ADM 1/403; Keith to Nepean, 10 Mar 1801, ADM 1/404; Keith to Abercromby, 3 Mar 1801, Meek MSS, KEI/47/2/131–33, 134; R. Anderson, *Naval Wars in the Levant*, 389; Clowes, *Royal Navy*, 4:447–48.

24. Rigault, *Menou*, 295.

25. Journal of the Fleet, 8 Mar 1801, ADM 50/36; John Moore, *Diary*, 6 Mar 1801 [misdated], 2:2–3; Nicol, *Life and Adventures*, 179.

26. Keith to Nepean, 10 Mar 1801, *KP*, 2:273–75; Inglis to Young, 8 Mar 1801, in Laughton, "Operations," 343–44; John Moore, *Diary*, 6 Mar 1801, 2:3; A. Anderson, *Journal*, 8 Mar 1801, 222.

27. Keith to Mary, 28 Feb 1801, entry for 9 Mar, NMM, KEI/46/243; Abercromby, General Orders, 9 Mar, entry for 8 Mar 1801, in A. Anderson, *Journal*, 224–26; Keith to Nepean, 10 Mar 1801, *KP*, 2:273–75.

28. Menou to Reynier, 7 Mar 1801, in Rousseau, *Kléber et Menou*, 398–99.

29. Keith to Paget, 5 Mar 1801, *Paget*, 1:324–25.

30. Keith to Spencer, 11 Mar 1801, *Spencer*, 4:147–49.

31. Keith to Abercromby, 12 Mar 1801, ADM 1/404.

32. Abercromby to Keith, 14 Mar 1801, NMM, KEI/18/7.

33. Keith to Abercromby, 14 Mar 1801, ADM 1/404.

34. Bonaparte to Ganteaume, 6 Mar, Bonaparte to Sahuguet, 6 Mar 1801, *CN*, 7:81, 86–87.

35. Governor of Cyprus to Keith, 20 Mar 1801, Gezar Pasha to Keith, 8 Jun 1801, NMM, KEI/15/1; Mustapha Bey to Keith, 15 Apr, 19 May 1801, NMM, KEI/15/3; Journal of the Fleet, 26–28 Mar, 26 Apr, 21 May 1801, ADM 50/36; A. Anderson, *Journal*, March 1801, 261.

36. Jackson to Keith, 10 Feb 1801, NMM, KEI/24/2; Fedorak, "Catholic Emancipation," 64.

37. Navy Board to Nepean, 26 May 1801, NMM, KEI/L/33/80–81; Keith to Nepean, 11 May 1801 and notes by Admiralty Board, ADM 1/404.

38. Hutchinson to Keith, 25 Mar 1801, NMM, KEI/18/7; Keith to Nepean, 1 Apr 1801, Meek MSS, KEI/47/3/177–80; Bonaparte to Forfait, 28 Feb 1801, *CN*, 7:64–65.

39. Keith to Mary, 21 Apr 1801, NMM, KEI/46/250; Warren to Keith, 30 Mar, Keith to Nepean, 23 Apr 1801, ADM 1/404; James, *Naval History*, 3:93.

40. Journal of the Fleet, 21, 22, and 29 Apr 1801, ADM 50/36; Meek MSS, KEI/47/3/209.

41. Menou to Forfait, 3 May 1801, in Rousseau, *Kléber et Menou*, 404; Bonaparte to Forfait, 18 Apr 1801, *CN*, 7:165; Rigault, *Menou*, 319; James, *Naval History*, 3:93.

42. Journal of the Fleet, 8–11 and 15 Jun 1801, ADM 50/36; Keith to [Mary], 17 Jun 1801, NMM, KEI/46/253; Bonaparte to Forfait, 11 Aug 1801, in Bonaparte, *Lettres inédites*, 1:33; James, *Naval History*, 3:94–95.

43. Cochrane to Keith, 24 Mar, Keith to Hutchinson, 25 Mar 1801, *KP*, 2:278–79; A. Anderson, *Journal*, 11 Apr 1801, 282.

44. Dundas to Abercromby, 6 Oct 1800, *KP*, 2:242–43.

45. Hutchinson to Keith, 27 Apr 1801, *KP*, 2:287; A. Anderson, *Journal*, 9 Apr 1801, 278.

46. Keith to Hutchinson, 29 Apr, Hutchinson to Keith, 4 May 1801, *KP*, 2:288, 290–91.

47. Wilson to Keith, 30 Apr 1801, NMM, KEI/18/7.

48. Stephenson to Keith, 27 May 1801, NMM, KEI/18/7; Keith to Stephenson, 15 May 1801, *KP*, 2:303.

49. Stephenson to Keith, 11 and 25 Jun 1801, NMM, KEI/18/7.

50. Meek MSS, KEI/47/3/394; Capitulation for the French under Belliard, 27 Jun 1801, in A. Anderson, *Journal*, 324–31.

51. Kapudan Pasha to Keith, 1 Jul 1801, NMM, KEI/15/3; Admiralty to Keith, 6 Oct 1800, Keith to Hutchinson, 5 Jul, Hutchinson to Keith, 13 Jul 1801, *KP*, 2:240–42; 327–31.

52. Keith to Mary, 11 Aug 1801, NMM, KEI/46/257.

53. Keith to Admiralty, 5 Aug 1801, ADM 1/405; Journal of the Fleet, 17 Aug 1801, ADM 50/36, pt. 2.

54. Keith to Cochrane, 23 Mar, 20 Apr 1801, NLS, MSS 2,569, 123–24, Cochrane to Keith, 20 Apr 1801, NLS, MSS 3,022, 20; Sailing Order, 17 May 1793, NMM, KEI/3.

55. Cochrane, Louis, and Martin to Keith, 9 May 1801, ADM 1/404.

56. Keith to Cochrane, Louis, and Martin, 10 May 1801, ADM 1/404; Captains of the Fleet to Keith, 11 May 1801, *KP*, 2:295. The captains were Alexander Cochrane, Thomas Louis, George Martin, Alexander Ball, William Hancock Kelly, John Elphinstone (no relation), Benjamin Hallowell, Will Hope, George Burlton, George Scott, and John Chambers White.

57. Keith to Captains of the Fleet, Captains of the Fleet to Keith, 11 May 1801, *KP*, 2:296–97.

58. Keith to Cochrane, 24 and 25 Mar, 12 May 1801, NLS, MSS 3,022, 24, 26, 42–43. The ravages of war made the purchase of cattle impossible (Gezar Pasha to Keith, 8 Jun 1801, NMM, KEI/15/1), but the Ottomans sent the British 100,000 lemons (Mustapha Bey to Keith, 15 Apr 1801, NMM, KEI/15/3).

59. Hallowell to Keith, 9 May 1801, ADM 1/404.

60. Hallowell to Keith, 9 May 1801, NLS, MSS 2,569, 133.

61. Keith to Nepean, 3 Nov 1801, ADM 1/405.

62. Hallowell to Keith, 11 May 1801, ADM 1/404.

63. Keith to Brown, 6 Jun, Brown to Keith, 6 Jun 1801, *KP*, 2:313–15.

64. Examination of Ault (Purser of the *Northumberland*), 7 Sep 1801, ADM 1/405; Sherwig, *Guineas and Gunpowder*, 133.

65. Keith to Nepean, 3 Nov 1801, ADM 1/405.

66. Nepean to Keith, 10 and 18 Nov 1802, NMM, KEI/L/33; Admiralty to Hollowell, 5 Jul 1804, Meek MSS, KEI/47/2/728.

67. Keith to Cochrane, 5 Jun 1801, NLS, MSS 2,569, 149–50; Cochrane to Keith, 5 Jun 1801, *KP*, 2:311–13.

68. Cochrane to Keith, 29 Aug 1801, ADM 1/405; Journal of the Fleet, 20 Jul 1801, ADM 50/36, pt. 2; Cochrane to Keith, 27 Aug 1801, NLS, MSS 2,569, 193.

69. John Elphinstone to Cochrane, 30 Jul 1801, NLS, MSS 2,569, 178.

70. Admiralty's note on letter from Keith to Nepean, 31 Jul 1801, ADM 1/405; Lavery, *Nelson's Navy*, 252.

71. Louis to Nepean, 30 Oct 1801, ADM 1/2068, L176; Martin to Nepean, 1 Nov 1801, ADM 1/2139, M66; St. Vincent to Keith, 4 Sep 1801, *LSV*, 1:221–23; St. Vincent to Markham, 27 Dec 1801, *Markham*, 2.

72. Keith to Markham, 23 Feb 1804, *Markham*, 153–54.

73. Keith to Mary, 2 Sep, 10 Nov 1801, NMM, KEI/46/258, 263; Cochrane's father to Cochrane's sister, 17 Dec 1801, NLS, MSS 2,569, 212–13.

74. Keith to Admiralty, 19 Feb 1802, Meek MSS, KEI/47/3/521–22; Nepean to Keith, 18 Nov 1802, NMM, KEI/L/33; St. Vincent to Markham, 27 Dec 1801, *Markham*, 2.

75. Keith to Markham, 13 Jun 1801, *Markham*, 102; Keith to Hutchinson, 5 Jul 1801, *KP*, 2:329–31.

76. Keith to Nepean, 27 Aug 1801, ADM 1/405; Coote to Keith, 22 Jul 1801, *KP*, 2:337.

77. Bickerton to Keith, 21 and 22 Aug 1801, *KP*, 2:344–45.

78. Bickerton to Cochrane, 22 Aug 1801, NLS, MSS 3,022, 69.

79. Keith to Nepean, 27 Aug, Ships in Alexandria, 2 Sep 1801, ADM 1/405; Articles of Capitulation, 30 Aug 1801, in A. Anderson, *Journal*, 373–84.

80. Keith to Nepean, 15 Sep 1801, ADM 1/405.

81. Keith to Nepean, 3 and 16 Sep 1801, ADM 1/405; *Journal of the Fleet*, 8, 11, and 13 Sep 1801, ADM 50/36, pt. 2; Saul, *Russia*, 153–57.

82. Keith to Nepean, 29 Oct 1801, ADM 1/405.

83. Nepean to Keith, 13 Dec 1801, NMM, KEI/L/33/157, 271; Mediterranean Fleet, 1 Oct 1801, ADM 8/82; Journal of the Fleet, 9 Mar 1802, ADM 50/36, pt. 2; Nepean to Keith, 30 Apr 1802, *KP*, 2:187.

84. Journal of the Fleet, 15 Apr 1802, ADM 50/36, pt. 2; Peace of Amiens, 27 Mar 1802, in Clercq, *Recueil des traités*, 1:484–94; Admiralty to Keith, 30 Apr 1802, *KP*, 2:187.

85. Keith to Mary, 24 Apr 1802, NMM, KEI/46/279; Dyott, *Diary*, 16 Oct 1801, 1:185.

86. Keith to Mary, 3 Apr 1802, NMM, KEI/46/275; St. Vincent to Nelson, 11 Aug 1801, *LSV*, 1:208.

87. Journal of the Fleet, 16 Jun, 3 Jul 1802, ADM 50/43, pt. 4; Marsden to Keith, 5 Jul 1802, NMM, KEI/L/33/283; Admiralty to Keith, 30 Apr 1802, *KP*, 2:187.

88. St. Vincent to Addington, 15 Nov 1801, *LSV*, 1:228; Cobbett, *Parliamentary History*, 35:1428–29, 36:191; Dyott, *Diary*, 6 Sep 1801, 1:174–75; Wilson, *Expedition to Egypt*, 149.

Chapter 7. "Such times require the ablest men that can be got": Keith in the North Sea (1803–7)

1. Keith to Mary, 30 Apr 1803, NMM, KEI/46/311. Quote in chapter title is from Keith to Markham, 21 Dec 1803, *Markham*, 121–22.

2. Meek MSS, KEI/47/3/578; St. Vincent to the King, 11 Mar 1803, *LCG3*, 4:84; Plymouth Report, 17 Mar 1803, *Naval Chronicle*, 9:245; Lavery, *Nelson's Navy*, 222.

3. St. Vincent to Keith, 31 Mar, entry 5 Apr 1801, *LSV*, 2:281–82.

4. Keith to [Mary], 20 Mar 1803, NMM, KEI/46/291; Plymouth Report, 24 Mar 1803, *Naval Chronicle*, 9:328; Albion, *Forests and Sea Power*, 316–23.

5. Keith to St. Vincent, 11 Mar 1803, *KP*, 3:13–14; Lavery, *Nelson's Navy*, 251.

6. St. Vincent to Dacres, 11 Mar 1803, *LSV*, 2:272–73.

7. St. Vincent to Keith, 11 and 19 Mar 1803, *LSV*, 2:273, 277–78.

8. Keith to [Mary], 19 Apr 1803, NMM, KEI/46/303; St. Vincent to Keith, 23 Apr 1803, *LSV*, 2:285–86.

9. Keith to [Mary], 8 May 1803, NMM, KEI/46/315; St. Vincent to Keith, 7 May 1803, *LSV*, 2:288; Admiralty to all Commanders-in-Chief, 15 May, Admiralty to Keith, 17 May 1803, *KP*, 3:14–15.

10. List of Ships in Keith's Command, 27 Jul 1804, BL, Add. MSS 41,081, 76–84; Secretary of the Admiralty to Keith, 10 Oct 1803, *KP*, 3:42–45; St. Vincent to Keith, 26 Jun 1803, *LSV*, 2:366–67; Lavery, *Nelson's Navy*, 246.

11. Monthly return of the North Sea Fleet, 1 Jan 1804, ADM 8/87; Keith to Markham, 23 Dec 1803, *Markham*, 124; Secretary of the Admiralty to Keith, 11 Oct 1803, *KP*, 3:42–45.

12. Keith to Markham, 24 Oct 1803, *Markham*, 110.

13. Keith to St. Vincent, 22 Jun, Markham to Keith, 19 Dec 1803, *KP*, 3:23, 59.

14. Keith to Markham, 13 Oct 1803, *Markham*, 108–9.

15. Keith to Markham, 25 Feb, 19 Mar 1804, *Markham*, 154–55, 163.

16. St. Vincent to Keith, 24 Nov 1803, *LSV*, 2:387–88; Keith to Markham, 24 Oct 1803, 22 Feb, 27 Mar 1804, *Markham*, 110, 153, 166.

17. Finers to Lake, 14 Jul, W. McDowal to his brother, 7 Jul 1803, *Letters Intercepted*, 34, 47–48.

18. Admiralty to Keith, 25 Jul 1803, *KP*, 3:187.

19. H. Barry to his brother, 25 Aug 1803, *Letters Intercepted*, 36.

20. Admiralty to Keith, 17 Oct 1803, ADM 2/1360; St. Vincent to Keith, 28 Jan 1804, *LSV*, 2:395; Keith to Secretary of the Admiralty, 20 Jul, Notice of Blockade, 14 Aug 1804, *KP*, 3:194–96; G. Rose, *Diaries*, 2 Oct 1803, 2:61.

21. Keith to Secretary of the Admiralty, 27 May–4 Jun 1803, ADM 1/535.

22. St. Vincent to Keith, 24 Jun 1803, *LSV*, 2:366.

23. Keith to Markham, 12 Nov 1803, *Markham*, 116–17.

24. Keith to Markham, 13 Oct 1803, 20 Mar 1804, *Markham*, 108–9, 164; St. Vincent to Keith, 23 Apr 1804, *LSV*, 2:238; Memorandum for the King and Cabinet, 11 Jan 1806, *Barham*, 3:108–18; Lavery, *Nelson's Navy*, 263.

25. Sous-commissaire de marine to Decrès, 14 Sep 1803, in Desbrière, *Projets et tentatives*, 3:218–19; Nepean to Keith, 29 Sep 1803, in Leyland, *Blockade of Brest*, 1:163–64.

26. Admiralty to Keith, 1 Oct 1803, ADM 2/1361; Keith to the Secretary of the Admiralty, 2 Oct, Owen to Keith, 7 Oct, *KP*, 3:41–42, 139–40.

27. Keith to Marsden, 12 Mar 1804, ADM 1/541; Keith to Duke of York, 21 Oct 1803, ADM 1/553; Keith to Markham, 11 Oct 1803, *Markham*, 108. These are the numbers in Keith's report. They differ slightly from the Admiralty's recommendation. (See Secretary of the Admiralty to Keith, 11 Oct 1803, *KP*, 3:42–45.) It should be assumed that Keith customized the deployment.

28. Thornbrough to Keith, 27 Jan 1804, ADM 1/540; Keith to Markham, 7 Jan, 19 Feb 1804, *Markham*, 132, 150–51; Keith to Duke of York, 21 Oct 1803, Keith to Thornbrough, 21 Feb, Intelligence Report, 9 May 1804, *KP*, 3:47–53, 70–71, 79.

29. Smith to Keith, 27 Dec 1803, General Observations by Keith to Marsden, 13 Feb 1804, ADM 1/540; Bonaparte to Davout, 6 Oct, Bonaparte to Bruix, 22 Nov, 3 Dec 1803, *CN*, 9:35–36, 127–28, 164.

30. Keith to Markham, 10 Nov 1803, 12 Jan 1804, *Markham*, 115, 135–37.

31. North Sea Report, 25 Mar 1804, *Naval Chronicle*, 11:340.

32. Keith to Markham, 9 Dec 1803, *Markham*, 118–19.

33. Owen to Keith, 26 Dec 1803, *Markham*, 128–31; Owen to Keith, 18 Apr 1804 (quote in text), *KP*, 3:72–74; McGuffie, "Stone Ships," 490–91.

34. Hobart to St. Vincent, 10 Feb, St. Vincent to Keith, 25 Apr 1804, *LSV*, 2:396–97, 406.

35. Keith to Markham, 18 Mar 1804, *Markham*, 162–63.

36. Keith to Hamond, 25 Feb 1804, ADM 1/540.

37. Margaron to Soult, 13 Apr 1804, Bruix to Napoleon, 13, 16 Apr 1804, in Desbrière, *Projets et tentatives*, 3:519–20, 558–61.

38. Keith to Nepean, 7 Jun 1803, ADM 1/535; MC to MH, 2 Aug 1803, *Letters Intercepted*, 83–84.

39. Board Minutes, 13 Jun 1803, ADM 3/147/696; Keith to Nepean, 30 Jun 1803, ADM 1/536; Keith to Marsden, 26 Jan 1804, ADM 1/540; Keith to Marsden, 18 Mar 1804, ADM 1/541; Hardyman to Keith, 15 Aug 1803, *KP*, 3:188–89.

40. Bonaparte to Bruix, 4 Oct, Decision, 11 Oct 1803, *CN*, 9:26–27, 61–62.

41. Keith to Marsden, 19 Apr 1804 (2 letters), ADM 1/541.

42. G. Rose, *Diaries*, 2 Oct 1803, 2:59.

43. Keith to Markham, 21 Dec 1803, 10 May 1804, *Markham*, 121–22, 175–76.

44. St. Vincent to Keith, 22 Apr 1804, *LSV*, 2:237; Montrose to Keith, 20 Apr 1804, *KP*, 3:212–13.

45. Keith to Melville, 19 Jun 1804, *KP*, 3:213.

46. Keith to Melville, 19 Jun 1804, *ibid.*, 3:213.

47. Keith's Remarks on queries proposed by Lord Melville, [May/June 1804?], BL, Add. MSS 41,081, 38–39.

48. Keith to Melville, 16 Nov 1804, NLS, MSS 9,733, 71–72.

49. Napoleon to Daugier, 2 Jul, Organization of the Flotilla, 3 Jul 1804, *CN*, 9:517–18, 524–29.

50. Melville to Keith, 6 Jun 1804, NLS, MS 9,733, 23–24.

51. Keith to Melville, 19 May 1804, BL, Add. MSS 41,081, 24; Gambier to Keith, 16 Jun 1804, NMM, KEI/26/1.

52. Melville to Keith, 23 and 26 May, Comparative view of the force under Keith's command, 11 May and 14 Sep 1804, BL, Add. MSS 41,081, 30–31, 36–37, 113.

53. Admiralty to Keith, 19 Jun 1803, *KP*, 3:21; Fulton to Pitt, 9 Aug 1805, *MCVC*, 5:86–87; Philip, *Robert Fulton*, 154–61. Philip says these weapons were known by such names as carcass, coffer, smack, hogshead, or torpedo; essentially, they were mines of up to two tons in weight that could be positioned against a target or in the proximity of one. Each was to be detonated by a clockwork mechanism (161).

54. Keith to Popham, 1 Oct 1804, BL Add. MSS 41,081, 135.

55. Keith to Secretary of Admiralty, 3 Oct, Popham to Keith, 4 Oct 1804, *KP*, 3:89–90, 93–94; Napoleon to Decrès, 6 Oct 1804, *CN*, 10:14–15; Bruix to Decrès, 3 Oct 1804, in Desbrière, *Projets et tentatives*, 4:139–41.

56. Keith to Melville, 5 and 8 Oct 1804, BL, Add. MSS 41,081, 148–49, 41,082, 10–11; Melville to Keith, 7 Oct 1804, *KP*, 3:95–96.

57. Keith to McMahon, 10 Apr 1805, *POW*, 5:208–9; Breihan, "Addington Party," 176–78; Harling, *Waning of 'Old Corruption,'* 82–88.

58. Harrowby to Bathurst, 21 Apr 1805, Camden to Bathurst, 22 Apr 1805, HMC, *Bathurst*, 45–48.

59. Barham to Keith, 1 May 1805 (two letters), NMM, KEI/26/1.

60. Barham to Keith, 25 Jul 1805, NMM, KEI/26/1; Admiralty to Keith, 22 Jul 1805, ADM 2/1363, 115–16.

61. Barham to Keith, [late July 1805], NMM, KEI/26/1; Barham to Keith, 31 Jul 1805 (two letters), *KP*, 3:112.

62. Keith to Barham, 1 Aug, Keith to Secretary of Admiralty, 15 Aug 1805, *KP*, 3:113–14; Napoleon to Marmont, 27 Jun 1805, *CN*, 10:698–700.

63. Hanson to Russell, received by Keith, 17 Aug, Keith to Marsden, 23 Aug 1805, ADM 1/552.

64. Keith to Melville, 28 Sep 1804, BL, Add. MSS 41,081, 129–30.

65. Barham to Keith, 24 Aug 1805, NMM, KEI/26/1; Keith to Marsden, 23 Aug 1805, ADM 1/552.

66. Napoleon to Marmont, 7 and 27 Jun 1805, *CN*, 10:611–12, 698–700.

67. Keith to Marsden, 11 Sep 1805, ADM 1/552.

68. Barham to Keith, 31 Aug, 4 and 9 Oct 1805, NMM, KEI/26/1.

69. Pitt to Castlereagh, 6 Oct 1805, *MCVC*, 5:117–18; Keith to Barham, 12 Oct 1805, *Barham*, 3:157–58.

70. Keith to Barham, 3 Oct 1805, *MCVC*, 5:112–13.

71. Keith to Smith, 14 Nov 1805, *KP*, 3:120; Keith to Smith, 5 Oct 1805, in Lloyd, "Congreve's Rockets," 4:431–32.

72. Smith to Castlereagh, 14 Oct 180[5], *MCVC*, 5:119–20.

73. Barham to Keith, [23 Oct 1805], *Barham*, 3:161–62.

74. Smith to Keith, 20 Nov 1805, in Lloyd, "Congreve's Rockets," 4:437–38. The British lost four wounded.

75. Barham to [Pitt], 18 Nov 1805, *Barham*, 3:170–71; Smith to Keith, 11 Dec 1805, in Lloyd, "Congreve's Rockets," 4:438.

76. Barham to Keith, 16 Oct 1805, NMM, KEI/26/1; Memorandum for the Consideration of the Cabinet, Sep 1805, Castlereagh to Keith, 18 Oct, 28 Nov 1805, *MCVC*, 6:6, 21, 58–60.

77. Keith to Barham, 1 Dec 1805, NMM, MID/1/60/38; Chronological Memorandum, 10 Oct–22 Dec 1805, *MCVC*, 6:36–37.

78. Castlereagh to Harrowby, 21 Dec 1805, List of the Eight Transports Wrecked, 15 Jan 1806, *MCVC*, 6:81–87, 125.

79. Castlereagh to Pitt, 23 Dec, Castlereagh to Keith, 29 Dec 1805, *MCVC*, 6:91–95.

80. Keith to Marden, 31 Dec 1805, ADM 1/552.

81. Keith to Marden, 24 Feb 1806, ADM 1/553; Castlereagh to Cathcart, 10 Jan, 4 Feb 1806, *MCVC*, 6:104–12, 127.

82. Keith to Barham, 2 May 1805, NMM, MID/1/60/2.

83. Barham to Keith, 18 Jul 1805, NMM, KEI/26/1.

84. Barham to Keith, 15 Oct 1805, NMM, KEI/26/1.

85. Keith to Thompson, 13 Nov 1805, NMM, MID/1/60/25.

86. Keith to Thompson, 29 Dec 1805, *Barham*, 3:178–79.

87. Barham to Keith, 8 Jan 1806, NMM, KEI/26/1; Barham, Memorandum for the King and Cabinet, 11 Jan 1806, *Barham*, 3:108–18; Keith to Barham, Dec 1804, *KP*, 3: 121–23.

88. Keith to Barham, 1 Feb 1806, *Barham*, 3:184.

89. Grenville to Keith, 4 Oct 1806, *KP*, 3:131–32.

90. Grenville to Keith, 3 and 20 Nov 1806, NMM, KEI/26/1; Board Minutes, 15 Oct, 15 Dec 1806, ADM 3/156/306, 673.

91. Dispositions of the North Sea Fleet, November 1805 to April 1807, ADM 8/90–93; Harvey, "Talents," 632–37.

92. Intelligence, 11 Jul 1806, ADM 1/4202; Keith to Secretary of Admiralty, 16 Jul 1806, *KP*, 3:130.

93. Congreve to Grenville, 8 Oct, Owen to Keith, 9 Oct 1806, in Lloyd, "Congreve's Rockets," 4:447–51.

94. Congreve to Grenville, 10 Oct 1806, ibid., 4:452–53.

95. Keith to Grenville, 21 and 24 Oct 1806, ibid., 4:454, 459.

96. Keith to Grenville, 24 Oct 1806, ibid., 4:459.

97. Hall, *British Strategy*, 153–56.

98. Keith to Secretary of Admiralty, 20 May 1807, *KP*, 3:132.

99. Lavery, *Nelson's Navy*, 246.

Chapter 8. "I lead a disagreeable life": Command of the Channel Fleet (1812–14)

1. Hyde, *Thrales*, 21, 276, 280–81.

2. Keith to Hester Lynch Piozzi, 1 Dec 1807, in Piozzi, *Letters*, 4:163–64.

3. Allardyce, *Memoir*, 348.

4. Mme d'Arblay [née Burney] to Waddington, 23 Sep 1813, in Burney, *Journals and Letters*, 7:182–87.

5. Hyde, *Thrales*, 280–81, 287. Keith invested a considerable sum in these estates. Although not all records are available, he paid £57,500 for Tullyallan in 1800, £3,750 for East Cliff in 1803, and £24,240 for Purbrook Park in 1806 (Jackson to Keith, 22 Apr 1800, 26 Dec 1803, NMM, KEI/24/2; Ledger Book, 30 Jun 1806, NMM, KEI/L/162).

6. Keith to Elliot of Willis, 26 Jan 1811, NLS, MSS 13,336, 189–90.

7. Keith to Speirs, 19 Jul 1811, NAS, GD 22/1/327; Charlotte to Margaret Mercer Elphinstone, 25 Sep 1811, in Aspinall, *Princess Charlotte*, 5–6.

8. Keith to Speirs, 19 Jul 1811, NAS, GD 22/1/327; Smith, *George IV*, 137–41.

9. Piozzi to Lady Keith, 29 Feb, Piozzi to John Salusbury Piozzi Salusbury, 29 Feb 1812, *Piozzi Letters*, 5:127–30; Admiralty to Keith, 24 Feb 1812, *KP*, 3:224; Krajeski, *Shadow of Nelson*, 190.

10. Keith to Fahie, 18 Mar 1812, NMM, KEI/L/57/20; List of French and British Forces, 29 Feb 1812, *KP*, 3:226.

11. King to Keith, 23 Mar, Durham to Keith, 23 Mar, Neale to Keith, 5 Apr 1812, ADM 1/148; Ferris to Keith, 11 Mar 1812, *KP*, 3:226–27.

12. Keith to Croker [Secretary of Admiralty], 20 Mar 1812, ADM 1/148.

13. Keith to Croker, 10 and 27 Apr 1812, ADM 1/148; Mme d'Arblay to Waddington, 18 Mar 1813, in Burney, *Journals and Letters*, 7:100–101.

14. Keith to Croker, 23 Apr 1812, NMM, KEI/L/55/167–68; Instructions to Keith, 24 Apr 1812, *KP*, 3:227–29.

15. Keith to Neale, 5 May, Keith to Durham, 5 May 1812, NMM, KEI/L/55/175–94.

16. Croker to Keith, 19 May 1812, NMM, KEI/43; Popham to Keith, 30 May 1812, *KP*, 3:267–68.

17. Herzog, "Salamanca Campaign," 63–64.

18. Diary of the Proceedings of the *Venerable* and Squadron, 22–28 Jun 1812, NMM, KEI/37/1.

19. Wellington to Popham, 4 Aug 1812, BL, Add. MSS 41,082, 118; Caffarelli to Marmont, 16 Jul 1812, in Marmont, *Mémoires*, 4:423–25.

20. Keith to Popham, 7, 30 Jul 1812, NMM, KEI/L/57/155–57, 170–72; Keith to Melville, 10 Aug 1812, BL, Add. MSS 41,082, 98.

21. Keith to Popham, 30 Jul, 9 Aug 1812, NMM, KEI/L/57/170–72, 184–86; Popham to Keith, 4 Aug 1812, NMM, KEI/37/2.

22. Melville to Keith, 18 Aug 1812, NMM, KEI/37/9; Keith to Melville, 28 Aug 1812, BL, Add. MSS 41,082, 101–2; Bathurst to Wellington, 8 Oct 1812, in Wellington, *Supplementary Despatches*, 7:446.

23. Keith to Popham, 5 Oct 1812, NMM, KEI/L/57/224–26.

24. Wellington to Popham, 12 Oct, NMM, KEI/37/2, Keith to Popham, 20 Oct 1812, NMM, KEI/L/57/241–42.

25. Popham to Keith, 7, 23 Dec 1812, NMM, KEI/37/2.

26. Keith to Salt [*Unicorn* (32)], 15 May 1812, NMM, KEI/L/57/92–93.

27. Melville to Keith, 11 Jun 1812, NMM, KEI/37/9.

28. Keith to Popham, 9 Aug 1812, NMM, KEI/L/57/181–83; Order in Council, 30 Jul 1812, Blackwood to Keith, 26 Feb, 3 and 12 Mar 1813, Neale to Keith, 14 Mar 1813, *KP*, 3:235, 237–39.

29. Keith to Croker, 13 Jul 1813, ADM 1/154. In detailing the British blockade of the United States between 1812 and 1815, Wade G. Dudley has emphasized the overextension of the British navy and its resulting inability to effectively blockade the American coast (*Splintering the Wooden Wall*, 2–5). In many respects the Channel Fleet, deployed much closer to Britain, faced a similar predicament even though this region had been a primary British theater of war for most of the previous two decades.

30. Keith to Melville, 28 Aug 1812, BL, Add. MSS 41,082, 101–2; Domett to Keith, 10 Feb 1813, NMM, KEI/37/9; Keith to Croker, 23 Jun 1813, ADM 1/154; Channel Fleet Dispositions, 1 Jul 1813, ADM 8/100.

31. Domett to Keith, 24 Nov 1812, Melville to Keith, 23 Aug 1813, NMM, KEI/37/9.

32. Keith to Melville, 8 May 1813, NLS, MSS 3,420, 100–101.

33. Keith to Croker, 23 Jun 1813, ADM 1/154; Official Summary of Instructions to Keith, 24 Apr 1812, *KP*, 3:227–29.

34. Keith to Melville, 13 Mar 1813, NLS, MSS 9,734, 7–8.

35. Collier to Keith, 21 Jun 1813, ADM 1/154; Wellington to Bathurst, 24 Jun, 2 Jul 1813, in Wellington, *Dispatches*, 10:458–59, 495.

36. Melville to Wellington, 28 Jul 1813, in Wellington, *Supplementary Despatches*, 8:144–47.

37. Keith to Croker, 23 Jun 1813, ADM 1/154.

38. List of Vessels under Collier, 21 Jul 1813, ADM 1/154; Keith to Wellington, 3 Jul 1813, *KP*, 3:293–94; Wellington to Collier, 22 Jul 1813, in Wellington, *Dispatches*, 10:561–62.

39. The best account of the siege is Herzog, "'Once More Unto the Breach.'"

40. Melville to Keith, 3 Sep 1813, NMM, KEI/37/9; State of Supplies carried into San Sebastián, 1 Jul–16 Aug (signed Songeon), Rey to Soult, 2, 15, 18, and 24 Aug, Depoge to Soult, 8, 18, and 19 Aug 1813, in Belmas, *Journaux des sièges*, 4:667, 677–79, 682–84, 691–98, 700–701; Collier to Graham, 21 Jul 1813, in Wellington, *Supplementary Despatches*, 8:98.

41. Wellington to Bathurst, 19 Aug 1813, in Wellington, *Dispatches*, 11:17–19.

42. Wellington to Melville, 21 Aug 1813, ibid., 9:26–28.

43. Keith to Collier, 31 Aug 1813, in Martin, *Letters and Papers*, 2:329–30.

44. Keith to Croker, 16 Jul, 15 Aug 1813, ADM 1/154; Wellington to Graham, 22 Aug 1813, in Wellington, *Dispatches*, 11:29.

45. Collier to Keith, 23 Aug, Melville to Keith, 24 Aug 1813, *KP*, 3:300–301.

46. Rey to Soult, 25 Aug 1813, Belmas, in *Journaux des sièges*, 4:709.

47. Keith to Collier, 14 Aug 1813, ADM 1/154.

48. Keith to Melville, 31 Aug 1813, NLS, MSS 9,734, 48–49.

49. Ibid.

50. Melville to Keith, 3 Sep 1813, NMM, KEI/37/9; Keith to Malcolm, 17 Aug 1813, ADM 1/154; Martin to Keith, 21 Sep, Martin's Observations involving Cooperation with the Army, 14 Sep 1813, in Martin, *Letters and Papers*, 2:385–89, 404–13.

51. Wellington to Bathurst, 24 Sep 1813, in Wellington, *Supplementary Despatches*, 8:272–75.

52. Domett to Keith, 2 Oct 1813, NMM, KEI/37/9; Keith to Collier, 6 Oct 1813, ADM 1/155.

53. Keith to Collier, 6 Oct 1813, ADM 1/155.

54. Keith to Croker, 10 Oct 1813, ADM 1/155.

55. Melville to Keith, 15 Oct 1813, NMM, KEI/37/9; Wellington to Bathurst, 1 Nov 1813, in Wellington, *Dispatches*, 11:238–41.

56. Keith to Croker, 18, 23, 27, and 30 Oct 1813, ADM 1/155; Hayes to Warren, 5 Feb 1814, *Naval Chronicle*, 33:423–24; Clowes, *Royal Navy*, 5:543–44.

57. Admiralty to Keith, 13 Dec 1813, ADM 2/1379/15; Hope to Keith, 8 and 29 Nov 1813, NMM, KEI/37/9; Napoleon to Decrès, 13 Jun 1813, *CN*, 25:446–47.

58. Keith to Croker, 18 Oct 1813, ADM 1/155.

59. French Frigates at Sea, 1814, NMM, KEI/40/4.

60. St. Vincent to Prince William Frederick, 11 Mar 1804, *LSV*, 2:356.

61. Melville to Keith, 18 Dec 1813, NMM, KEI/37/9; Dispositions on the North Coast of Spain, 5 Feb 1814, NMM, KEI/40/4; Collier to Keith, 10 Jan 1814, *KP*,

3:309–10; Wellington to Bathurst, 24 Sep 1813, in Wellington, *Supplementary Despatches*, 8:272–75.

62. Keith to Melville, 17 Jan 1814, NLS, MSS 3,420, 107–8; Penrose to Keith, 9 Feb 1814, NMM, KEI/37/12.

63. Melville to Keith, 27 Mar 1814, NMM, KEI/37/9.

64. Melville to Keith, 31 Mar 1814, NMM, KEI/37/9; Penrose to Keith, 7 Apr 1814, NMM, KEI/43, Memorial annex L; Penrose to Keith, 26 Mar 1814, *KP*, 3:250.

65. Letter of Termination of Hostilities, 30 Apr 1814, *KP*, 3:253–54.

66. Keith to Wellington, 16 May 1814, ADM 1/158; Keith to Melville, 10 Jun 1814, NLS, MSS 3,420, 109–10; Keith to Mary, 23 Jun 1814, NMM, KEI/46/330.

67. Keith to Mary, 27 Jun 1814, NMM, KEI/46/331.

68. Keith to Mary, 16 May 1814, NMM, KEI/46/328.

69. Keith to Croker, 20 and 29 Jul 1814, ADM 1/158; Allardyce, *Memoir*, 353.

Chapter 9. "I am doing my best to nab Nap!": The Fates of Keith and Napoleon (1815–23)

1. Piozzi to Alexander Leak, 16 Mar 1815, in Piozzi, *Letters*, 5:336–37. Quote in chapter title is from Keith to Lady Keith, 20 Jul 1815, *FN*, 152.

2. Admiralty to Keith, 28 Apr 1815, ADM 2/968/377; Melville to Keith, 22 May 1815, NMM, KEI/37/9.

3. Admiralty to Keith, 23 Jun 1815, ADM 2/1382/86; Keith to Lady Keith, 21 Jun 1815, *FN*, 142–43.

4. Admiralty General Order, 21 Jun 1815, ADM 2/166/540; Melville to Keith, 17 Jun 1815, NMM, KEI/37/9; Memorandum to Keith's Captains, 25 May 1815, NLS, MSS 9,734, 149.

5. Croker to Keith, 5 Jul 1815, NMM, KEI/37/9; Memorandum of Proceedings from June 24 to . . . Aug 17 1815, *KP*, 3:338–44; Keith to Lady Keith, 30 Jun 1815, *FN*, 146.

6. Admiralty to Keith, 30 Jun 1815, ADM 2/1382/125.

7. Keith to Lady Keith, 6 Jul 1815, *FN*, 148.

8. Croker to Keith, 14 Jul 1815, *KP*, 3:353.

9. Hotham to Keith, 3 Jun 1815, *KP*, 3:344; Marchand, *In Napoleon's Shadow*, 280–81; Las Cases, *Memorial de Sainte-Hélène*, 1:21.

10. Bertrand to Maitland, 14 Jul 1815, ADM 1/159; Marchand, *In Napoleon's Shadow*, 282; Las Cases, *Memorial de Sainte-Hélène*, 1:22; Gourgaud, *Journal de Sainte-Hélène*, 11, 14 Jul 1815, 1:40, 44.

11. Maitland to Keith, 18 Jul 1815, in Maitland, *Buonaparte*, 102–4.

12. Keith to Secretary of Admiralty, 22 Jul 1815, *KP*, 3:361–62; Napoleon to Prince Regent, 13 Jul 1815, in Maitland, *Buonaparte*, 56–57.

13. Maitland to Keith, 24 Jul 1815, *KP*, 3:363.

14. Melville to Keith, 25 Jul 1815, *FN*, 157–58; Las Cases, *Memorial de Sainte-Hélène*, 1:32.

15. Keith to Melville, 27 Jul 1815, *KP*, 3:369–70.

16. Proceedings (see note 5); Marchand, *In Napoleon's Shadow*, 316; Montholon, *Napoleon at St. Helena*, 1:43.

17. Keith to Margaret Mercer Elphinstone, 28 Jul 1815, *FN*, 159.

18. Proceedings (see note 5).

19. Memorandum on the Conference between Bunbury, Keith, and Napoleon signed by Bunbury, 31 Jul 1815, in C. Bunbury, *Memoir*, 297–304.

20. Enclosure, Keith to Melville, 31 Jul 1815, *FN*, 164–65.

21. Keith to Margaret Elphinstone, 3 Aug 1815, *FN*, 167–68. Although none of the French sources provides as many details of the meeting as Keith's letter and Bunbury's memorandum, they largely substantiate the information in the British documents; see Marchand, *In Napoleon's Shadow*, 317; Montholon, *Napoleon at St. Helena*, 1:44; Gourgaud, *Journal de Sainte-Hélène*, 31 Jul 1815, 1:49; Las Cases, *Memorial de Sainte-Hélène*, 1:33.

22. Keith to Margaret Elphinstone, 3 Aug 1815, *FN*, 167–68.

23. Proceedings (see note 5).

24. Keith to Margaret Elphinstone, 30 Jul 1815, *FN*, 162–63.

25. Proceedings (see note 5).

26. Melville to Keith, 10 Aug 1815, *KP*, 3:404. Melville's analysis appeared accurate, for Mackenrot was a West Indies merchant who had suffered through difficult times, and he blamed his financial problems on the Cochrane family. In 1814 he had published a volume entitled *Secret Memoirs of Cochrane Johnston and Sir Alex. Cochrane* in which he claimed that Alexander Cochrane, an admiral, committed fraudulent acts. This naval officer responded by charging Mackenrot with libel, and the West Indies merchant called Napoleon as a witness (*KP*, 3:334).

27. Keith to Lady Keith, 5 Aug 1815, *FN*, 168–69.

28. Proceedings (see note 5); Melville to Keith, 2 Aug 1815, *KP*, 385.

29. Mackenrot to Keith, 4 Aug 1815, in Allardyce, *Memoir*, 390; Keith to Melville, 5 Aug 1815, *KP*, 3:392.

30. Keith to Melville, 6 Aug 1815, *KP*, 3:393.

31. Admiralty to Keith, 2 Aug 1815, ADM 2/1382/192; Keith to Lady Keith, 5 Aug, Keith to Margaret Elphinstone, 5 Aug 1815, *FN*, 168–69; Maitland, *Buonaparte*, 168–70; *Journals of the House of Commons*, 12 Mar 1816, 71:185–86; ibid., 4 Apr 1816, 71:269, 289.

32. Keith to Melville, 7 Aug 1815, *FN*, 171–73; Marchand, *In Napoleon's Shadow*, 320, 329.

33. Las Cases, *Memorial de Sainte-Hélène*, 1:42–43.

34. Montholon, *Napoleon at St. Helena*, 1:46.

35. Keith to Margaret Elphinstone, 13 Aug 1815, *FN*, 175–77. The *Tonnant* was one of the prizes taken by Nelson at Aboukir Bay in 1798. Strangely enough, the *Bellerophon* was one of Nelson's ships at Aboukir Bay.

36. Proceedings (see note 5).

37. Keith to Margaret (see note 35).

38. Melville to Keith, 14 Aug 1815, in Allardyce, *Memoir*, 412.

39. Keith to Margaret (see note 35).

40. Keith's Journal, 19 Aug 1815, *ibid.*, 177.

41. Note attached to file, NMM, KEI/46; Hyde, *Thrales*, 299, 319.

42. Lieven to Alexander Benckendorff, 8 Dec 1814, in Lieven, *Letters*, 11–12.

43. Aspinall, *Princess Charlotte*, xii, xxi; Stacton, *Bonapartes*, 16–17, 258. The illegitimate son was Auguste, duc de Morny. A half brother to Louis Napoleon, he served prominently during the Second Empire (Stacton, *Bonapartes*, 258, 287–88).

44. Lieven to Alexander Benckendorff, 9 Jan 1816, in Lieven, *Letters*, 21–23; Guedalla, *Secret*, 58.

45. Keith to Mary, 28th [?], NMM, KEI/46/336; d'Arblay to Mme d'Arblay, 14 Jun, 22 Jul 1817, in Burney, *Journals and Letters*, 10:469, 575.

46. Keith to Mary, 5 Jun 1817, NMM, KEI/46/335.

47. Keith to Mary, 3 Jun 1817, NMM, KEI/46/334; Guedalla, *Secret*, 58–59.

48. Lieven to Alexander, 1 Jul 1817, in Lieven, *Letters*, 32–33.

49. Keith to Melville, 15 Jun 1815, NLS, MSS 9,734, 161–62; Burney, *Journals and Letters*, 9:310. The couple returned to France after the formation of the July Monarchy in 1830, and the comte de Flahaut served both Louis Philippe and Napoleon III primarily as an ambassador. This included an appointment to the Court of St. James's in 1860. She died leaving five daughters but no sons (*Burke's Peerage*, 2:1637).

50. Mme d'Arblay to H.R.H. Princess Elizabeth, 27 Feb 1819, in Burney, *Journals and Letters*, 11:57–66.

51. Lady Keith to Mme d'Arblay, 3 Apr 1823, BL, Eg. 3,698, 198–99.

52. Lady Keith to Mme d'Arblay, 19 Feb, 3 Apr 1823, BL, Eg. 3,698, 194–95, 198.

53. Lady Keith to Mme d'Arblay (see note 51); Hyde, *Thrales*, 319, 323. Charles Elphinstone Fleming was the second son of John, 11th Lord Elphinstone, Keith's eldest brother.

54. Obituary, *Gentleman's Magazine*, March 1823, 273.

Conclusion. "He has generally stood high in estimation, as an officer"

1. Hotham, *Pages and Portraits*, 2:32. Quote in chapter title is from Admiral William Young, 12 Jan [1801], BL, Add. MSS 46,712, 17.

2. G. K. Elphinstone to Charles Elphinstone, 9 May 1764, NAS, GD 156/6/8/2.

3. Nelson to Ball, 22 Oct 1804, *DLN*, 6:250.

4. Keith to Mary, 21 Jan 1797, NMM, KEI/46/89.

5. Jackson to Keith, 6 May 1800, Statement of Prize money and Freight Money, 30 Nov 1799–11 Nov 1801, *KP*, 2:394, 3:218.

6. Jackson to Keith, 15 Sep 1812, NMM, KEI/37/9.

7. Account of Keith with John Jackson, 1795–1807, NMM, KEI/L/165; Pay for Admiral Lord Keith, 19 May 1803–24 Feb 1807, ADM 24/001, 40.

8. Rose to Keith, 13 Jul 1814, NMM, KEI/42.

9. This amount may actually be closer to half a million pounds. It is very difficult to ascertain the exact figure. Keith held many commands, and the distribution of the money occurred very slowly. Keith dealt with several prize agents, essentially lawyers skilled in the workings of Admiralty Prize Courts who handled the collection and distribution of the money. Keith's papers in the National Maritime Museum do not contain complete records from every prize agent. Information on freight money is likewise incomplete. Freight money was the payment Keith received for the shipment of specie. A captain usually received 1 percent of its value, and the commander in chief received one-third of the captain's share (N.A.M. Rodger, *Wooden World*, 318).

10. Collingwood to his sister, 1 Jan 1805, in Collingwood, *Correspondence*, 169.

11. Jackson to Keith, 22 Apr 1800, NMM, KEI/24/2.

12. Lieven to Alexander, 1 Jul 1817, in Lieven, *Letters*, 32–33.

13. Meek MSS, KEI/47/1/6.

14. Keith to William Elphinstone, 28 Mar 1800, NMM, KEI/46/206.

15. Anonymous letter to Keith, 8 May 1813, NMM, KEI/37/9.

16. Hotham, *Pages and Portraits*, 2:32.

17. Keith to Markham, 22 Dec 1803, *Markham*, 123.

18. Keith to Jones [*Ville de Paris*], 23 Jul 1813, ADM 1/154.

19. This supports the contention made by Brian Lavery that "his historical reputation rests on his meticulous organisation of complex fleets . . . and in his expertise on amphibious warfare" ("George Keith Elphinstone," 399).

20. Cleghorn to Hobart, Dec 1796–Jan 1796, in Cleghorn, *Papers*, 239.

Bibliography

Archival and Unpublished Sources

BRITISH LIBRARY, LONDON (BL)

Barrett Collection. BL, Egerton MSS 3,698.
Melville, 1st and 2nd Viscounts. Correspondence with George Keith Elphinstone, Viscount Keith, 1797–1821. BL, Add. MSS 41,081–82.
Paget, Arthur. Paget Papers. BL, Add. MSS 48,397.
Young, G. F. Young Papers. BL, Add. MSS 46,712, 46,714.

INDIA OFFICE, LONDON (IO)

Elphinstone, William. William Elphinstone Papers. IO, European Manuscripts, MSS EUR F/89/131.

THE NATIONAL ARCHIVES [FORMERLY PUBLIC RECORD OFFICE], LONDON

Admiralty Office Papers (ADM).

NATIONAL ARCHIVES OF SCOTLAND [FORMERLY SCOTTISH RECORD OFFICE], EDINBURGH (NAS)

Cunninghame Graham Muniments. Section 19–Legal and Financial Documents. NAS, GD/22.
———. Section 39–Title Deeds and Estate Papers. NAS, GD/22.
Elphinstone Muniments. Juvenile Letters of George Keith Elphinstone. NAS, GD/156/6/8.
Robertson of Lude Muniments, 1448–1923. Family Provision and Inheritance. NAS, GD/132/338.

NATIONAL LIBRARY OF SCOTLAND, EDINBURGH (NLS)

Cochrane, Alexander. Correspondence and Papers of Admiral the Hon. Sir Alexander Cochrane, 1801–1804. NLS, MSS 2,569, 3,022.
Elliot, Gilbert, 1st Earl Minto. Minto Local Affairs, 1811. NLS, MSS 13,336.
Elphinstone, George Keith, 1st Viscount Keith. Miscellaneous Correspondence, 1813–1815. NLS, MSS 3,420.
Graham, Thomas, Lord Lynedoch. Correspondence. NLS, MSS 3,595, 3,598, 3,600–602.

Melville, 1st and 2nd Viscounts. Correspondence with Related Papers 1797–1815 between Henry Dundas, 1st Viscount Melville, and Robert Saunders Dundas, and Viscount Melville, as First Lords of the Admiralty, and Admiral George Keith Elphinstone, Viscount Keith, largely during his commands in the Mediterranean, 1798–1802, and North Sea and Channel 1803–1815. NLS, MSS 9,733–34.
Stuart, Sir Charles. Letters with Lord Keith, 1798–99. NLS, MSS 7,199.

NATIONAL MARITIME MUSEUM, GREENWICH (NMM)

Elliot, Gilbert, 1st Earl Minto. Minto Naval Papers (1751–1814). NMM, ELL/139.
Elphinstone, George Keith, 1st Viscount Keith. Keith Manuscripts. NMM, KEI.
Meek, James. MSS Meek's Draft on the Life of Keith. NMM, KEI/47.
Middleton, Charles, 1st Baron Barham. The Papers of Charles Middleton, Lord Barham. NMM, MID.
Nepean, Sir Evan, 1st Baronet. Papers of Sir Evan Nepean, bart. NMM, NEP/4–7.
Stephenson, Thomas. Papers of Captain Thomas Stephenson. NMM, STE/2.

WILLIAM R. PERKINS LIBRARY, DUKE UNIVERSITY, DURHAM, N.C.

Hamond, Sir Andrew Snape. Andrew Snape Hamond Papers.

Published Sources

Acerra, Martine, José Merino, and Jean Meyer, eds. Les Marines de guerre européennes, XVII–XVIIIe siècles. Paris: Presses de l'Université de Paris–Sorbonne, 1985.
Albion, Robert Greenhalgh. Forests and Sea Power: The Timber Problem of the Royal Navy, 1652–1862. Cambridge, Mass.: Harvard University Press, 1926.
Allardyce, Alexander. Memoir of the Honourable George Keith Elphinstone, K.B., Viscount Keith, Admiral of the Red. Edinburgh: William Blackwood, 1882.
Anderson, Æneas. A Journal of the Forces, which sailed from the Downs, in April 1800, . . . through all the subsequent transactions of the army under the command of the Right Hon. General Sir Ralph Abercromby, K.B. in the Mediterranean and Egypt . . . London: J. Debrett, 1802.
Anderson, R. C. Naval Wars in the Levant, 1559–1853. Princeton: Princeton University Press, 1952.
Arthur, Charles B. The Remaking of the English Navy by Admiral St. Vincent: Key to the Victory over Napoleon; The Greatest Unclaimed Naval Revolution (1795–1805). Lanham, Md.: University Press of America, 1986.
Aspinall, A., ed. Correspondence of George, Prince of Wales, 1770–1812. 8 vols. New York: Oxford University Press, 1963–71.

————, ed. *The Later Correspondence of George III.* 5 vols. Cambridge: Cambridge University Press, 1962–70.

————, ed. *Letters of the Princess Charlotte, 1811–1817.* London: Home and Van Thal, 1949.

Bain, James, Jr., ed. "The Siege of Charleston: Journal of Captain Peter Russell, December 26, 1779 to May 2, 1779." *American Historical Review* 4 (1890): 478–501.

Balderston, Marion, and David Syrett, eds. *The Lost War: Letters from British Officers during the American Revolution.* New York: Horizon, 1975.

Barham, John Middleton, Baron. *Letters and Papers of Charles, Lord Barham, Admiral of the Red Squadron, 1758–1813.* Edited by John Knox Laughton. 3 vols. London: Navy Records Society, 1907–11.

Barnard, Anne Lindsay. *The Letters of Lady Anne Barnard to Henry Dundas, from the Cape and Elsewhere, 1793–1803.* Edited by A. M. Lewin Robinson. Cape Town: A. A. Balkema, 1973.

Barras, Paul. *Memoirs of Barras: Member of the Directorate.* Edited by George Duruy. Translated by Charles E. Roche. 4 vols. New York: Harper and Brothers, 1895–96.

Barrow, John. *The Life and Correspondence of Admiral Sir William Sidney Smith.* 2 vols. London: R. Bentley, 1848.

Belmas, Jacques V. *Journaux des sièges faits ou soutenus par les Français dans la péninsule, de 1807 à 1814: Rédigés d'après les ordres du Gouvernement, sur les documents existant aux Archives de la guerre et au Dépôt des fortifications.* 4 vols. and atlas. Paris: Firmin Didot, 1836–37.

Bonaparte, Napoleon. *Correspondance de Napoleon 1er: Publiée par ordre de l'empereur Napoleon III.* 32 vols. Paris: Imprimerie Imperiale, 1858–69.

————. *Lettres inédites de Napoléon Ier (An VIII–1815).* Edited by Léon Lecestre. 2 vols. Paris: E. Plon, Nourrit, 1897.

Breihan, John R. "The Addington Party and the Navy in British Politics 1801–1806." In *New Aspects of Naval History: Selected Papers Presented at the Fourth Naval History Symposium, United States Naval Academy. 25–26 October 1979,* edited by Craig L. Symonds et al., 163–89. Annapolis, Md.: Naval Institute Press, 1981.

Brown, David J. "'Nothing but Strugalls and Corruption:' The Commons Elections for Scotland in 1774." *Parliamentary History* 15 (1996): 100–119.

Bruijn, Japp R. *The Dutch Navy of the Seventeenth and Eighteenth Centuries.* Columbia: University of South Carolina Press, 1993.

Brun, Vincent-Félix. *Guerres maritimes de la France: Port de Toulon, ses armements, son administration, depuis son origine jusqu'à nos jours.* 2 vols. Paris: Henri Plon, 1861.

Bunbury, Charles J. F., ed. *Memoir and Literary Remains of Lieutenant-General Sir Henry Edward Bunbury, Bart.* London: Spottiswoode, 1868.

Bunbury, Henry. *Narratives of Some Passages in the Great War with France (1799–1810).* 1854. London: Davies, 1927.

Burke's Peerage and Baronetage. Edited by Charles Mosley. 106th ed. 2 vols. London: Fitzroy Dearborn, 1999.

Burney, Fanny. *The Journals and Letters of Fanny Burney (Madame D'Arblay).* Edited by Joyce Hemlow et al. 12 vols. Oxford: Clarendon Press, 1972–84.

Carlan, J. M. *Navios en secuestro: La Escuadra Española del Océano en Brest (1799–1802).* Madrid: Instituto Histórico de Marina, 1951.

Chadwick, French Ensor, ed. *The Graves Papers and Other Documents Relating to the Naval Operations of the Yorktown Campaign July to October, 1781.* New York: De Vinne, for the Naval History Society, 1916.

Chandler, David G. *The Campaigns of Napoleon.* New York: Macmillan, 1966.

———. *Dictionary of the Napoleonic Wars.* New York: Macmillan, 1979.

Christie, Ian R. "The Anatomy of the Opposition in the Parliament of 1784." *Parliamentary History* 9 (1990): 50–77.

Clark, William Bell, et al., eds. *Naval Documents of the American Revolution.* 10 vols. Washington, D.C.: Government Printing Office, 1964–.

Clay, Christopher. "Marriage, Inheritance, and the Rise of Large Estates in England, 1660–1815." *Economic History Review,* 2nd ser., 21 (1968): 503–18.

Cleghorn, Hugh. *The Cleghorn Papers, a Footnote to History: Being the Diary, 1795–1796, of Hugh Cleghorn of Stravithie.* Edited by William Neil. London: A. and C. Black, 1927.

Clercq, A. de, ed. *Recueil des traités de la France.* 23 vols. Paris: A. Durand et Pédone-Lauriel, 1880–1917.

Clinton, Henry. *The American Rebellion: Sir Henry Clinton's Narrative of His Campaigns, 1775–1782, with an Appendix of Original Documents.* Edited by William B. Willcox. New Haven, Conn.: Yale University Press, 1954.

Clowes, William Laird, with Clements Markham, A. T. Mahan, H. W. Wilson, Theodore Roosevelt, and L. Carr Laughton. *The Royal Navy: A History from the Earliest Times to the Present.* 7 vols. London: Sampson Low, Marston, 1897–1903.

Cobbett, William, ed. *Cobbett's Parliamentary History of England.* 36 vols. London: R. Bagshaw (vols. 1–7); Longmans (vols. 8–36), 1806–20.

Cochrane, Thomas, 10th Earl of Dundonald. *The Autobiography of a Seaman.* 1860. London: Maclaren, n.d.

Cokayne, George E. *The Complete Peerage of England, Scotland, Ireland, Great Britain and The United Kingdom, Extant, Extinct or Dormant.* 13 vols. London: St. Catherine Press, 1910–59.

Colledge, J. J. *Ships of the Royal Navy: An Historical Index.* 2 vols. New York: A. M. Kelley, 1969.

Collingwood, Cuthbert. *The Private Correspondence of Admiral Lord Collingwood.* Edited by Edward Hughes. London: Navy Records Society, 1957.

Colombos, C. John. *The International Law of the Sea.* 6th ed. London: Longmans, 1967.

Crook, Malcolm. *Toulon in War and Revolution: From the Ancien Régime to the Restoration, 1750–1820.* Manchester: Manchester University Press, 1991.

Davies, K. G., ed. *Documents of the American Revolution, 1770–1783 (Colonial Office Series).* 21 vols. Shannon: Irish University Press, 1972–.

Delavoye, Alexander Marin. *Life of Thomas Graham, Lord Lynedoch.* London: Richardson, 1880.

Derry, John W. *Politics in the Age of Fox, Pitt and Liverpool: Continuity and Transformation.* Basingstoke, Hants: Macmillan, 1990.

Desbrière, Édouard. *1793–1805, Projets et tentatives de débarquement aux Îles britanniques.* 4 vols. Paris: Libraire Militaire R. Chapelot, 1900–1902.

Deutsch, Phyllis. "Moral Trespass in Georgian London: Gaming, Gender, and Electoral Politics in the Age of George III." *Historical Journal* 39 (1996): 637–56.

Dictionary of National Biography. Edited by Leslie Stephen and Sidney Lee. 1885–1901. 22 vols. London: Oxford University Press, 1949–50.

Douin, Georges. *La Campagne de Bruix en Mediterranée, mars–août 1799.* Paris: Société d'éditions géographiques, maritimes et coloniales, 1923.

Dudley, Wade G. *Splintering the Wooden Wall: The British Blockade of the United States, 1812–1815.* Annapolis, Md.: Naval Institute Press, 2003.

Dugan, James. *The Great Mutiny.* New York: Putnam, 1965.

Dunfermline, James Abercromby, Lord. *Lieutenant-General Sir Ralph Abercromby, K.B., 1793–1801: A Memoir.* Edinburgh: Edmonston and Douglas, 1861.

Dyott, William. *Dyott's Diary, 1781–1845: A Selection from the Journal of William Dyott, Sometime General in the British Army and Aide-de-Camp to His Majesty King George III.* Edited by Reginald W. Jeffery. 2 vols. London: A. Constable, 1907.

Ehrman, John. *The Younger Pitt.* 3 vols. Stanford, Calif.: Stanford University Press, 1983–96.

Ewald, Johann. *Diary of the American War: A Hessian Journal.* Translated and edited by Joseph P. Tustin. New Haven, Conn.: Yale University Press, 1979.

Fedorak, Charles J. "Catholic Emancipation and the Resignation of William Pitt in 1801." *Albion* 24 (Spring 1992): 49–64.

Fortescue, John W., ed. *The Correspondence of King George the Third from 1760 to December 1783.* 6 vols. London: Macmillan, 1927–28.

Fraser, William. *The Elphinstone Family Book of the Lords Elphinstone, Balmerino and Coupar*. 2 vols. Edinburgh: T. and A. Constable at Edinburgh University Press, 1897.

Furber, Holden, ed. *A Private Record of an Indian Governor-Generalship: The Correspondence of Sir John Shore, Governor-General, with Henry Dundas, President of the Board of Control, 1793–1798*. Cambridge, Mass.: Harvard University Press, 1933.

Gachot, Édouard. *Histoire militaire de Masséna: Le Siège de Gênes (1800); la guerre dans L'Apennin; journal du blocus; les opérations de Suchet*. Paris: Plon-Nourrit, 1908.

Ginter, Donald E. "The Financing of the Whig Party Organization, 1783–1793." *American Historical Review* 71 (1966): 1–40.

———, ed. *Voting Records of the British House of Commons, 1761–1820*. 6 vols. London: Hambledon, 1995.

———, ed. *Whig Organization in the General Election of 1790: Selections from the Blair Adam Papers*. Berkeley and Los Angeles: University of California Press, 1967.

Gourgaud, Gaspard, Baron. *Journal de Sainte-Hélène, 1815–1818*. Edited by Octave Aubry. 2 vols. Paris: Flammarion, 1944.

Graham, Murray. "A Footnote to the Elphinstones in Catherine the Great's Navy." *Mariner's Mirror* 85 (February 1999): 92–93.

Guedalla, Philip. *The Secret of the Coup d'État: Unpublished Correspondence of Prince Louis Napoleon, MM. de Morny, de Flahault, and others, 1848 to 1852*. New York: Putnam, 1924.

Guillon, Édouard. *La France et l'Irlande pendant la Révolution: Hoche et Humbert*. Paris: Colin, 1888.

Habakkuk, H. J. "Marriage Settlements in the Eighteenth Century." *Transactions of the Royal Historical Society*, 4th ser., 32 (1950): 15–30.

Hall, Christopher D. *British Strategy in the Napoleonic War, 1803–15*. Manchester: Manchester University Press, 1992.

———. "The Royal Navy and the Peninsular War." *Mariner's Mirror* 79 (November 1993): 403–18.

Harding, Richard. "Sailors and Gentlemen of Parade: Some Professional and Technical Problems Concerning the Conduct of Combined Operations in the Eighteenth Century." *Historical Journal* 32 (1989): 35–55.

Harling, Philip. *The Waning of 'Old Corruption': The Politics of Economical Reform in Britain, 1779–1846*. Oxford: Clarendon Press, 1996.

Harlow, Vincent T. "The British Occupations, 1795–1806." In *The Cambridge History of the British Empire*, vol. 8, *South Africa, Rhodesia and the High Commis-*

sion Territories. Edited by A. P. Newton, E. A. Benians, and Eric A. Walker. New York: Macmillan, 1936.

Harvey, A. D. "The Ministry of All the Talents: The Whigs in Office, February 1806 to March 1807." *Historical Journal* 15 (December 1972): 619–48.

Hatch, Marie M., ed. "Letters of Captain Sir John Jervis to Sir Henry Clinton, 1774–1782." *American Neptune* 7 (1947): 87–106.

Herzog, Richard T. "'Once More Unto the Breach': Military and Naval Operations Around San Sebastian, June–September 1813." M.A. thesis, Florida State University, 1991.

———. "The Royal Marine and Insurgent Operations in the Salamanca Campaign, 1812." In *Proceedings, 1992: Consortium on Revolutionary Europe, 1750–1850*. Edited by Gordon C. Bond, 62–69. Tallahassee: Institute on Napoleon and the French Revolution, 1993.

Hibbert, Christopher. *George IV*. Vol. 1, *Prince of Wales, 1762–1811*. London: Longman, 1972.

Hill, Richard. *The Prizes of War: The Naval Prize System in the Napoleonic Wars, 1793–1815*. Stroud, Glos.: Royal Naval Museum, 1998.

Historical Manuscripts Commission. 30th series. *The Manuscripts of J. B. Fortescue, Esq., preserved at Dropmore*. 10 vols. London: HMSO, 1892–1927.

———. 59th series. *Report on American Manuscripts in the Royal Institution of Great Britain*. 4 vols. London: HMSO, 1904–9.

———. 76th series. *Report on the Manuscripts of Earl Bathurst Preserved at Cirencester Park*. London: HMSO, 1923.

Horward, Donald D. "British Seapower and Its Influence Upon the Peninsular War (1808–1814)." *Naval War College Review* 31 (Fall 1978): 54–71.

Hotham, William. *Pages and Portraits from the Past: Being the Private Papers of Sir William Hotham, GCB, Admiral of the Red*. Edited by A.M.W. Stirling. 2 vols. London: H. Jenkins, 1919.

Hyde, Mary, ed. *The Thrales of Streatham Park*. Cambridge, Mass.: Harvard University Press, 1977.

Ingram, Edward. *Commitment to Empire: Prophesies of the Great Game in Asia, 1797–1800*. Oxford: Clarendon Press, 1981.

———. "Geopolitics of the First British Expedition to Egypt—Part I: The Cabinet Crisis of September 1800." *Middle Eastern Studies* 30 (July 1994): 435–60.

James, William. *The Naval History of Great Britain, From the Declaration of War by France . . . 1793, to the Accession of George IV . . .: A New Edition, with Additions and Notes, and An Account of the Burmese War and the Battle of Navarino*. Edited by Captain [Frederick] Chamier. 6 vols. London: Richard Bentley, 1837.

Jenkins, E. H. *A History of the French Navy: From Its Beginnings to the Present Day*. London: MacDonald and Jane's, 1973.

Jensen, Merrill, ed. *American Colonial Documents to 1776.* New York: Oxford University Press, 1955.

Jonquière, Clément de la. *L'expédition d'Égypte, 1798–1801.* 5 vols. Paris: H. Charle-Lavauzelle, 1899–1907.

Journals of the House of Commons. 1774–75, 1780–81, 1796, 1816.

Kerry, Henry William Edmund Petty Fitzmaurice, Earl of, ed. *The First Napoleon: Some Unpublished Documents from the Bowood Papers.* Boston: Houghton Mifflin, 1925.

King, Dean. *A Sea of Words: A Lexicon and Companion for Patrick O'Brian's Seafaring Tales.* 2nd ed. New York: Henry Holt, 1997.

Knight, R.J.B., ed. *Guide to the Manuscripts in the National Maritime Museum.* Vol. 1, *The Personal Collections.* London: Mansell, 1977.

Krajeski, Paul C. *In the Shadow of Nelson: The Naval Leadership of Admiral Sir Charles Cotton, 1753–1812.* Westport, Conn.: Greenwood, 2000.

Las Cases, Emmanuel. *Memorial de Sainte-Hélène: Journal of the Private Life and Conversations of the Emperor Napoleon at Saint Helena.* 3 vols. Boston: Wells and Lilly, 1823.

Laughton, John Knox, ed. "Extracts from the Papers of Samuel, First Viscount Hood." In *The Naval Miscellany,* 1:221–58. London: Navy Records Society, 1902.

———, ed. "Operations on the Coast of Egypt, 1801." In *The Naval Miscellany,* 2:333–49. London: Navy Records Society, 1912.

Lavery, Brian. "George Keith Elphinstone, Lord Keith, 1746–1823." In *Precursors of Nelson: British Admirals of the Eighteenth Century.* Edited by Peter Le Fevre and Richard Harding, 377–99. Mechanicsburg, Pa.: Stackpole, 2000.

———. *Nelson's Navy: The Ships, Men, and Organisation, 1793–1815.* Rev. ed. Annapolis, Md.: Naval Institute Press, 1994.

Lawson, Phillip. "Grenville's Election Act, 1770." *Bulletin of the Institute of Historical Research* 53 (1980): 218–28.

Letters Intercepted on Board the Admiral Aplin, Captured by the French. Translated from the French. London: A. Wilson, 1804.

Lewis, Bernard. "The Impact of the French Revolution on Turkey." *Journal of World History* 1 (1953): 105–25.

Leyland, John, ed. *Dispatches and Letters Relating to the Blockade of Brest, 1803–1805.* 2 vols. London: Navy Records Society, 1899–1902.

Lieven, Doroteya Khristoforovna. *Letters of Dorothea, Princess Lieven, During Her Residence in London, 1812–1834.* Edited by L. G. Robinson. London: Longmans, 1902.

Lloyd, Christopher, ed. "Congreve's Rockets." In *The Naval Miscellany,* 4:428–61. London: Navy Records Society, 1952.

Londonderry, Charles Vane, Marquess of, ed. *Memoirs and Correspondence of Viscount Castlereagh*. 12 vols. London: H. Colburn, 1848–53.

Lyon, David. *The Sailing Navy List: All the Ships of the Royal Navy—Built, Purchased and Captured, 1688–1860*. London: Conway Maritime Press, 1993.

Mackesy, Piers. *British Victory in Egypt, 1801: The End of Napoleon's Conquest*. London: Routledge, 1995.

———. "'Most Sadly Bitched': The British Cadiz Expedition of 1800." In *Les Empires en guerre et paix, 1793–1860*. Edited by Edward Freeman, 41–57. Vincennes: Service Historique de la Marine, 1990.

Maitland, Frederick Lewis. *Narrative of the Surrender of Buonaparte and of His Residence on Board H.M.S. Bellerophon: With a Detail of the Principal Events That Occurred in That Ship, Between the 24th of May and the 8th of August, 1815*. 2nd ed. London: H. Colburn, 1826.

Manwaring, George Ernest, and Bonamy Dobrée. *The Floating Republic: An Account of the Mutinies at Spithead and the Nore in 1797*. London: Geoffrey Bles, 1935.

Marchand, Louis-Joseph-Narcisse. *In Napoleon's Shadow: Being the First English Language Edition of the Complete Memoirs of Louis-Joseph Marchand, Valet and Friend of the Emperor, 1811–1821*. Edited by Jean Bourguignon and Henry Lachouque. San Francisco: Proctor Jones, 1998.

Markham, Clemens, ed. *Selections from the Correspondence of Admiral John Markham during the Years 1801–4 and 1806–7*. London: Navy Records Society, 1904.

Marmont, Auguste-Frédéric-Louis Weisse de. *Mémoires du maréchal Marmont, duc de Raguse, de 1792 à 1841, imprimés sur le manuscrit original de l'auteur*. 2nd ed. 9 vols. Paris: Perrotin, 1857.

Marshall-Cornwall, James Handyside. *Marshal Massena*. London: Oxford University Press, 1965.

Martin, Thomas Byam. *Letters and Papers of Admiral of the Fleet Sir Thos. Byam Martin, G.C.B.* Edited by Richard Vesey Hamilton. 3 vols. London: Navy Records Society, 1898–1903.

Masséna, André. *Mémoires d'André Masséna, duc de Rivoli, prince d'Essling, maréchal d'Empire*. Edited by Jean-Baptiste Koch. 7 vols. 1848–50. Paris: J. de Bonnot, 1966.

McCahill, William W. "The Scottish Representative Peers and Parliamentary Politics, 1787–1793." In *Peers, Politics and Power: The House of Lords, 1603–1911*. Edited by Clyve Jones and David Lewis Jones, 283–308. London: Hambledon, 1986.

McCranie, Kevin D. "Admiral Keith at Genoa: A Success and Failure of Coalition Warfare." In *Proceedings, 1997: Consortium on Revolutionary Europe, 1750–1850*.

Edited by Donald D. Horward, 368–76. Tallahassee: Institute on Napoleon and the French Revolution, 1997.

———. "The Floating Diplomats: The Role of British Naval Officers in the Convention of El Arish, 1800." In *Proceedings, 1998: Consortium on Revolutionary Europe, 1750–1850*. Edited by Donald D. Horward, 139–48. Tallahassee: Institute on Napoleon and the French Revolution, 1998.

———. "'He shall be properly taken care of': Lord Keith, Patronage, and the Royal Navy, 1761–1823. In *Proceedings, 1999: Consortium on Revolutionary Europe, 1750–1850*, edited by Donald D. Horward, 393–402. Tallahassee: Institute on Napoleon and the French Revolution, 1999.

McGuffie, T. H. "The Stone Ships Expedition against Boulogne, 1804." *English Historical Review* 64 (October 1949): 488–502.

Montholon, Charles-Tristan de. *History of the Captivity of Napoleon at St. Helena.* 4 vols. Philadelphia: Carey and Hart, 1847.

Moore, James Carrick. *The Life of Lieutenant-General Sir John Moore, K.B.* 2 vols. London: J. Murray, 1834.

Moore, John. *The Diary of Sir John Moore.* Edited by J. F. Maurice. 2 vols. London: E. Arnold, 1904.

Morriss, Roger, and Richard C. Saxby, eds. *The Channel Fleet and the Blockade of Brest, 1793–1801.* Aldershot: Ashgate, for the Navy Records Society, 2001.

Naish, George P. B., ed. *Nelson's Letters to His Wife, and Other Documents, 1785–1831.* London: Routledge and Kegan Paul, for the Navy Records Society, 1958.

Namier, Lewis, and John Brooke. *The House of Commons, 1754–1790.* 3 vols. London: Oxford University Press, for the History of Parliament Trust, 1964.

Naval Chronicle. Periodical. 40 vols. London: J. Gold, 1799–1818.

Nelson, Horatio. *The Dispatches and Letters of Vice Admiral Lord Viscount Nelson.* Edited by Nicholas Harris Nicolas. 7 vols. London: H. Colburn, 1845–46.

Nicol, John. *The Life and Adventures of John Nicol, Mariner.* 1822. Edited by Tim Flannery. New York: Atlantic Monthly Press, 1999.

O'Gorman, Frank. *The Whig Party and the French Revolution.* London: Macmillan, 1967.

Oman, Charles. *History of the Peninsular War.* 7 vols. Oxford: Clarendon Press, 1902–30.

Paget, Arthur. *The Paget Papers: Diplomatic and Other Correspondence of the Right Hon. Sir Arthur Paget, G.C.B: 1794–1807.* Edited by Augustus B. Paget. 2 vols. London: W. Heinemann, 1896.

Parkinson, Cyril Northcote. *War in the Eastern Seas, 1793–1815.* London: Allen and Unwin, 1954.

Parry, Clive, ed. *The Consolidated Treaty Series.* Vol. 55, *1799–1801.* Dobbs Ferry, N.Y.: Oceana, 1969.

Parsons, G. S. *Nelsonian Reminiscences: Leaves from Memory's Log*. London: Saunders and Otley, 1847.

Perrin, W. G., and Christopher Lloyd, eds. *The Keith Papers: Selected from the Papers of Admiral Viscount Keith*. 3 vols. London: Navy Records Society, 1927–55.

Petrie, Donald A. *The Prize Game: Lawful Looting on the High Seas in the Days of Fighting Sail*. New York: Berkley Books, 2001.

Pettigrew, Thomas Joseph. *Memoirs of the Life of Vice-Admiral Lord Viscount Nelson K.B. Duke of Bronté . . .* 2nd ed. 2 vols. London: T. and W. Boone, 1849.

Philip, Cynthia Owen. *Robert Fulton: A Biography*. New York: F. Watts, 1985.

Philips, Cyril H. "East India Company 'Interest' and the English Government, 1783–4." *Transactions of the Royal Historical Society*, 4th ser., 20 (1937): 83–101.

———. *The East India Company, 1784–1834*. 2nd ed. Manchester: Manchester University Press, 1961.

Phipps, Ramsay Weston. *The Armies of the First French Republic and the Rise of the Marshals of Napoleon I*. 5 vols. London: Oxford University Press, 1926–39.

Piozzi, Hester Lynch. *The Piozzi Letters: Correspondence of Hester Lynch Piozzi, 1784–1821 (Formerly Mrs. Thrale)*. Edited by Edward A. Bloom and Lillian D. Bloom. 6 vols. Newark: University of Delaware Press, 1989–2002.

Richards, Gerda C. "The Creations of Peers Recommended by the Younger Pitt." *American Historical Review* 34 (October 1928): 47–54.

Rigault, Georges. *Le Général Abdallah Menou et la dernière phase de l'expédition d'Égypte, 1799–1801*. Paris: Plon-Nourrit, 1911.

Robinson, John. *Parliamentary Papers of John Robinson, 1774–1784*. Edited by William Thomas Laprade. Camden, 3rd ser., no. 33. London: Royal Historical Society, 1922.

Rodger, Alexander Bankier. *The War of the Second Coalition, 1798 to 1801: A Strategic Commentary*. Oxford: Clarendon Press, 1964.

Rodger, N.A.M. *Naval Records for Genealogists*. 3rd ed. Public Record Office Handbook no. 22. Kew: PRO Publications, 1998.

———. "Patronage and Competence." In Acerra et al., *Marines de guerre*, 237–48.

———. *The Wooden World: An Anatomy of the Georgian Navy*. London: Collins, 1986.

Rose, George. *The Diaries and Correspondence of the Right Hon. George Rose*. Edited by Leveson Vernon Harcourt. 2 vols. London: R. Bentley, 1860.

Rose, J. Holland. *Lord Hood and the Defence of Toulon*. Cambridge: University Press, 1922.

Ross, R. D. "The Naval Officer, 1793–1815: His Efficiency, Conditions of Service, Prospects and Handicaps." *Army Quarterly and Defence Journal* 78 (1959): 71–95.

Rousseau, François, ed. *Kléber et Menou en Égypte depuis le départ de Bonaparte (août 1799–septembre 1801)*. Paris: A. Picard et Fils, 1900.

Ryan, Anthony N. "The Royal Navy and the Blockade of Brest, 1689–1805: Theory and Practice." In Acerra et al., *Marines de guerre*, 175–93.

Sandwich, John Montagu, 4th Earl of. *The Private Papers of John, Earl of Sandwich, First Lord of the Admiralty, 1771–1782*. Edited by G. R. Barnes and J. H. Owen. 4 vols. London: Navy Records Society, 1932–38.

Saul, Norman E. *Russia and the Mediterranean, 1797–1807*. Chicago: University of Chicago Press, 1970.

Saxby, Richard C. "The Blockade of Brest in the French Revolutionary War." *Mariner's Mirror* 78 (February 1992): 25–35.

———. "The Escape of Admiral Bruix from Brest." *Mariner's Mirror* 46 (May 1960): 113–19.

Scully, Denys. *The Catholic Question in Ireland and England 1798–1822: The Papers of Denys Scully*. Edited by Brian MacDermot. Dublin: Irish Academic Press, 1988.

Serle, Ambrose. *The American Journal of Ambrose Serle, Secretary to Lord Howe, 1776–78*. Edited by Edward H. Tatum Jr. San Marino, Calif.: Huntington Library, 1940.

Shaw, Stanford J. *Between Old and New: The Ottoman Empire under Sultan Selim III, 1789–1807*. Cambridge, Mass.: Harvard University Press, 1971.

Sherwig, John M. *Guineas and Gunpowder: British Foreign Aid in the Wars with France, 1793–1815*. Cambridge, Mass.: Harvard University Press, 1969.

Smith, E. A. *George IV*. New Haven, Conn.: Yale University Press, 1999.

Smyth, W. H. *The Life and Services of Captain Philip Beaver, Late of His Majesty's Ship Nisus*. London: J. Murray, 1829.

Spencer, George John. *Private Papers of George, Second Earl Spencer, First Lord of the Admiralty, 1794–1801*. Edited by Julian S. Corbett and H. W. Richmond. 4 vols. London: Navy Records Society, 1913–24.

Stacton, David. *The Bonapartes*. New York: Simon and Schuster, 1966.

St. Vincent, John Jervis, Earl of. *Letters of Admiral of the Fleet the Earl of St. Vincent whilst the First Lord of the Admiralty, 1801–1804*. Edited by David Bonner Smith. 2 vols. London: Navy Records Society, 1922–27.

———. *Memoirs of Admiral the Right Hon. the Earl of St. Vincent*. Edited by Jedediah Stephens Tucker. 2 vols. London: R. Bentley, 1844.

Sunter, Ronald M. *Patronage and Politics in Scotland, 1707–1832*. Edinburgh: John Donald, 1986.

Syrett, David. "Admiral Rodney, Patronage and the Leeward Island Squadron, 1780–2." *Mariner's Mirror* 85 (November 1999): 411–20.

————. *The Royal Navy in American Waters, 1775–1783*. Aldershot, Hants.: Scolar Press, 1989.

————. *The Royal Navy in European Waters During the American Revolutionary War*. Columbia: University of South Carolina Press, 1998.

————. *Shipping and the American War, 1775–83: A Study of British Transport Organization*. University of London Historical Studies 27. London: Athlone Press, 1970.

Theal, George McCall. *History of South Africa*. 11 vols. Reprint, Cape Town: C. Struik, 1964.

————, ed. *Records of the Cape Colony*. 36 vols. London: Government of the Cape Colony, 1897–1905.

Thiébault, Paul. *Journal des opérations militaires et administratives des siège et blocus de Gênes*. New ed. 2 vols. Paris: J. Corréard, 1846–47.

Thorne, R. G. *The House of Commons, 1790–1820*. 5 vols. London: Secker and Warburg, for the History of Parliament Trust, 1986.

Thursfield, H. G., ed. *Five Naval Journals, 1789–1817*. London: Navy Records Society, 1951.

Tilley, John A. *The British Navy and the American Revolution*. Columbia: University of South Carolina Press, 1987.

Tone, William Theobald Wolfe, comp. *Life of Theobald Wolfe Tone*. 1826. Edited by Thomas Bartlett. Dublin: Lilliput, 1998.

Tunstall, Brian. *Naval Warfare in the Age of Sail: The Evolution of Fighting Tactics, 1650–1815*. Edited by Nicolas Tracy. London: Conway Maritime Press, 1990.

Uhlendorf, Bernhard A., ed. and trans. *The Siege of Charleston, With an Account of the Province of South Carolina: Diaries and Letters of Hessian Officers from the von Jungkenn Papers in the William L. Clements Library*. Ann Arbor: University of Michigan Press, 1938.

Weinzierl, John F. "The Military and Political Career of Claude-Victor Perrin." Ph.D. diss., Florida State University, 1997.

Wellington, Arthur Wellesley, Duke of. *The Dispatches of Field Marshal the Duke of Wellington, during His Various Campaigns in India, Denmark, Portugal, Spain, the Low Countries, and France, from 1799 to 1818*. Edited by John Gurwood. 13 vols. London: J. Murray, 1837–39.

————. *Supplementary Despatches, Correspondence and Memoranda of Field Marshal Arthur, Duke of Wellington, K.G.* Edited by his son, the Duke of Wellington. 15 vols. London: J. Murray, 1858–72.

Wells, Roger. *Insurrection: The British Experience, 1795–1803*. Gloucester: A. Sutton, 1983.

Willcox, William B. "Arbuthnot, Gambier, and Graves: 'Old Women' of the Navy." In *George Washington's Opponents: British Generals and Admirals in the American Revolution.* Edited by George A. Billias, 260–90. New York: William Morrow, 1969.

Wilson, Robert T. *The British Expedition to Egypt: Containing a Particular Account of the Operations of the Army under the Command of Sir Ralph Abercrombie . . . Carefully Abridged from the Account of Robert Thomas Wilson.* London: R. Milliken, 1803.

Index

Abercromby, Gen. Sir Ralph, 89; arrived in the Mediterranean (1800), 92; and the British Cádiz operation (1800), 93–95; and the failure at Cádiz (1800), 97–100, 184; relationship with Dundas, 99; expectations for Egypt (1801), 101; and preparations for Egypt, 104–107; decision on location for Egyptian landings, 108–109; disagreed with Keith, 109; mortally wounded (1801), 110

Aboukir Bay (Egypt): battle (1798), 65–66, 83, 110, 176, 224n35; as landing site for British (1801), 105–106; anchorage for British fleet, 107–108; British landings at (1801), 108–109

Active (32)(HMS), 19

Adam, William (politician and Keith's brother-in-law), 26–28, 31, 40

Addington, Henry, 134

Admiralty, Board of, 42–43; and decision to split Eastern Seas command, 51; and the mutinies (1797), 58–59; decision to remove Keith from the Channel Fleet (1797), 63; opinion on Nelson's actions (1799), 77; ordered Keith to command in the Mediterranean Fleet (1799), 80; gave permission for Nelson's return to Britain (1800), 83; denied replacement for the *Queen Charlotte*, 85; on the British Cádiz operation (1800), 94, 99; on lack of sailors in the Mediterranean Fleet (1801), 106; sent squadron after Ganteaume (1801), 108; responded to problems between Keith and captains (1801), 120; set peacetime strength of Mediterranean Fleet (1802), 122; restricted Keith's independence, 128;

ordered the bombardment of French invasion ports (1803), 130; decided on deployments for the North Sea fleet, 131; ordered Keith to the Channel Fleet (1812), 151–53; provided Keith with new instructions (1812), 153; and operations on the north coast of Spain, 154–55, 161; and the frigate shortage (1812–13), 157; and San Sebastián (1813), 159–60; unable to reinforce Channel Fleet (1813), 161–62; reappointed Keith to command of the Channel Fleet (1815), 167; approved of Keith's actions to find Napoleon (1815), 168

Agamemnon (64)(HMS), 34

Aigle (44)(HMS), 23–24

Ajax (74)(HMS, launched 1798), 96, 115–16, 118

Ajax (74)(HMS, launched 1809), 159–60

Alessandria, convention (1800), 89–91

Alexander (74)(HMS), 82, 103, 111

Alexander I (tsar of Russia), 121

Alexandria, Egypt, 65, 104, 106; blockade of, 107–109, 111; surrounded by the British, 120; surrender of (1801), 121

Allardyce, Alexander (author), 3, 201n63

Allemand, Vice Admiral Zacharie J., 151–52

Amboyna (Moluccas), 49–51

America (64)(HMS), 43, 46, 48, 50

American colonies, 9–24

American Prohibitory Act (1775), 12

Amiens, Peace of, 122, 124

Antigua. *See* English Harbor

Antwerp, Belgium, 162, 165

Arbuthnot, Vice Admiral Marriot, 17, 19

Arcturus (tender)(HMS), 7

Arniston (Indiaman)(British), 43, 46

Digby, Rear Admiral Robert, 22–23
Dinah (victualer)(British), 12
Dockyards (British), 125
Downs (England), 130, 145, 148
Duckworth, Rear Admiral John Thomas,
    65, 70, 75, 81
Dudley, Wade G. (author), 220
Duff, Rear Admiral Robert, 10
Dunbartonshire: Parliamentary elections,
    9, 25–27, 31
Duncan, Admiral Adam, 59, 65, 77
Dundas, Henry (later 1st Viscount Mel-
    ville): role in Elphinstone's appoint-
    ment to the Eastern Seas (1795), 42–43;
    patronage of, 56, 63–64, 80–81, 95, 99,
    182; role in creating Elphinstone an Irish
    peer, 56–57; and the Prince of Wales
    (1797), 57–58; dealt with the aftermath
    of the British Cádiz operation (1800),
    99; and plans for Egypt, 101; out of
    office (1801), 110; appointed First Lord
    of the Admiralty (1804), 134; micro-
    management of the North Sea Fleet
    (1804–1805), 135–36; on technological
    innovations (Fulton, Congreve), 136–38;
    on lax conversation among officers,
    137–38; resigned as First Lord (1805), 138
Dundas, Sir Lawrence, 25
Dundas, Robert Saunders, 2nd Viscount
    Melville: appointed First Lord of the
    Admiralty (1812), 153–54; on the war
    with the United States (1812), 156; and
    San Sebastián (1813), 159–60; chooses
    replacement for Collier (1814), 163;
    ordered Keith to the Gironde (1814),
    163–64; ordered Keith to Plymouth
    (1815), 167; on Napoleon being sent to
    St. Helena (1815), 170; opinion on the
    Mackenrot episode (1815), 173, 223n26;
    complemented Keith (1815), 176
Dungeness, England, 130, 145
Dunkirk, France, 131
Durham, Rear Admiral P.C., 153
Dutch (navy): Lucas's expedition to

the Cape Colony, 50–52; surrender
    of squadron at Saldanha Bay (1796),
    52, 60–61; quality of sailors, 52, 186,
    200n47; squadron in the Texel, 143–44

East Cliff, England: as Keith's headquar-
    ters, 129, 145, 150, 183, 219n5. *See also*
    Margate; Ramsgate
East India Company (English), 4, 7,
    42–43, 151
Echo (16), 43, 46, 48–49, 51
Edgar (60)(HMS), 19–20
Edmonstone, Sir Archibald, 25–26
Egyptian campaign (British)(1801), 101–121
Elbe River, 126, 131, 143
Elphinstone, Charles, 10th Lord (Keith's
    father), 4, 25, 40, 65
Elphinstone, Charles (Keith's brother), 4
Elphinstone, Eleonora (Keith's sister), 27
Elphinstone, Admiral Sir George Keith,
    (later Viscount Keith)
—Career: near engagement off Cádiz
    (1799), 1; list of fleet commands, 2;
    aboard the *Gosport* (1762), 6; aboard the
    Juno, 6–7; aboard the *Lively* (1763), 7;
    aboard the *Arcturus* (1765), 7; employed
    by East India Company (1767) 7;
    aboard the *Emerald*, 8; aboard the *Stag*
    (1769), 8; as lieutenant in the East
    Indies (1769), 8–9; in command of the
    Scorpion (1772), 9; in command of the
    Romney (1776), 10, 26; in command
    of *Perseus* (1776–1780), 10–19; and the
    Dinah affair, 12; off Charleston, 13–14; in
    temporary command of the *Pearl* (1777),
    13; at St. Augustine, 14–15; captured the
    La Thérèse (1779), 16; at the capture of
    Charleston (1780), 17–19; in command
    of the *Warwick* (1780–82), 19–24, 26; cap-
    tured the *Rotterdam* (1780), 20; captured
    the *Aigle* (1782), 23–24; in command of
    the *Robust* (1793), 33; at Toulon (1793),
    34–39; returned to Britain (1794), 39; in
    the Channel Fleet (1794), 41–42; selected

Hotham, Rear Admiral Sir Henry, 168–69, 181, 185
Howe, Vice Admiral Richard, Lord, 10, 12, 39, 41–42
Howick, Viscount. See Grey, Charles
Hutchinson, General. See Hely-Hutchinson, Maj. Gen. John
Hyères, islands of, 39

Île d'Aix: French ships at, 151, 153
Impatiente (44)(French), 55
Impétueux (74)(HMS), 76–77
Impressment, 13–14
India, 7, 49–50
Inglis, Capt. Charles, 102
Istanbul. See Constantinople
Italian Peninsula: state of affairs in (1800), 92

Java, 51
Jervis, Capt. John (later Admiral the Earl of St. Vincent; later First Lord of the Admiralty), 2; as captain of the Gosport, 5–6; created earl, 64; relationship with Keith, 64, 109–10, 181–82; in command of the Mediterranean Fleet, 64; description of British ships, 66; approved of Keith's actions at Cádiz (1799), 69; and pursuit of Bruix (1799), 69–70, 76, 78; commanded fleet from Minorca (1799), 70–74; relinquished command of Mediterranean Fleet (1799), 74; concerned for Minorca (1799), 72–75, 77; became First Lord (1801), 110–11; on problems in Keith's Mediterranean Fleet (1801), 118–19; compared with Spencer, 122; appointed Keith port admiral at Plymouth (1803), 124; and poor state of the navy (1803), 125; appointed Keith to the North Sea Fleet, 125, 182; and problems with officers, 127–28; on expanding number of blockaded ports (1803), 128; on the stone ship expedition, 132–33; out

of office (1804), 134; appointed Commission of Naval Inquiry, 138
Johnson, Dr. Samuel, 149
Joint operations (British): Charleston (1780), 17–19; Cape of Good Hope (1795), 43–48; nature of command in, 93; at Cádiz (1800), 93–100; during the Egyptian expedition (1801), 101–105, 108–14, 120–21, 123; in northern Germany (1805–1806), 143–44; on the north coast of Spain (1812–14), 154–61, 163–64; overview of Keith's abilities involving, 187–88
Juno (32)(HMS), 6–7
Jupiter (50)(HMS), 50

Kapudan Bey, 105
Kapudan Pasha, 105, 107, 110, 114, 121
Keith, George Skene, 179
Keith, Lady. See Thrale, Hester Maria
Keith, Admiral Lord. See Elphinstone, Admiral Sir George Keith
Keith Manuscripts (National Maritime Museum, Greenwich), 3
Kelly, Capt. William Hancock, 213n56
King, Admiral Sir Richard, 60
Kingsmill, Vice Admiral Sir Robert Brice, 200n55

Lapoype, Gen. Jean, 36–37
Las Cases, Emmanuel de, 169–70, 172, 174–76
Laughton, John Knox (author), 3
Lavery, Brian (author), 191n5, 225n19
Leith, Scotland, 126, 145, 148
Lieutenant's exam, 6, 8
Lincoln, Gen. Benjamin, 19
Lindsay, Commodore Sir John, 8
Lion (64)(HMS), 23, 82
Lively (20)(HMS), 7
Liverpool, Robert Banks Jenkinson, 2nd Earl of, 153, 174
Livorno, Italy, 84, 92

Kevin D. McCranie is assistant professor of history at Brewton-Parker College in Mount Vernon, Georgia.